BRAVING THE WORLD

Adventures in Travel and Retirement

Pam Saylor

\

Braving The World: Adventures in Travel and Retirement

Copyright ©2021 Pam Saylor

All Rights Reserved.

Cover design by Kate Rado

Editing by Victoria Hanley

ISBN: 978-1-7360731-1-7

DEDICATION

THIS BOOK is dedicated to Dave, my loyal partner in travel and in life who more than once kept me from jumping on the wrong train, bus, or tram. This book would not exist if it weren't for his computer skills, patience and help with all the details of turning a manuscript into what you now hold in your hands.

Table of Contents

INTRODUCTION

THIS IS NOT a typical guidebook because there are plenty of those on the market. Does the world really need another book telling you how to spend 36 hours in a foreign city? My husband Dave and I retired and then spent one entire year living in Europe.

When we left for Italy, we were newly retired and needed to figure out our post-retirement life. What new shape would life take? It wasn't all smooth sailing and we struggled along the way. Retirement was an adjustment for us, individually and as a couple, and we realized just how different from each other we had become over the years. It was a big change for us to leave behind our 9 to 5 lives and suddenly be alone together all day, every day.

As a Type 1, insulin1-dependent diabetic, living in Europe came with a steep learning curve for me. When we left the U.S., I didn't know how I would find insulin to manage my diabetes, or if it would be affordable. All of my research and planning before the trip began couldn't prepare me for the reality of managing diabetes in a foreign country.

Still, despite worries, we had talked about and dreamed about our "Bel Sogno," our Beautiful Dream trip for years. We wanted to settle into Italy and live, temporarily, like locals. We wanted to get to know a neighborhood, to eat where the locals ate, learn new things, and watch one season replace another. We longed to plunge into a place and not just dip our toe in and then leave. Retirement gave us the time to make our dream come true.

I hope reading about our experiences will inspire others to try traveling for longer periods. In my opinion, the non-stop eight-day jaunts to three cities are crazy. On our way home from our year of travel, we spent a few days in Paris. We were sitting in a park outside the Louvre having an impromptu picnic, complete with glasses of wine. A sweaty, panting couple came and sat next to us, gobbling their sandwiches, and as we chatted with them, they explained they were part of a tour group and would only be in Paris one day. They split their morning between two sites, and in the afternoon, they thought they could cram in two more before they rejoined the tour group. That sort of travel is what Dave and I came to call the "Tourist Death March." It is hurried, hectic, and rushed with no time to breathe.

Maybe travel doesn't have to be a jam-packed sprint. There is a lot to be said for settling into a place and getting beyond the surface instead of racing to the Top Ten Attractions touted in every guidebook and every blog. I truly believe you get a better sense of Paris sitting in a park drinking a glass of wine or walking along the Seine or trying pastry at a patisserie than you do rushing to get to the Arc de Triomphe or the Eiffel Tower.

Not everyone can travel for weeks or months at a time. Still, even if you only have a few days, my advice is to spend less time rushing and at least part of the time just walking, sitting, following whatever street looks interesting, and stopping for a coffee at any café with an open table in the sun. Go to the tourist spots, but on the way, stop and soak it in a little, dawdle, loiter and linger. A trip should make time for deliberation and daydreaming. I love Virginia Woolf's idea of real travel:

"By hook or by crook, I hope that you will possess yourselves of money enough to travel and to idle, to contemplate the future or the past of the world, to dream over books and loiter at street corners and let the line of thought dip deep into the stream."

IN THE BEGINNING

My first ever trip overseas was to London in 1999 at age 38 with my then boyfriend. I was thrilled with my new, blank passport. Three years later, I made another overseas trip, this time all alone, after breaking up with my boyfriend. Deep down, it terrified me to go to a foreign country by myself, but I was determined. Since middle school, I had dreamed of Venice after finding a magazine article showing a Venice full of old palazzos, bridges, churches, pigeons, gondolas, canals, piazzas, dark alleys, and most of all, water—sparkling bright water. I wanted to see Venice for myself before it sank into the lagoon it was built on. Growing up in a small Midwestern town, far from the ocean, I almost couldn't believe such a place could be real. My first trip to Venice lasted only four short days because that was all I could afford. Once there, I wandered, got lost in the labyrinth of alleys, and saw the canals' shimmering water reflecting the sky and the clouds. I didn't want to leave this storybook land. I was in love.

In 2004 when Dave and I got married, a second marriage for both of us, we began traveling overseas together, starting with a honeymoon in Paris. Dave was eager to use *his* new, blank passport for his first trip out of the country. We traveled to Rome, Florence, Munich, and one year we went to Venice so I could share my favorite city with my husband. He loved it almost as much as I did. Dave and I traveled well together. Neither of us cared about the hotel (as long as it was clean) because the hotel was just the place to sleep. Both of us could eat and drink anything and were eager to try new foods. We agreed that the real fun of any trip was to see and do things.

However, as much as I liked to travel, I wasn't genuinely adventurous or brave. For me, every trip involved hours of research, guidebooks, and maps to keep all risks to a minimum. I made sure to carry a folder that included details of every flight, every hotel reservation, and every planned event of the trip. I made lists. Dave was the calm one when we traveled because he knew I had prepared and double-checked every element of the journey.

For years, in between our short trips overseas, Dave and I started talking about a different *kind* of trip, a long-term trip. Both of us loved the food, wine, and people of Italy, and we began talking/dreaming about someday living in Italy for an entire year. We named this dream our Beautiful Dream—our "Bel Sogno."

In 2009 we had just returned from a short trip to Florence when I opened a bottle of wine and took it out to the patio where Dave was sitting.

"Florence was amazing. We crammed a lot into a short trip," I said, pouring wine for each of us.

"Yeah, every single day was a rush. It wasn't a relaxing trip, but with only five days, there isn't time to relax."

"Exactly. Every short trip we take makes me dream even more about our Bel Sogno.

Dave smiled. "No jet lag!"

"We would have time to relax, to linger, to explore, to just be. I twirled my wineglass, picturing this potential life. After years of reading every travel memoir book I could get my hands on, I dreamed of staying in one place and becoming known to neighbors and to shopkeepers where I bought groceries. I wanted to experience different cities and countries below the surface and not just skim along the top. I imagined discovering the small neighborhood restaurants tourists never had time to find.

"Where would we live for our year?" Dave said, interrupting my fantasy. I brought my mind back to reality and picked up the wine bottle to pour a little more wine.

"I don't know. Let's figure out the details with our next bottle of wine. It will be years before we have to decide."

But change came sooner than either of us expected. In 2016 Dave became eligible for early retirement and was offered a buyout from his job. It was a hard decision to make. We could have kept working and building up our retirement funds. That would have been the wise thing to do. That would be the advice of most financial planners. But my scripted life had already lurched out of control in 2013 when I found out I had Type 1 diabetes. Now my days involved multiple insulin shots, visits with an endocrinologist, and lots of supplies and equipment. The good health I had taken for granted my whole life vanished, leaving me to learn how to manage a chronic condition. It was challenging. People lived for decades with diabetes, so it wasn't a death sentence, but now time felt more precious, life more fragile, and I didn't want to waste one second of whatever active time I had left. Despite my diabetes, I was still reasonably young and healthy. Early retirement would give us a chance to do the things the two of us had been dreaming about for years.

So the decision was made.

We dusted off the Bel Sogno plan and plunged into a year of turning it into reality. At our "mature" age, we were ready to shake up the routines and put our everyday lives on hold, surprising our blended family of five grown children, who questioned us closely about our plans. Of course, I made sure we started out with a plan and a detailed list. We agreed to leave the U.S. in September 2017 and go to Rome in central Italy for six months to spend the fall and winter. Then in 2018, as the weather warmed up, we would move north for six months to Venice to spend the spring and summer before returning to the U.S. in 2018.

Like giddy kids, we bought two one-way tickets to Rome.

§   §   §

Almost immediately, I felt overwhelmed. I had taken Italian language classes off and on for years, but I was not at all fluent. Can reading dozens of guidebooks and travel memoirs really prepare you for this? We would be far from friends and family for an entire year. Would we get homesick? A lot could go wrong. What do you do with your mail for months at a time, and how do you refill your prescriptions in a foreign country? Our usual doctors and pharmacies would not be available. Complications from diabetes had landed me in the hospital emergency room twice. If that happened in Italy, it could be dangerous. There could be other sudden health emergencies, accidents, or illnesses. What would it be like to live in a small space with Dave, completely alone together, 24/7? Our everyday lives began to look more and more warm, comfortable, and safe.

Now that we were leaving everything behind, I realized how much I liked my habits, schedules, and routines. Spontaneous, powerless, messy situations usually made me nervous and uncomfortable. On this trip, I wouldn't be able to control very much. We were upending our lives, by choice, and I couldn't clearly see what would replace our norms. Would we even like this new life in a foreign country, or would we want to return home after a month? When it came right down to it, our dream trip felt like falling off a cliff.

So we held hands and walked over the cliff.

PART I: PREPARATIONS

• THE LIST-an overview •

Since I am a confirmed list maker, organization nerd, and planner, obviously when we first began preparing for our adventure, Dave and I sat down together at the kitchen table, with a glass of wine, and began brainstorming a gigantic "to-do" list. Each of us took turns naming every single little detail we could think of that we would need to accomplish before leaving the country.

"What will we do with our townhome?" Dave wondered.

"I don't know who will watch the dog for a year."

"The mail…."

"Should we keep the cars?"

"Will our phones work over there?"

"Can we find an affordable apartment in Rome?"

Taking a deep breath, I paused and looked at the very long list in front of me. Gazing around our sunny living room, I thought about all the effort that went into renovating and decorating this light-filled, warm, and comfortable room. It would be hard to leave. Dave poured more wine, and I turned back to our list.

There were medical to-dos like stockpiling medication, getting doctors' visits, checkups, and shots. We needed to figure out how to access our health insurance overseas and we would both need to get prescriptions refilled. I needed to have insulin and other diabetes supplies.

It was essential to have access to our money while overseas without paying hefty bank fees. Dave notified our bank, credit card companies, and everyone else we would be traveling for a year. Our homeowner's insurance policy had to be changed to a rental insurance policy. We hired an accountant to file our taxes while we were out of the country and arranged to pay our bills online.

We had to rent out our townhome, find a home for our dog, store our furniture, find an apartment in Italy and sell our cars. The list was daunting. As the weeks passed and we crossed things off our list, more questions came up. More and more often, my typical morning began at 3 a.m. much like this:

Me: wide awake and staring at the ceiling with my mind spinning with new questions. Will we like the food; will we get sick; will I be able to buy insulin at local pharmacies; will we have enough money; will we lose our passport; will we be homesick; how will I do laundry?

The first time this happened, after tossing and turning, I eventually fell back asleep, exhausted. The next morning I went to hug Dave and began unloading all the new worries from my 3 a.m. fear fest. He put his arms around me and listened but didn't say a word, his face pale and eyes staring off across the room.

"What's wrong?" I asked.

"That sounds like my brain at 2 a.m.," he said. "What if our phones don't work, or we don't have Wi-Fi, or we can't pay bills online." Dave tended to worry about tech.

There were a lot of questions, and I controlled none of the answers. If there was a time to back out, this was it. But in the daylight, after our miserable nights' sleep, and after talking together, our determination returned along with the feelings of excitement and adventure that surrounded the dream. So, we pushed ahead.

• FATE OR LUCK •

What to do with our townhouse and our dog for a year? These were important questions. The property management company we met with could rent and manage our three-bedroom townhome. The rent would cover our monthly mortgage and HOA fees, and leave us with $400 extra to use to pay someone to board our dog for a year and to pay for a storage unit for our furniture.

Shelby, our 12-year-old blue heeler, had issues. She was very attached to me and followed me everywhere. She didn't like other dogs, and we assumed she didn't like cats. All of our family members already had pets, so Shelby couldn't go to them. A local blue heeler rescue group seemed willing to connect me with a foster family to keep Shelby for a year, for a fee, but then my contact at the rescue group inexplicably stopped returning my phone calls. In a way, it was a relief that I wouldn't have to leave Shelby with strangers, but I was back to square one.

Then fate intervened and we got very lucky. My friend Aliciah and I met almost every week to go to the movies, drink wine, and talk about general life stuff. She had heard all of our trip planning ups and downs, and I'd heard her debates about moving or not moving in September when her apartment lease expired. Eventually, I made the connection between our move to Italy in September and Aliciah's lease ending.

"What if Aliciah rented our townhouse for a year?" I asked Dave.

"I like Aliciah," Dave said.

"Even Shelby likes Aliciah," I said.

So I floated the idea to Aliciah to rent our townhouse and keep our dog, and she agreed. We kept the rent low, just enough to cover our monthly mortgage and HOA fees. Aliciah would save on rent and speed up her plans to be able to buy her own place. We would leave some of our furniture for Aliciah to use, and the rest we could store in our garage. I loved not paying for furniture storage. More importantly, it was a relief to know we could spend our year in Europe without worrying about Shelby or our townhouse. I knew Aliciah would take good care of both. For us, this solved two critical hurdles, and the rest of our planning moved forward.

> *TIP: Taking care of our mail for the entire year was another priority. We didn't want to burden our family or friends with it. First, I registered with ecocycle.org to get rid of junk mail. I made everything paperless—banks, brokerage, insurance, etc. Before leaving the country, I notified the Post Office to forward our mail to a company called PostScan Mail (postscanmail.com) at an address in California. For $15.00 per month, the mail service sent us scans of all of our mail envelopes. For a small additional fee, they would scan the contents or forward the mail to us. It worked perfectly. I only had to remember to renew our mail forwarding order with the Post Office when it expired after six months.*

• JUGGLING MONEY OVERSEAS •

It was important to access our money while overseas. Because many small businesses in Europe don't accept credit cards, we planned to use cash most of the time. Our U.S. bank charged hefty foreign ATM fees, so I began looking for another option.

Both Capital One and Schwab offered accounts that could work overseas, and they didn't charge foreign ATM fees, transaction fees, or currency conversion fees. After setting up an online account with Capital One, we linked it to our existing U.S. bank account. Dave's monthly retirement check was direct deposited into our U.S. bank account, and we would go online to transfer money to the Capital One account as needed. On the Capital One website, there were hundreds of ATMs in Rome, with many more scattered around Europe.

Even if we didn't plan to use credit cards very often, they still had to be available. We took credit cards from two separate companies—Dave carried one and I carried the other. Unless both of us lost our wallets or unless some cunning thief simultaneously pickpocketed both of us, we would always have one credit card to use. We also asked for the PIN numbers for our credit cards to get cash advances—flexibility was key. Having a financial Plan A, Plan B, and Plan C helped me feel more in control of the uncontrollable future.

We added my daughter Vanessa to our U.S. bank accounts so she could handle whatever money issues arose while we were gone. All of our monthly bills were set up to be paid by automatic payment. If necessary, we could go online and have checks sent out for unexpected bills.

After all of this, it felt like we could cross banking and money off the to-do list. The real test of all our plans would begin when we arrived in Rome.

TIP: To free up money in our budget, we sold one car a few months before we left and the other car we donated to a charity just two days before leaving—no storage fees, taxes, license, or insurance fees. When we returned to the U.S., we planned to buy only one car and see if our post-retirement life together would work with a shared vehicle.

• APARTMENT IN ROME •

When it came to finding an apartment in Rome, I tried everything. I looked at expensive Airbnb apartments. Sites like VRBO.com, Homeaway.com, and Cribrentalsrome.com, didn't have very many rentals when I was searching, and the fees they charged were confusing. There were places for rent on Craigslist, Facebook, and Rome newspapers, but that seemed risky. There would be no recourse if something went wrong.

"You could try Spotahome." This suggestion came from a friend I met in Italian class. She had just returned from a visit to Rome, and we were drinking coffee at Barnes & Noble while practicing our Italian together. She opened her phone and showed me pictures of the rental she had used in Rome. "Spotahome sends people to check every apartment they have listed to make sure there are no surprises. I loved my apartment." Her apartment did look nice, it was in a good area, and the rent was very reasonable.

Dave and I picked an evening and sat down with a bottle of wine and a computer. After hours of research, I had narrowed the apartment choices down to only four, and it was time to make a decision.

"I like this one." Dave pointed to an apartment with a small balcony. I liked the balcony, but the rooms looked dark to me.

I pointed to another picture. "This place has an oven, but it is a little far out of the city center," I said. I jotted down a list of "pros" and "cons" for each apartment. *What will it feel like to live in such a different place, a different unfamiliar culture?* I worried.

15

There was great natural light in one apartment, but our other choice was a little larger. Finally, both of us agreed on a small apartment that I really liked in Trastevere, a neighborhood just a few miles south of the Vatican, and signed on for a six-month lease with Spotahome. It didn't have an oven but was near the center of everything. I raised my wine glass. "Cheers! To an apartment in Rome!"

We paid the first month's rent online, and after arriving in Rome, we would have to pay an additional €1,200 damage deposit. I began showing everyone the picture of "our" apartment in Rome. *This is actually going to happen*, I thought. *The dream becomes a reality.*

• INSURANCE, DOCTORS, DENTISTS, AND DRUGS •

Our health insurance was very unusual because it would cover overseas accidents, injuries, or illnesses. All foreign doctors and hospitals were "in-network." I obtained a "proof of coverage" letter from our health insurance company to give to the Italian consulate in Chicago when we went to get our visa. We wouldn't need to buy a travel medical insurance policy.

When we filled prescriptions overseas, we would pay out of pocket and then submit claims to our insurance carrier for reimbursement. I changed our insurance mailing address to my daughter Vanessa's address so medical reimbursement checks could be mailed directly to her. I also made sure everything else with the insurance company was paperless. Before leaving the country, both of us got our annual flu shots and pneumonia shots. The Center for Disease Control recommended Hepatitis A and B shots for anyone traveling to Italy, so we got those too. Finally, I made a list of English-speaking doctors in Rome and Venice using the U.S. State Department website.

In the final months before leaving, we arranged for last-minute appointments with all of our doctors, who turned out to be full of questions. My endocrinologist for the last few years especially peppered me with a lot of questions about my diabetes arrangements. She seemed envious and skeptical at the same time. I wouldn't say she was worried, but she wanted to make sure I had thought everything through. I tried to appear calm and full of answers as I sat in the chair in her office and hid the tremors in my stomach.

"Do you have enough insulin pumps? Will the company ship more to you in Europe?" she asked.

"No," I replied. "They won't."

At the time we left the U.S., I had been a Type 1 diabetic for four years. During the first few years, I had given myself multiple daily needle shots of insulin. For the last few years, I'd switched to an insulin pump system from Omnipod consisting of small individual pumps (about the size of a large strawberry) called Pods. In the U.S., Omnipod shipped a supply of Pods to me every three months, but they would *not* ship Pods to Europe. I arranged for Pods to be mailed to my daughter in the U.S. and she would send them to Europe.

Every three days, I filled a new Pod with insulin before attaching it to my body. A small cannula from the Pod inserted just slightly under my skin so that the Pod could automatically give me continuous low doses of insulin. I took another dose before a meal to cover the carbs I planned to eat or drink, and a "correction" dose of even more insulin if my blood sugar was stubborn and stayed high. My endocrinologist worked out the doses and recommended changes to my pump regime, and I saw her several times a year. To control the Pods and the delivery of insulin (as well as pump settings and calculations), I used a small black plastic device called a Personal Diabetes Manager (PDM) that I carried *everywhere* I went. The PDM was the center of my life.

All in all, the routine was simple and pain-free. Okay, maybe not simple, but I had gotten used to the insulin pump, and the only alternative was to give myself multiple daily shots with a needle.

"I've been stockpiling Pods for months," I reassured my doctor. "I quit using the pumps for a few months and went back to giving myself shots so that I could have extra Pods for this trip. I have a six-month stockpile of Pods/pumps ready to go. My daughter will ship more when I need them."

The doctor seemed reassured, but she had more questions. "What backup supplies do you have? In case the pump or the PDM stop working and you go back to daily injections?" She and I both knew that for daily injections, I would need needles, insulin pens of *long*-acting insulin, and insulin pens of *slow*-acting insulin. I packed a supply of lancets (to prick my fingers), glucose tablets (in case my blood sugar went low), and an emergency glucagon kit in a bright red plastic case (in case my blood sugar went really, seriously, dangerously low, and I was unconscious and could not chew or swallow). The glucagon kit held a vial of glucagon (a hormone) and a syringe with a long needle. Even though I had been diabetic for years, I had never once used an emergency glucagon kit. I just made sure I bought a new kit every year after the old, unused one expired. Add in the test strips, backup blood glucose meter, cotton balls, batteries, and alcohol swabs, and I had accumulated a lot of supplies.

I tried to put the doctor's mind, and mine, at rest. "My monthly prescriptions of insulin vials, insulin pens, and test strips are really about a six-week supply. For months I've been getting prescriptions filled every 30 days. The extra, unused monthly supplies have gone into my stockpile."

My hand went to the medical ID necklace I always wore, and I twisted it anxiously as I waited for the next question. She scanned my records on the computer screen as she thought. She was thorough. "Will any of your supplies expire before you can use them?" she asked.

"I've checked all the vials and pens in my stockpile. The insulin won't expire." As my stockpiles grew, I made sure the expiration date on everything was within our trip time frame. Expired insulin doesn't work, and if I used it, I could end up in the emergency room.

As I stood to leave her office, she printed off paper copies of all of my prescriptions and a letter confirming I was diabetic and listing the supplies I needed. I planned to translate this letter into Italian and wave it in front of any security or customs officers who questioned my suitcase full of medication and supplies.

I left her office feeling like the police had grilled me, but also feeling good. If she didn't see any holes in my plans, then I must have thought of everything. To be comfortable, I just needed to fill in one more piece of the puzzle. I really wanted to know if I could take paper prescriptions, written in English, and get them filled at a pharmacy in Rome or if I would need to see an Italian doctor and get all prescriptions translated to Italian. I turned to the experts.

As I researched living in Italy, I found a group on Facebook called Expats Living in Rome. (They also have a website: www.expatslivinginrome.com.) It was the perfect travel porn site with restaurant tips and recommendations, yoga and language classes, meet-ups, services, and notice boards. When I posted a question about buying insulin in Rome, the expats unanimously agreed I wouldn't be able to get English prescriptions filled at regular pharmacies in Rome. But I could get insulin at the Vatican City pharmacy in Rome. It was a relief to have that question solved.

When we left the U.S., my carry-on bag was full of nothing but stockpiled insulin supplies—enough to last six months and get me halfway through the trip. Since it was crucial to keep all of the insulin cold, I also traveled with a small soft-sided beer cooler full of insulin and ice packs. I was as ready as I possibly could be.

TIP: Most experts recommend buying a travel insurance medical plan when traveling outside the country. Online comparison sites like Squaremouth.com, travelinsurance.com, and insuremytrip.com make shopping easy. Most travel insurance policies do not include coverage for pre-existing health conditions. Policies that cover pre-existing conditions exist, but make sure you know what you are buying.

• MAKING **IT WORK—ELECTRONICS IN EUROPE •

Of course, it was essential to have our phones in Europe. Our phone service provider in the U.S. offered an international plan costing $10 per day. This was not practical for our year-long stint in Europe, so I delegated the job of "making electronic shit work" in Europe to Dave. I would call myself "I.T. challenged," and since Dave worked in the tech world his entire career, he was the undisputed tech expert in our marriage. He was very good at finding lost files and fixing all the snarls I managed to create on the computer. This trip would simply not work unless Dave could keep our phones and other electronics working so we could pay bills and stay in touch with our family.

For all the techie's and non-techies out there, here is my simplified translation of what Dave did before we left the U.S. to get our phones and computers ready for our year-long adventure.

About a year before leaving the country, we needed to replace our older phones with something a little newer. Knowing we planned to go to Europe for a year, Dave made sure he bought "unlocked" phones from our service provider. An unlocked phone is one that can be used on any carrier's network. Dave also made sure the phones he bought were compatible with the mobile phone technology used in Europe. In Europe, they use GSM (Global System for Mobiles) mobile phone technology while in the U.S., phones use both GSM technology and CDMA (Code

Division Multiple Access) technologies. The new phones he bought were unlocked, and they used both GSM and CDMA technology.

A few months before we were due to leave, Dave commandeered my phone to do upgrades. After a few hours of intense work, he finished. "Here you go," he said, handing me my phone. "Ready to go."

"What did you do to it?" I asked.

"I added an app called Viber. We will be able to call our family in the U.S. from Europe. The app uses VOIP and takes analog audio signals and turns them into digital data that can be transmitted over the internet." Dave was beaming with pride as he said this.

"Do I want to know what VOIP is? You know this is gibberish to me."

"VOIP is Voice over Internet Protocol."

"Still gibberish." If Dave thought this would work, I would keep my fingers crossed.

We did not want to lose our U.S. phone numbers while we were out of the country. Dave discovered we could "port" our phone numbers to Google Voice, for no fee, and keep our existing U.S. phone numbers. He downloaded the Google Voice app to our phones and, after our phone numbers ported to Google, which didn't happen until the day we left the country, we could receive texts on the app. Any phone messages we received would be changed into texts using Google's voice-to-text technology.

Dave researched European phone companies and chose Vodafone over Tim or Wind because it would work everywhere in Italy and it had good online reviews. Once in Italy, we would need to buy Italian SIM cards for each of our phones for €10 (about $12) each, and after that, we would only pay €20 every four weeks for each phone. This plan would give us unlimited data, and there were no activation or set-up fees. We typically paid more than $100 per month in the U.S. to get service for our two phones, so we were thrilled to pay less for unlimited data, and hopefully, great service.

Finally, our computer had to be secure since we would use it to handle some financial matters online. We would need to move money between bank accounts, check credit card and bank balances, and pay some bills. With our phones, we could always check email and Facebook, but we didn't want our private financial information going through an unsecured server. Our apartment in Rome came with Wi-Fi, but we didn't know what firewalls were on the landlord's server or how secure it was. Dave signed up for a two-year contract with a Virtual Private Network (VPN) and loaded it onto our computer. With every login, the VPN would create a secure, encrypted connection between our computer and a VPN remote server.

At this point, all we could do was wait and hope that all of our phone and computer plans would work for our trip.

TIP: Be prepared for periods of ambivalence and doubt, mixed with a little fear and terror. Most days felt like a game of whack-a-mole. Problems kept appearing, and we kept pounding them down. Planning our "dream trip" wasn't dreamy—it was messy and emotionally exhausting. Some indecision is reasonable and our plans changed multiple times. Selling our cars, for example, was a surprisingly hard decision. There is no "one size fits all" list of how to travel for weeks, months, or a year. But the anticipation, excitement, and a bit of courage kept us going.

• PACKING •

It was a hot day in July, and I stood in front of my closet, contemplating my clothes. *Should I be packing now?* It was still a full two months before we would be jumping on a plane to Rome, and I knew it was too early, but I was itching to begin. What if there was something to shop for, some gap in my clothing supply that required immediate shopping? This dilemma is something women will understand. Dave is a procrastinator and tends to wear the same clothes over and over, so he waited until the last week before leaving and then carefully rolled his favorite t-shirts and jeans into small, neat bundles and loaded them into his suitcase.

In everyday life, I am pretty good at thinning out clothes. How many black t-shirts does one person need? I do like buying shoes, but my one and only clothes closet is less than five feet long, and it isn't a walk-in. My folded clothes go in a separate armoire and it isn't full.

This project should have been easy, considering I didn't have many clothes to begin with, but it quickly got out of hand. This was going to be a year-long journey across four seasons. I started pulling out what I thought I would need and sorted it on the bed:

- five to six pairs of jeans
- five to six sweaters and button-up long sleeve shirts
- an assortment of thin T-shirts and sleeveless shirts (also good for layering)
- one cardigan sweater

- one long vest with pockets
- one sweatshirt
- heavy warm pajamas (only one set)
- one set of winter yoga clothes (also serving as backup pajamas)
- one swimsuit
- one heavy-ish black coat with hood
- one denim jacket
- one lightweight rain type jacket with hood
- one shawl (black)
- three scarves
- one black dress (lightweight and would work with the shawl or denim jacket)

When I finished, there was a mountain of clothes piled on the bed. This pile didn't include shoes, underwear, socks, or bras.

We planned to take only four suitcases between the two of us. I would only have one larger checked bag and one smaller carry-on bag. The checked bag had to weigh less than 50 pounds. Clearly, all the clothes I'd pulled out weren't going to fit into my one checked suitcase. I couldn't add anything to my carry-on suitcase because it would be full of my diabetes medicine and supplies.

I flopped down on one empty sliver of the bed and looked at everything. Part of one pile started to slide off the bed, and I grabbed it quickly. Something would have to go. I pulled one pair of jeans out of the pile, then another, finally pulling out all but three pairs. I eliminated all but one heavy sweater. *How cold will it be in Rome?* I ran to the computer and checked temperatures in Rome: in September, the average temperature was 70 degrees, and in October, the temperature was still averaging 60 degrees. I personally tend to run hormone hot, so I kept only two long sleeve shirts, two T-shirts but kept all three sleeveless shirts (to be worn under everything else I planned to take). *Layers, layers, layers*, I reminded myself. Nearly everything I packed was black, white, or beige so I could mix and match clothes.

Dave walked into the room and gave the pile of clothes the side-eye. "What are you doing?"

"Trying to decide what to pack. I think I might need more shoes."

"I could have guessed that."

I kicked Dave out of the room. I couldn't leave things lying on the bed for two months, so I piled everything into a suitcase and heaved it into the spare room, out of the way. The suitcase was overflowing, but I knew Dave, the expert packer, would work his magic later and get it all to fit. Packing now kept me from second-guessing myself for the next two months and probably shopping for more and more clothes.

I realized all the blogs and websites I'd spent hours researching, the ones giving sample wardrobes for travel in Europe, the blogs and websites that sounded so authoritative and certain about what clothes to pack, were just *guessing*. There was no magic packing list for a year in Europe. It would be fine to pack fewer clothes, and I could always shop. There wasn't a lot of room in the budget for shopping, but I already planned to find the perfect pair of Italian black leather boots in Rome. If I also needed to buy a few other items to round out my wardrobe, I could live with that.

• BEL SOGNO
PLAN A - GETTING A VISA •

In the year leading up to our departure, in between sorting out banking, insurance, insulin, and phones, I jumped into the work of figuring out how to get a visa. If we wanted to be ordinary tourists, to stay 90 days or less in Italy, we wouldn't need a visa. Since we planned to stay in Italy for a whole year, we needed a long-term stay visa, specifically an "Elective Residence Visa." Italy is part of the Schengen Area—a zone of 26 European countries[1] with open borders—so getting a visa from Italy would allow us to travel and stay, long-term, in any one of those 26 countries.

My visa research began online. A lot of information was about getting student or work visas, but we weren't studying or working. Most blogs, books, and websites I read were useless and generally glossed over visa issues entirely. Getting a visa came with a steep learning curve.

There are 10 Italian consulate offices in the U.S., and each one has jurisdiction over specific areas of the U.S. Since we lived in Denver, we would go to Chicago to get our visa. In-person interviews were required,

---

[1] Besides Italy, the Schengen countries include Austria, Belgium, Czech Republic, Denmark, Estonia, Finland, France, Germany, Greece, Hungary, Iceland, Latvia, Liechtenstein, Lithuania, Luxembourg, Malta, Netherlands, Norway, Poland, Portugal, Slovakia, Slovenia, Spain, Sweden, and Switzerland.

and it was impossible to get a visa online. The Italian consulate website in Chicago was helpful, and provided a list of the paperwork required for an Elective Residence Visa.

It was clear right away that the biggest obstacle to acquiring a visa would be the "proof of lodging" rule. According to the consulate website, they required a *"lease of a house or an apartment in Italy for the entire period requested. Please note that the lease must be for one house/apartment only. Multiple bookings of houses/hotels cannot be accepted for this type of visa."* This housing requirement was a problem because we did not want to stay in one place for our entire year in Italy. We planned to live for six months in Rome and then six months in Venice. Maybe we would change things up and live in Florence for a little while. We wanted to be flexible and move around.

The website of the Italian consulate in Houston didn't even mention lodging as a visa requirement. In Philadelphia, the Italian consulate website only asked for proof of "available accommodation to be chosen as a residence, owned or rented, with a signed contract." Why didn't the Philadelphia or the Houston consulate have the same rules as the Chicago consulate? Why didn't they require a 12-month lease in one location? It didn't matter. We could only deal with the consulate in Chicago.

We were holding one-way tickets to Rome, leaving in September 2017, and, as recommended by the consular website, I scheduled our in-person interviews with the Chicago consulate for July 2017. I spent the weeks before our appointments rifling over and over through the documents I had gathered for the visa. There were five copies of everything. We had an apartment in Rome that we had rented for our first six months in Italy, and I had a one-page letter from the rental company confirming our rental. The letter looked more and more insubstantial as the consular appointment neared. It wasn't for a full 12 months. It was just a letter, not a signed lease. The visa/lodging problem became another issue waking me up at around 3 a.m.

Once again, I contacted the Expats Living in Rome Facebook group I had found months earlier and posted a question about my lodging problem, hoping they could help me.

> ME: Hello, everyone. I am new to this page, but my husband and I will be living in Italy for a year starting in September. Problem: The Chicago Italian consulate expects us to have a one-year lease on a rental in Rome to get a visa! We plan to move around Italy for the entire year. What can I do?
>
> Marco: The Italians love making rules. They do not expect you to follow them. Do not worry.
>
> Sienna: I moved here from Australia, and I showed the consulate my hotel reservation. No problems!
>
> Patrick: You will love Rome. Just flyover and worry about visa later.

I received a lot of replies, and they mostly broke down into two camps 1) don't worry—be happy, and 2) I did "X," and it worked perfectly— even though "X" did not match my fact situation. I also got an offer of help from "P," who was involved in running the Rome expats group.

> "P" : I have seen people in your situation before. I have a large apartment in Rome with an empty bedroom. I can write a letter for you, confirming that you have rented my extra room for 12 months. I have written such letters before for others.

Me: What if the consulate finds out we are lying. Will we be kicked

out of the country?

"P" promised she would speak to the consulate if they called to confirm our lease. Dave and I talked it over. Her fee for providing this letter was €150 (about $182.00).

"I want to do it. The 12-month lodging rule is just arbitrary and pointless. It is paperwork for the sake of paperwork," I argued. Dave wasn't sure what to do and thought it could be a rip-off. I saw an opportunity to fix a problem, so I went ahead and paid "P," and she sent our letter. I felt better, and my panic subsided a little. My stack of papers now included a letter as written "proof" that we had 12 months of lodging in one location in Rome, which I hoped would satisfy the Italian consulate in Chicago. A letter isn't a signed lease, but it was close.

It was July 2017, and Dave and I arrived together a half-hour early at the consular office in downtown Chicago for *my* in-person interview. Dave's separate appointment was scheduled for two days later, something I set up intentionally in case I needed time to fix any problems that came up during my interview.

As we waited, I sat in my chair, jiggling my leg and resisting the urge to bite my fingernails. I watched intently as two other visa applicants walked up to the thick bullet-proof glass with handfuls of paperwork and chatted with the consular staff officer. They quickly got fingerprinted for their visas. There were mistakes on a few of their papers, but the staff officer helped them fix the issues, and they were approved. I felt my neck relax. This felt promising.

When my turn came, the staff officer first said, "I don't want you to be nervous, but this is the hardest visa to get."

"Now, I am more nervous!" I said.

He began examining my documents. The visa application was fine. The proof of health insurance coverage was fine. The proof of income was fine. We were flying right through my stacks of paperwork.

When he got to the letter confirming our 12-month rental in Italy, he said, "No, this will not work. My supervisor requires a registered lease."

"What?"

In all my searching, researching, and reading, I had never before seen the phrase "registered lease." It wasn't on any one of the 10 Italian consular websites I'd looked at, not on any blog, not in any book, not on any web page.

"A registered lease is a lease that has been registered with the Agenzia delle entrate—the tax authorities of Italy," the staff officer explained.

"But your own website says nothing about a registered lease!" I exclaimed.

He was "sorry they were short-staffed and did not have time to update the website," but nonetheless, they needed a registered lease before they would issue an Elective Residence Visa.

We could only leave. There was nothing more to accomplish by continuing to question the staff officer. As I gathered up the stacks of paper, some slithered off onto the floor, and Dave and I scrambled to pick them up. I felt sick. My head was pounding and I was in a panic.

"What are we going to do now?" Dave asked. His face was worried, and he could tell how frantic I was. I honestly didn't know what to do. All my carefully researched plans had just blown up in our faces.

We walked to a nearby café, and Dave wanted to help, so I sent him to get a coffee for us, although caffeine was the last thing I needed. I sat looking as people walked past me, but I wasn't seeing anyone. My mind was racing. Finally, I dug out the contact information for the management company that had rented us an apartment in Rome. I called, hoping they could convert our lease to a "registered" one, but they couldn't help us. They didn't offer registered leases.

I dialed "P" in Rome and luckily reached her immediately. "The consulate rejected us. Do you know anything about the Agenzia delle Entrate? Is your lease registered with the tax authorities?"

"I've lived in Rome for years, but I don't know how my landlord handles the lease I sign. Maybe it is registered." She promised to check with her landlord and call me back. Dave and I sat at the small café talking and waiting for "P's" call. In less than an hour, she called with more information.

"My lease is not registered," she said. "My landlord didn't even want to talk to me about it. Tax authorities make Italians nervous."

Damn.

"Dave and I have talked," I said. "The only idea we can come up with is for you to sign a simple lease. A lease would be more official than a simple rental letter, even though it won't be registered with the tax authorities."

I found a simple lease form online, and I faxed it to "P" in Rome, who signed and returned it quickly. Maybe when we returned to the consulate for Dave's appointment, a kinder, gentler consular staff officer would overlook the registered lease rule and let us slide.

That evening in Chicago, I did more research on Italian registered leases. If we somehow found a landlord who would give us one, the price of our monthly rent would be significantly higher. The taxes on the rental income were 20-22%, so the landlord would charge us at least 5% of the total rental cost as an additional fee for registering the lease. Plus, there were stamps and other miscellaneous fees the landlord would expect us to

34

share. Italian landlords disliked registered leases because they were forced to actually pay taxes on the income (what a thought) and because the registered lease gave the tenant more rights and protections. Basically, the consulate was putting us in charge of making sure their citizens paid their taxes. We just wanted to live in Italy.

Two days later, we returned together to the consulate for Dave's appointment, along with our unregistered lease, and the consulate rejected us again. Later "P" refunded the €150 fee she charged to give us a rental letter.

At least we had tried again. I would have always wondered if maybe a second try at the consulate would have worked. Now we were forced to make a decision about what to do.

TIP: As of July 25, 2020, the Italian Consulate office website in Chicago still does not specify that a registered lease is required to obtain an Elective Residence Visa.

• EUROPE PLAN B - NO VISA •

After being rejected for a visa in Chicago by the Italian consulate, we went home to Denver to regroup. All the elements of our Bel Sogno plan were in place. We held one-way plane tickets to Rome, leaving in two months, and had an apartment rented in Rome. We had rented our home in Denver, made arrangements for our dog, our finances were in order, and we'd begun selling and packing extraneous things. Shortening the trip or staying home were not options.

Since we'd been denied a visa from Italy and only had two months before we left the U.S., there was no time to try to get a visa from a different Schengen country. (I learned later that Poland approved 90% of all visa requests.) The rules were clear. Without a visa from a Schengen country, we would have to leave the Schengen area after 90 days, and we could not return to *any* country within the Schengen area until a full 90 days elapsed. Our post 911 world is computerized, and officials were looking more closely at visas. I had no intention of trying to break the rules and overstay our visa (although some in the Expats Living in Rome group urged us to do that).

So *Europe* Plan B began to emerge from the wreckage of Plan A. In September, we would leave the U.S. as planned and spend 90 days in Rome—no visa required. (Our landlord in Rome was very accommodating and changed our rental to only three months when I told her about our visa problems.) Then we would spend the rest of our year.....somewhere. We hauled out a large atlas of the world and spread it out on the kitchen table.

"We can go to Greece, can't we?" I asked. Dave checked the Schengen list.

"Nope. Greece is part of the Schengen zone," he said.

"I want someplace warm," I mused out loud, moving my finger around the map. Spain. Portugal. Malta. No and no and no. Leaving Europe entirely didn't appeal to either of us. We wanted Europe. One by one, we ruled out the countries we couldn't go to. Then I saw Croatia, just east of Italy, on the Adriatic Sea.

Although it joined the European Union in 2013, Croatia was not yet part of the Schengen Area. Under Croatian law, we could stay in Croatia for 90 days without obtaining any special visa. "Croatia?" I looked at Dave with my eyebrow raised in question. We quickly agreed on Croatia for the winter portion of our trip—December, January, and February. Croatia would be less expensive so that we could save up a little money. It was more of a southerly country, and maybe the winter would be warmer there.

The rest of Europe Plan B quickly fell into place. We would go to expensive London for the spring—March, April, and May—when the weather there improved a little. I had visited London once, but Dave had never been. Great Britain was not part of the Schengen Area.

For the final 90 days of our year-long adventure—June, July, and August of 2018, after being out of the Schengen area for six months—we would return to Italy and live in Venice. Italy would be the beginning and the ending of our one-year adventure. This wasn't the same dream trip we spent years imagining, and I had some hesitation as we penciled in a rough draft of our future lives, but it was too late for second thoughts. We were going forward.

• MOVING DAY •

With only four days to go until departure, we began moving some furniture out of our house and into our two-car garage where we planned to store it for the year we would be gone. I was keeping an eye on the budget, and using the garage for storage saved us expensive storage fees. Every penny we didn't spend in the U.S. was extra money we would have available to spend in Europe.

Our camper was going to be stored in half the garage, along with some of our furniture. Dave made sure there was enough room for Aliciah to park her car. Loading the garage with furniture was a fun challenge for Dave, who thought of himself as a Tetris master when it came to fitting lots of things into a small space. It took us a long time to get it exactly the way he wanted, and there was still the entire house left to clean. The day started with a lot of progress but ended badly.

I was mopping the living room, and as Dave walked by, he grabbed the mop bucket and headed to the bedroom. I wiped my sweaty forehead and walked after my mop bucket.

"I wasn't finished with this. Can't you just wait?" I snapped at him. I knew I was unreasonable and that he was just trying to help, but at the same time, my head was pounding, I felt hot, sweaty, and hungry, and we had just started cleaning. That would take all day. I especially wanted it perfect because my friend was moving in, and I didn't want so much as a stray hair on the sink. Dave didn't say a word as he grabbed the vacuum cleaner and went downstairs, leaving me alone with my mop bucket. We didn't talk for hours.

As I cleaned, I felt more and more guilty and sad. It started in my toes and moved up into my chest until I thought it would drown me. We had spent all these months planning and implementing this move. It was all stressful. There was a long list of things to do. We were trying to think of everything. Neither of us wanted to forget something we would be unable to fix once we moved overseas.

We had been taking turns waking up in the middle of the night with another new thought about something we should do before leaving. In the mornings after a bad night's sleep, we would regale each other with our nighttime worries and try to sort out what was an important worry versus an unimportant one. It was a big step to pack up our lives and live out of suitcases for a year.

As I mopped, I thought about how we each reacted to stress. Dave withdrew into silence and kept his worries inside. I handled stress by talking more and making even longer lists. Silence, predictably, drove me crazy, and so I talked more. I didn't want to spend our year arguing. I wanted our life in Europe to be perfect. Once we got to our destination, would the stress let up a little?

At the end of the day, I apologized for being a hopeless grump, and we talked about the last few months of anxiety and tension and excitement. We were back on the same team again. At this point, we were both on the same wild, out-of-control, bucking ride called "don't you want to live in Europe for a year?" and the ride wasn't over yet.

• ALMOST DEPARTURE DAY •

The day before leaving, I tried to print boarding passes and got an error message. "An error has occurred. Please check-in at the airport." This was not what should happen the day before we left the U.S. with our entire lives packed into four suitcases. I called the company that had booked the airline, and after checking the computer, they assured me we were checked in. I still couldn't relax, so I also called the U.S. airline in charge of getting us from Denver to Boston, and they agreed we were checked in but didn't know why I couldn't get our boarding passes. Finally, I called the foreign airline and they gave me the same answer. We were checked in and would just need to go to the airport to get boarding passes. Panic subsided.

Now just hours from leaving our lives behind for a year, I thought about all the things we wouldn't do: We wouldn't see our family for a year. We probably wouldn't drive a car or operate a clothes dryer. Apartments we saw online often included clothes washers, but it was extremely unusual to find one with a dryer, and of course, we would cook and eat differently too.

Our old life began to feel like a dream, a memory, but our new life hadn't started.

After everything we've been through just to get to this point, I wonder how our lives will be different when we return from our year of travels.

PART II: ROME

• DEPARTURE DAY •

The day before we left the U.S., we had taken the time to weigh our suitcases, and each of our carry-ons was almost double the 17-pound airline weight limit. "The airlines never weigh carry-on luggage." That argument didn't even convince me. *What if this is the one and only flight where the airline weigh carry-ons?* I began pulling last-minute things out of each bag.

While Dave re-checked the weight, I looked critically at our ten-year-old scuffed and stained suitcases.

"These old things look bad. The wheel on my carry-on is pretty dodgy. It goes every direction except straight."

Dave stood considering the suitcases. "The best thing about these suitcases is that no one will want to steal them."

"True, and we can spend the hundreds of dollars we save on new luggage on wine in Italy." Being basically cheap when it came to spending money meant we had talked ourselves out of new suitcases.

The night before we left, I spent hours tossing and turning in bed— constant worries. Would we oversleep? Would the alarms go off? My stomach was churning from a mixture of anticipation, anxiety, excitement, and terror.

As soon as the alarm went off, both of us jumped up, started dressing, and began final packing. We took our suitcases out to the sidewalk to wait for the Uber driver. More worries. Would the Uber driver show up? Would he be late? Would he get a flat tire on the way to the airport? Every possible problem bounced around inside my head.

We arrived at the airport by 7:15 a.m. for our 10:23 a.m. flight. The airline check-in desk wasn't even open yet. After breakfast, when we walked back to the check-in desk, there were only three people in line, and when our turn came, there were no problems. Happily, the friendly ticket agent printed all of our boarding passes for each leg of our trip, so we wouldn't need to wait in more lines along the way.

As we waited to get through Denver airport security, I tensed up, anticipating the first test of our trip—would I be able to get my beer cooler full of insulin through security? My insulin stockpiles added up to a lot more than three ounces of liquids. In my hand, I had a letter from my endocrinologist, documenting my diabetes, and I planned to fight to take every ounce of insulin onto the plane. When my cooler was flagged and pulled off of the security conveyor belt, I stepped up to the TSA. official who was opening it.

"Is this yours?" he asked.

"Yes. I am diabetic and need my insulin."

He lifted the ice packet on the top and pulled out a vial of insulin and read the box label. He was tall with a short buzz cut. His uniform was well ironed, and his pants had a sharp crease. He wasn't smiling and gave off an "I play by the book" vibe. I watched him intently, saying nothing. When he put down my insulin without saying another word, zipped the bag, and handed it to me, I gave a silent sigh of relief. No problems.

Our plane from Denver left on time, and we arrived in Boston with two hours to spare. My heart dropped when we boarded the plane in Boston, and I saw our seats for the long Boston to Lisbon portion of our flight. They were terrible seats. On this plane there were two seats down the left side of the plane, two seats down the right side, and four seats side by side in the middle. Our seats were in the middle of the section of four.

We would have to climb over people to get in and out. We would be forced to share armrests. Since I had paid an extra $40 per seat to get "bulkhead" seats, I was not happy. The bulkhead is the dividing wall between cabins on long-haul flights. Bulkhead seats have almost an extra foot of legroom. Our seats were not in the bulkhead row. I wondered if the plane we were on was the same design as the plane I had seen when I initially booked online, months earlier. But this plane was full, and I didn't know how they could have moved us, so we climbed into our seats without complaint. At least the seats themselves were reasonably large, with a fair amount of leg space. There were many movies to choose from and the food turned out to be was semi-decent for airline food. We would survive.

After arriving in Lisbon, we had only one hour to get to our connecting flight to Rome. This had been worrying me for months. Dave and I rushed off the plane as quickly as possible and, in the airport, paused only a second to scan the monitors and find our gate for the Rome flight. We ran through the airport, zigging and zagging around people and obstacles, turned around a corner, then slammed to a stop in a long passport control line.

The line wasn't moving at all. I kept glancing at my watch, and each time I did, I felt my blood pressure skyrocketing. After five minutes of standing in line, I was too anxious just to wait there and tried to think of something I could do to keep my head from exploding. There was an airport official nearby wearing a cheap yellow plastic vest with an ID around his neck, and I left Dave in the motionless line to ask him about getting to our gate.

"We have a flight to Rome in one hour!" My voice came out in a breathless screech. The official opened up one section of the retractable belt divider and waved me, Dave, and another couple to the front of the passport line. As soon as we had passport stamps, we began running again for our gate. I was breathless, gasping, and dragging my carry-on suitcase while the unreliable wheel kept trying to flip the suitcase over. At least we were moving.

Then we plowed into *another* line, a slow-moving security line with everyone peeling off their jackets and piling luggage onto the scanners. I found another official in a yellow plastic vest and waved my boarding pass at him (Running out of time, dude!!), and he waved us to the front of the security line. I have never thrown off my jacket and shoes so fast.

After security, we both grabbed our suitcases and continued running for our gate. Rounding a corner, we skidded to a stop at our gate in the Executive Members line just as the plane was boarding. We barely made it. Dave was carrying his belt, and my shoes weren't tied, but we were going to Rome.

As I entered the plane, prepared to enjoy the perks of the $290 upgraded "Executive" class passes I had purchased, the attendant handed all of us, both Executive and non-Executive passengers, identical boxes of food. The Executive upgrade on this two-hour flight from Lisbon to Rome consisted of a grey curtain the attendant pulled together to separate us "Executives" from the lowly non-Executive passengers in the back of the plane. The attendant didn't bring us anything to drink and only gave me coffee and water after I asked for it. I was silently fuming because I had paid an extra $290 just so that we could sit on the plane in front of the grey curtain. Closing my eyes and leaning back, I tried to rest. It was impossible. My body was still full of adrenaline from our sprint through the airport. Giving up, I sat and looked out the window at the soft pink sunrise, envious of all the sleeping people around me.

TIP: Every time I traveled on a plane, I worried security would confiscate my insulin, but I never once got more than a routine question before guards waved me through security along with my cooler bag of insulin. I did keep all of my insulin and other prescriptions in their original boxes with the prescription labels even though this added to the bulk of everything crammed into the cooler.

• CHAOS aka ARRIVAL IN ROME •

Rome's Fiumicino airport is like most airports the world over—follow the luggage signs and wait in passport control lines. This time there was no hurry to get through the lines, and we could finally relax. I was exhausted and exhilarated at the same time. *This is it. It is all starting now.* As we waited to collect our checked bags we high-fived each other, and I resisted the urge to do a little dance of glee.

We bought train tickets on the Leonardo Express train to travel from the airport to Rome's central train station. I used the airport Wi-Fi to email our landlord and tell her we had arrived in Rome. We couldn't call or text with our phones since our phone numbers were ported (transferred) over to Google Voice, and we needed to buy new Italian SIM cards for our phones before they would work in Italy. We planned to buy the SIM cards at Stazione Termini, the train station in central Rome.

As soon as we arrived at Termini train station, we launched into our "to-do" list. We were so organized. I had thought of all of this for months. I silently congratulated myself on my incredible planning and detailed list-making skills. Dave went to Vodafone to get two Italian SIM cards for our unlocked U.S. phones. I went to the tabacchi shop inside the train station to buy our monthly bus passes. Then I walked downstairs to the ATM to get cash with my Capital One ATM card—and the card didn't work. The message on the ATM screen said the "card is not valid for international transactions." I felt like somebody had punched me in the stomach. This was bad, very bad.

Back upstairs, I found Dave, still at the Vodafone store, working with the phone rep to get our phones up and running. He looked like a refugee, surrounded by our suitcases, backpacks, and my beer cooler of insulin.

"Small problem." My voice was deliberately casual. "My ATM card didn't work. Let me take your ATM card."

"That shouldn't make any difference," Dave said, handing over his card. "Both cards are on the same account and work the same way."

"Hey, I don't know what else to do. I'll be right back." I took the stairs back to the ATM machine and waited in line again, but Dave's card didn't work either. I pulled out my credit card and fed it into the machine to get an ATM cash advance, but that didn't work either. The line behind me waiting for the ATM was getting long, and I was tired, flustered, and confused. My head was aching, and I really needed water. I trudged back upstairs, and Dave and I talked about what to do next.

"Come downstairs. You try the machine. Maybe I'm doing something wrong," I said.

We went downstairs together, waited in line, and watched other people using the ATM machine and getting cash. No one else was having problems. When our turn came, both of us tried both of our ATM cards and credit cards. Nothing worked. We couldn't go to our apartment until we could get enough cash to pay the €1,200 damage deposit. We had brought some euros with us, saved from our last trip to Europe years ago, but it was not enough. There weren't many choices.

"Should we go outside the terminal and look for a different ATM?" Dave asked. I looked around the terminal, crowded with people pushing their way through. There were three exits from the terminal and we didn't know which one led to an ATM. We were dragging four suitcases, two backpacks and a beer cooler full of insulin. It was confusing and overwhelming and we were both exhausted.

"No. Let's just get to our apartment and drop our stuff. Then look for another ATM."

Dave and I reluctantly took a credit card and found a currency exchange office inside Termini and paid what amounted to $1,131 to get just €800. With the other euros we brought with us, we would be able to pay our apartment damage deposit, but these fees would kill us if our ATM card refused to work.

After getting our cash together, I tried to use the Wi-Fi at the train station to email the landlord and tell her we were coming immediately to the apartment, but the Wi-Fi at Termini did not work on our phones.

"Why did the Wi-Fi at the airport work but not the Wi-Fi here at the train station?" I asked tech man Dave. My mood was sinking into a sleep-deprived cranky mode. Dave didn't know what was wrong, and that irritated me. At this point, we were both tired and frazzled—frightened our ATM cards were somehow defective—and more than a little ready for a gallon of coffee, a shower, and sleep.

At least Italian SIM cards were in our phones and we could make calls immediately. I dug through my folder of important papers and found the landlord's phone number.

"Donata?" I asked tentatively when I got an answer. "This is Pam. We are in Rome. Can you meet us at the apartment now?"

"Now I am not in Rome," Donata said. "You call Ruby to get in apartment." She gave me Ruby's number. After emailing the landlord for months to confirm our trip plans, it stunned me that she had never mentioned she wouldn't be there when we arrived to let us in, and she had never given me Ruby's number. The lack of sleep was catching up with me, and I felt overly confused.

So I called Ruby and got some guy who only knew enough English to say, "I am not Ruby. I send number," before he hung up. We collapsed onto seats in a café at the station to drink coffee, and thankfully I received a text with a new phone number for Ruby. That number actually reached Ruby, who spoke English, and who was at the apartment waiting for us. Finally, something in this day of chaos was going our way.

We took a taxi to the apartment and met Ruby, who took our deposit, gave us a receipt, and walked us through how everything in the apartment worked. We needed to know the Wi-Fi password, how to handle trash and recycling, how to operate appliances, and how to find the local grocery store. I eyed the tiny Moka pot used to make coffee. A small coffee pot would definitely not work for us—we both took our morning caffeine very seriously. Ruby gave us an emergency contact number in case of a serious malfunction in the apartment. Fire or flood? Ruby promised to bring us a clothing rack to hang our washed clothes to dry and left us alone in our apartment.

By now, it was about 2 p.m. local time, and even though the bed was calling, jet lag would be a little easier if I could get my body on local time as quickly as possible. If I sat, I would sleep. Staying in motion was the answer.

"I could easily crash now and sleep forever, but I am worried about the ATM card," I said to Dave. "I'm going to splash water on my face, and then we need to find another ATM machine. And we need to pray it works." When I came out of the bathroom, Dave had used the apartment Wi-Fi and his phone to find a nearby ATM machine, so we left the apartment and began walking.

"Every bone and joint in my body is tired and sore." I couldn't help moaning as we walked.

"In college, not sleeping for 24 hours was easy. Now I'm too old for that."

"How far is this ATM?" I asked, collapsing onto the stone steps of a building.

Dave consulted his phone. "I think there?" He turned the phone sideways and looked doubtfully across a busy street.

"Here. Give me the phone." He handed it over, and I squinted at it. "We need to cross this busy street and go to the right. It is a little way down the street."

We began walking again and found the ATM machine. I held my breath as Dave inserted his ATM card. Success! He withdrew the maximum daily cash allowed and jammed the wad of euros into his wallet. After a very early dinner at a restaurant close to the ATM, we trudged wearily back toward our apartment for showers and a very early bedtime. For the first time in weeks, both of us slept deeply and soundly.

P.S.   We never had another problem with our ATM cards during our entire year of travel and never solved the mystery of why the ATM card didn't work at the train station.

51

• SETTLING IN •

The next day we needed groceries for our apartment, but instead we walked to Vodafone. Our phones were still not working. A Vodafone store was not far away, but there was so much to see on the way that it took us over an hour to walk there. We stopped at a little bakery and ordered coffee and a pastry for breakfast. Walking along, Dave and I both kept stopping to look at stores, churches, and shops, marveling at how different everything was. Along the way, we found a grocery store and ducked inside briefly to check out the food options. We continued walking and, after a few wrong turns, finally arrived at Vodafone. At first, the lady working there didn't acknowledge us. When we finally got her attention, she didn't acknowledge me, only Dave. Well, my Italian was limited to general language skills and I didn't speak "phone tech."

"Yes?" she questioned us abruptly. Good. She spoke English.

Dave was the phone guy, so he took over. "We bought SIM cards at the train station yesterday, but our phones are still not working." She took the phone out of his hand and tossed her hair over one shoulder. She was making eye contact with Dave while ignoring me.

She pulled the SIM card out of the phone and I wandered away to look at the store displays. After a brief conversation with her, Dave came over to find me.

"She says our phones are not "unlocked" phones and that we can't use them in Italy."

"What! We deliberately bought new unlocked phones for *this* trip, to use in Italy, and they are wrong?"

"She says we have to buy an Italian phone. They have one for €19," Dave said. We walked over to look at the phones and took the one she offered us, the cheapest phone in the store, which rang up for €90. This was the first time we ran into a common Italian misunderstanding or mispronunciation of the words nineteen and ninety, seventeen and seventy, sixteen and sixty. Actually, they do sound an awful lot alike.

So we bought the €90 Italian phone and left. Just outside the store, Dave used the new Italian phone to call Verizon in the U.S. to complain about our phones not working in Italy. Verizon insisted our phones were unlocked, as promised, and advised us to go into settings on our phones and change the Access Point Name (APN) to the APN of Vodafone. We went back inside Vodafone and explained the APN problem to a different employee who quickly understood the problem and fixed our U.S. phones. They worked immediately. The rude Vodafone lady didn't know what she was talking about. By this time, there was a long line of people waiting for phone help, so we decided to box up the €90 phone at our apartment and return it the next day.

As we walked back to our apartment, it was lunch-time, and we stopped to grab lunch and a glass of wine at a sidewalk café. *Time to celebrate*, I thought. For the first time in months, I felt truly relaxed. We'd done it. We'd made the leap and were *living* in Rome.

"What is the plan for tomorrow?" Dave asked. "Colosseum?"

I sat back in the chair, crossed my legs, and let the afternoon sun soak into my shoulders as I listened to the people near me speaking Italian. Italian! On this one warm afternoon in Rome, I didn't feel the need to plan or try to control anything.

We ate lunch and drank a second glass of wine and talked about making a stop at the grocery store before going home. I asked for the check ("vorrei il conto"), and Dave pulled out his credit card and handed it to the waiter.

"Uh, no, this does not work. No cards," the waiter said, handing back the credit card. The waiter wandered off, and Dave pulled out his wallet. Inside was a lone €10 note.

"Do you have any cash?" he asked.

"Not on me. Where is all the cash we pulled from the ATM yesterday?"

"At home."

When the waiter returned, Dave handed him the €10 note and promised to return to pay the balance. I was embarrassed, but the waiter smiled and casually waved us away. We walked home, and Dave went back to the café with the additional cash to pay the bill. *How trusting these Romans are*. It was an excellent start to our stay in Rome after the fiasco of the day we arrived.

The following day we walked back to return the €90 Italian phone to Vodafone—no refunds. Again the rude lady waited on us, and imagine her surprise when Dave told her all we needed to make our phones work was the APN for Vodafone. All of us learned something here, only it cost us €90, and she got to keep being rude to people.

During the next few weeks, we spent a lot of time learning our way around and shopping for groceries and household goods for our apartment. Becoming comfortable using the bus and metro would take some time. I became the family navigator and relied heavily on Google Maps and its section on public transportation showing bus and train lines. I also downloaded the Moovit app because it told me when buses would be arriving. I could check Moovit from our apartment, and we would either fly out the door to catch the next bus or, if there was time, hang out and finish our coffee. For our little apartment, we needed a decent knife (only one steak knife in the rental), more towels (we brought two, and the apartment came with none), a bath mat, spatula, and ice cube trays for the shoe-box sized freezer. Our friendly Expats Living in Rome group directed me to a home goods store called Satur. Dave and I made a trip there one morning.

The building was on a corner, small, but once we walked inside, I saw that the shelves were jam-packed with goods. I couldn't understand how the store was organized and found rugs next to coffee cups.

"Let's split up," I said, after wandering together down one disorganized aisle.

Dave moved to the next aisle. I edged slowly through the store, picking up anything useful. I found the towels we needed next to an assortment of candles and picked up both. A bath mat was in the aisle with glassware, and I grabbed a vase for flowers. I sidled sideways through some parts of the narrow, overflowing aisles, and my arms were getting full. Carts were not available and wouldn't fit in the aisle anyway. I saw Dave at the end of my aisle and went to catch up with him.

"What did you find?" I looked at the assortment of goods in his hands.

"A French press coffee pot, wine glasses, and two potholders."

"I didn't know we needed all that."

"You haven't been doing the cooking." It was true. Since I was learning to navigate the city, scanning guidebooks, maps, and apps, Dave had volunteered to do the grocery shopping and cooking. He knew the kitchen better than I did.

We went to the cashier to pay, and behind the counter, I saw knives. We added one to our pile of home goods and paid the cashier. The store didn't have shopping bags, so we left to walk home with some things tucked into Dave's backpack and the rest in our arms.

"Okay, so we need to keep looking for a spatula and ice cube trays," I said, grabbing the bath mat that was slipping out of my arms.

Dave nodded. "And I need to add a shopping bag to my backpack. This isn't the first store that expected us to have our own shopping bags."

After arriving home and putting things away, I lit a candle and mentally added "cut flowers" to my shopping list. After only a few weeks in Rome, it was already beginning to feel like home.

• MONEY, MONEY, MONEY •

Before leaving the country and even as we traveled, people would ask us how we could afford our trip. "Did you win the lottery?" a friend of Dave's asked him.

People were curious about exactly *how* we would pay for an entire year in Europe. I was curious about that myself. For non-lottery winners, like us, who want to live overseas, this is how we dealt with money.

When we first started planning our trip, both of us were determined only to spend our monthly retirement income in Europe. Using up our savings or running up credit card bills was not in the plan. Tracking spending would keep us on budget, but I didn't want to spend time counting every penny. We intended to mostly use cash as we traveled, so the "daily cash spending allowance" was born.

At home, budgeting was my job, and so I took over budgeting money for our trip. Naturally, I began by creating a list. I listed our U.S. income and our U.S. fixed expenses on the top of page one of our budget sheet. Our U.S. fixed expenses included our mortgage, HOA fees, life insurance, and camper payment. By selling our cars, we got rid of insurance, taxes, and license fees. We got rid of cable TV, magazine, and newspaper subscriptions. We avoided furniture fees by using our garage for storage. As we packed, we sold off odds and ends of excess furniture and electronics. The last year before leaving, we were very frugal with money and added every penny possible to our savings by eliminating every expense we could.

After deducting our U.S. expenses from our U.S. income, we had a certain number of dollars available to spend in Europe. I converted the leftover dollars into euros, and I also added *that* number on page one of the budget sheet. (At the time we left for Italy one U.S. dollar was equal to 0.85 euros so $100 equaled €85. The conversion rate fluctuated daily but not by very much.) Next, I deducted our Italian fixed expenses from this euro amount. In Italy, we paid rent each month, paid our monthly cell phone bills with Vodafone, and paid for monthly transportation passes. I built extra travel money into our Rome budget so we could take short trips around Europe.

After carving out 20% for miscellaneous expenses, I took the 80% remainder and divided it by 30 (days per month), and voilà, I had our "daily cash spending allowance." This figure was the amount we could spend each day without jeopardizing our ability to pay all of our monthly bills, without using up our savings, and without running up credit card bills.

If this sounds complicated, it really isn't. For example, using made-up numbers:

Total U.S. income:	$5,000
Minus total U.S. expense	$1,000
Remainder in dollars	$4,000
Convert dollars to euros	€3,400 ($4,000 x 0.85)
Minus total Italian expenses	€2,000
Remainder in euros	€1,400
20% set aside for miscellaneous expenses	€280
80% for "daily cash spending allowance	€1,120
Calculation of daily spending Allowance (€1,120 divided by 30 days per month)	€37.3

In Rome, we went to the ATM every eight to ten days and pulled out cash to keep at home. Each day we would pull our spending allowance out of the cash stash at home and spend it as we went around the city. Dave carried the daily cash and paid for meals, groceries, or museum admissions. I carried some back-up euros and a credit card. I could spend money, but it was easier to stick to the budget if we spent just the daily cash allowance. If there was money leftover on one day, it carried over to the next.

The 20% I set aside for miscellaneous expenses came in handy when we moved from one country to another. The first few days in a new place were always expensive. A new country meant a big "stock up" at the grocery store. We ate out more until we could buy groceries. There were always small household things missing from the rental apartment that we needed to buy.

Still, we needed a way to keep track of credit card charges and ATM withdrawals. It was easy to forget a €60 dinner we splurged on when it was two weeks ago. So I created a second page of our budget, with four columns, to track credit card spending and ATM/cash withdrawals.

This was what the second page of our budget looked like:

DATE	CREDIT CARD SPENDING	DESCRIPTION	ATM/ CASH
1st	23.00	Lunch	
2nd			500.00
3rd			

I could look at this second page, and it was easy to see our spending for the month, to run some preliminary totals, and determine if we needed to cut back a little or if everything was on track. Creating the daily allowance and the two-page budget list satisfied my need to monitor the money and keep our budget on track, but I didn't feel like watching the budget was a burden.

To keep expenses down while in Europe, we didn't get particularly nice apartments. Our apartments were functional and in a good location, which sometimes meant they were a little scruffy around the edges. The one in Rome could have done with a new paint job and an updated kitchen. The latch on a window shutter was broken, and Dave taped it with some heavy-duty tape to keep it from popping off in our hands. We didn't have large apartments with a balcony or outdoor space, but our apartments were always clean and in safe neighborhoods.

We really only held onto two hard and fast requirements for any apartment we rented over the course of the year. It had to have a washing machine (no laundromats for me), and it had to have a separate bedroom. Being together on this trip for hours every day, day after day, was going to be a challenge in itself. Before retirement, Dave and I lived like most working couples—alongside each other, but busy in our separate ways. Of course, we were together evenings and weekends, but we spent our work-days with co-workers. At home, there was room to spread out and we each had our own way of doing things. We had our separate routines, schedules, and hobbies. Spending every day, all day crammed on top of each other in a small studio apartment did not sound appealing. Even though we could have saved money with a studio apartment, it wasn't going to happen.

Every step of the way, both of us tried to look for ways to make our trip affordable. Being able to travel to Europe for an entire year was like winning the lottery, but budget-wise it was essential to watch our spending and keep it within our income.

TIP: *After going to the ATM and getting extra cash to use for daily expenses, we needed to find someplace to keep it in the apartment. It wasn't a good idea to walk around town carrying hundreds of euros. We didn't know how secure our apartment was, if spare keys were floating around from past renters or if anyone would break-in. Our apartment in Rome was pretty bare-bones, and there were not a lot of hiding spaces. Finally, I thought of the box of cereal in the kitchen. I pulled out the paper bag of cereal from inside the cereal box, dropped our passports and cash inside, and put the paper bag back in the box. I had been robbed years before in the U.S., and the robbers tore my home office, bedrooms, and living space apart, looking for cash and jewelry. I didn't think a thief would rifle through our food looking for money or valuables. We never experienced a problem with theft in Europe, and I never worried about leaving money and passports in the apartment when we were gone for the day.*

• DAILY LIFE •

Once we arrived in Rome, stocked up on groceries, and learned our way around by bus at least a little, we launched into daily life. Our apartment worked very well. It was small, only about 350 square feet. From a quiet alley, barely wide enough for two cars, a short flight of stairs led to our apartment. Behind a thick steel door was our living room. There was a daybed/couch in the living room, and a pretty antique table pushed up against the wall became our dining table. Behind the wall on the right was our small kitchen with a washing machine, a two-burner electric stove, and a dorm-sized fridge. Even though I knew in advance about the small fridge, seeing it in person was a shock. My insulin alone would take up a chunk of space. The apartment did not include a clothes dryer, an oven, dishwasher, toaster, or microwave.

On the left was the doorway to the bedroom which had a giant wall of closets for storing our clothes and suitcases. Past the bedroom was a small TV area with one comfortable chair and room for the clothes rack, where our clothes hung to dry, and then the bathroom. The bathroom was tiny, small enough that in the shower I bumped my elbows on the glass walls as I shampooed my hair, but it managed to fit both a toilet and a bidet. Nothing says, "you're not in America anymore," quite like a bidet.

The entire apartment was painted bland beige and was a little scruffy, but the floors were warm wood parquet. There were heavy green wooden shutters on the windows. Every morning I opened the shutters, leaned out, and looked at the narrow cobblestone alley and the clotheslines crisscrossing it. At night, closing the shutters always ended the day in our new country. There were no pictures on the apartment walls, but I bought a large poster of the cityscape of Rome to tack onto one wall, and with our few books on the shelves, some flowers, and a scented candle on the table, the rooms became our home away from home.

Almost our first stop after arriving was to go to the grocery store. On our walk to Vodafone to sort out our phone problems, we found our small neighborhood grocery store. It was easy to miss being on the first floor of a large stone building with no signage out front. On our first trip there to stock up, the two of us went together with extra cash. After walking inside, I could see that although this tiny store had aisles of produce, meat, and frozen foods, there the resemblance to an American grocery store ended.

"Do we need one of these?" Dave asked, indicating a small plastic cart with wheels. Glancing around, I saw others pulling carts around the store.

"Yes. Today we need a lot of things. Definitely a cart."

The first section of the store was produce. "We need fruit, lettuce for salads, potatoes, onions, and garlic." I read from the list I had put together at home. Dave reached for some apples.

"Hold it," I said quickly. "You can't touch the produce with your hand."

"Why not?"

"It isn't considered hygienic or clean. You need a glove."

Standing to one side, I watched a few customers in the produce section and then made my move. I took a thin plastic glove from a dispenser and put it on. Each item of produce was in a plastic bin with the name of the produce, the price, and a two or three-digit number on the front. I needed that number. I put each item of produce in a separate plastic bag and took them one at a time over to the nearby scale. After I placed my produce on the machine, numbers 1 to 100 popped up on the screen, and I selected the number corresponding to the number on the bin of my produce. The machine spit out a sticky label, which I attached to the plastic bag.

Dave dragged the cart to the next aisle as I followed behind him, trying to read labels. There were only four aisles left. The entire store was no larger than the bakery section of my U.S. grocery store. *Would we even find everything here?* I wondered. The next aisle was personal and cleaning supplies. I saw some familiar brands of shampoo and soap, but the selection was minimal. If you didn't like one of the three shampoos on offer, you were out of luck. Cleaning and laundry supplies were not familiar brands, and I examined them while Dave pulled out his phone to use Google Translate.

"What is this?" I asked, handing Dave a plastic jug of (maybe) laundry detergent. He examined the bottle and fed the name into Google Translate. Grocery shopping was taking a long time.

"That is laundry detergent," he said, reading the translation from his phone. I put it in our cart.

Although the store was tiny, one whole side of an aisle was full of nothing but pasta. Pasta created a diabetic dilemma for me. Like all diabetics, I controlled my blood sugar by limiting carbohydrates. All day long, I estimated the number of carbs in the food and drink I consumed (with the help of the Fat Secret app on my phone) and then took insulin to offset the carbs. Pasta was high in carbs, but this was Italy, and pasta was everywhere. Even this mini grocery store offered dozens and dozens of different sizes and shapes. Tonnarelli? Chitarra? These pastas were all new to me. My cart was full of salad and vegetables from the produce aisle, but pasta would be a big part of my food options in Italy, and I would just have to adjust the amount of insulin I took.

"Here you go. Take this." I handed Dave two packages of pasta and some ready-made pasta sauce to put in the cart before moving on to the olive oil section.

Dave picked up a bottle of olive oil. "Will you look at this? Have you ever seen so many olive oils?" he asked. I stood beside him and examined the dozens of labels. There were almost as many olive oils as there were kinds of pasta. I had no idea which one to buy, but we needed oil right away, so I chose a middle-priced, extra virgin olive oil.

It took me a long time to find eggs—finally noticing them, un-refrigerated, at the end of an aisle. Eggs make the perfect low-carb diabetic-friendly breakfasts, so I grabbed two packages. Since my insulin took up a lot of space in our tiny fridge, it was good that the European eggs could sit out on the counter. My love affair with European eggs began with that first carton. The yolks were thick, dark yellow, and they tasted rich and, well, like eggs.

We finished up our shopping with some other staples, including a few bottles of wine for just €3 each, and then prepared to lug our supplies over the bridge to our apartment. On our first trip to the grocery store, examining everything and translating labels took well over an hour. Future trips would be much easier when we weren't stocking up and when the brands became more familiar. All the new food choices at my fingertips were thrilling.

TIP: If you get to the cashier and don't have stickers on your fruits and vegetables, the cashier will curse quietly in Italian, all the people in the grocery store line will curse softly, and you will be sent back to do it right.

• A ROMAN STYLE PUB CRAWL •

Every day after breakfast, we set out to explore the city. We began at the usual tourist sites like the Trevi Fountain and Spanish Steps, but even in September, Rome was overwhelmed with tourists. And it was hot, lacking any hint of cooler autumn air. The cobblestone streets and thick stone buildings soaked in the sun. I decided to get off the tourist path and explore away from the crowds for a few weeks until the tourists left, and we had the city to ourselves. Beer seemed an obvious place to begin.

In Denver, I had taken Italian language classes with the Dante Alighieri Society at Our Lady of Mt. Carmel Church. The Society also gave cultural talks and lectures, so Dave and I had attended a lecture on Italian craft beers offered by two guys, Bryan Jansing and Paul Vismara. I thought of Italy as strictly wine country, but we talked to Bryan and Paul after the lecture, and when they learned about our plan to be in Rome for three months, they gave us the names of a half dozen places to get craft beer. Before leaving the U.S., I studied Bryan and Paul's beer book, stunned to see that our apartment was, coincidentally, just blocks from several of the beer pubs they recommended. When we arrived in Rome, their book was in my suitcase.

There were definitely no tourist hordes at our first beer pit stop, Bir & Fud. We walked out of our apartment around the corner and only about 50 yards down the road to get there. The bar was a long narrow room with easily a dozen beers on tap. We found a table outside on the patio.

"What do you want?" Dave asked as he examined the beer list.

"You know me, the fruitier the beer, the better."

Besides Italian craft beers, they offered a few typical European beers, and Dave picked a craft beer for each of us. Dave likes to think of himself as a beer expert and tried dozens of craft beers in the short time we lived in Denver. I am a wine person and tend to stick to fruity beers while Dave tries not to judge my limited taste. Sometimes if fruity beers are not available, Dave will pick a super thick, dark beer for me to try, and when I don't want to finish it, he polishes it off for me. He thinks I don't see through his trick.

"Where to now?" Dave asked after we finished our beers.

"Now, we go....there." I pointed across the alley from Bir & Fud to an even smaller bar called Ma Che Siete Venuti a Fà (translated as "What the hell did you come here for?" Some kind of rude comment typical of Rome, we were told.) The space in Ma Che Siete was even smaller than our tiny Roman apartment, the walls solid stone. No windows, and the dark coolness reminded me of my Grandma's basement. Outside it was hot and humid, but the thick walls made the room feel 10 degrees cooler.

"There are no fruity beers here. At least, I don't think so," Dave said, opening the beer menu on the table and checking Google Translate. Finally, he picked a Papa Nero thick, dense black stout for himself and something lighter for me, and we sat sipping them as I surveyed the room. There wasn't an empty seat at any of the handful of tables inside the bar. A TV attached to the wall showed a soccer match, and the small crowd cheered from time to time. It was cool and comfortable inside, and I considered staying longer, but after the beers, I needed food. Leaving the bar, we pushed through crowds of drinkers and smokers on the street outside. More proof this was not America—public drinking in the streets.

It was almost dark as we trekked our way across the Ponte Sisto Bridge toward our next stop at Open Baladin, a 10-minute walk away, just off the busy Via Arenula. The cobblestones radiated heat back into the evening air, and I didn't think the city would cool off for hours.

Baladin was huge compared to the two beer spots we'd been in, and I immediately felt at home. On one wall of the large room, a chalkboard listed dozens of current beers on tap. I focused on the available fruity beer, and Dave picked some dark thick local beer to try. Most of the tables in the brightly painted, modern room were full of people eating and drinking.

"This is my new favorite beer—Cherry Lady—I love it." I belched slightly.

"I may have to cut you off," Dave said, rolling his eyes.

When our food arrived, I took one bite of my BBQ chicken wings and moaned with pleasure. In our short time in Rome, we'd already eaten a lot of pasta and pizza, so the food at Baladin was a fabulous surprise.

"I'll trade you half of my wings for half of your burger," I said.

"Sure." Dave handed over the half burger. We ate in silence, enjoying the familiar flavors and the homemade chips. Dave ordered more beer when the waiter came over.

On the way home, I linked arms with Dave. "We really, really have to go back there," I said. "Once a week."

"I'll never turn down beer." There were no arguments from Dave.

Of course, every day couldn't be a craft beer hunt, although we made it to Baladin quite often. During our three-months in Rome, our daily life included trips to the usual tourist spots, The Vatican, St. Peter's Square and Basilica, the Sistine Chapel, Colosseum, Trevi Fountain, Spanish Steps, the Roman Forum, Piazza Navona, Borghese Gallery, Circo Massimo, catacombs, Campo dei Fiori, and the Pantheon. There are shelves full of books written about each and every one of these places so I won't describe them again. Support writers and buy a book.

I liked to plan our days and would schedule our week in advance, carefully cross-checking the guidebook, bus schedules, and weather forecast, but some days all my plans fell apart. Sometimes we would run across flyers taped to the lampposts in Rome and decide to see the Picasso exhibit at the Scuderie del Quirinale before it closed down. Or maybe I noticed on the Wanted in Rome website that the Roseto Comunale, the municipal rose garden, was open but only for a few weeks. Interesting things popped up and caught my attention, so all my plans changed. At first, I hated changes and held onto my carefully crafted schedules. I had made a list of everything to do in Rome, and it felt satisfying to tick things off the list. I wasn't sure if I liked this new way of doing things, this new way of being. Adaptable. Flexible. Not my usual style, but maybe I could learn.

TIP: We were able to go to the Eurhop! Roma Beer Festival in October. The festival was in an outer suburb of Rome, held in a vast hall with dozens of stalls, each selling different craft beer. Dave drank many, many, many craft beers—including a dark coffee-flavored stout he really loved brewed by Menaresta and a dark imperial stout by Birrifico. It was impossible to pick a favorite. As the designated bus navigator responsible for getting us home, I sipped one sweet fruity beer called a Raspberry Lychee Foeder. I had no idea what a Foeder was but the beer was great. Craft beer festivals are on the rise throughout Italy, and if you like beer, they offer a once in a lifetime chance to try dozens of beers that are unavailable in the U.S. Bryan Jansing and Paul Vismara's book Italy: Beer Country is an excellent guide to all things in Italian craft beer or check out www.craft-beer-italy.it/en/.

• POMPEII—Don't Do What We Did •

One of the benefits of living in Europe was the excellent public transportation available between different regions. Europe is crisscrossed with trains and buses, both public and private, and there is a good selection of low-cost airlines. Rome was going to be our base for short trips around Italy and the rest of Europe. After only two weeks in Rome, I began planning a trip to Pompeii, the famous archaeological site. Unfortunately, the name of our trip to Pompeii should be *"Don't do what we did."*

First, we had to get there:

"I see this bus tour that will pick us up in the center of Rome and drive us to Pompeii. But it is €150 for each of us. That is a little pricey." I scanned the online tour website.

"It is, but what other choice is there? I don't want to drive in Italy. These people are crazy," Dave said. Both of us had almost been run over in Rome. We saw a woman knocked to the ground by a motorcycle. Even nuns crossed the streets in groups.

"We could do the train?" I said questioningly. We were both silent, contemplating the train. We knew the pitfalls of trains very well. On a trip to Florence years earlier, we traveled by train to Cinque Terre. It was great until we tried to get back to Florence, and there were no trains. We were stranded. The station agent calmly explained there was a train strike but, not to worry, it would be over in an hour. It was actually *many* hours later before a train came and we got back to Florence. Not a good memory.

I shook my head to get the bad train memories out of my brain. That was then. This was now. Now I was much more experienced in the ways of travel in general and Italian trains in particular. I knew to check the local newspaper that announced transportation strikes in advance. Also, I had found more train and travel websites with useful tips. (*TIP: See www.Seat61.com; www.loco2.com; www.thetrainline.com.*)

After reading all of the websites and blogs I could find on trains to Pompeii, it was clear we needed to get a train from Rome to Naples and then change to the Circumvesuviana train line to continue on to Pompeii. I even watched a YouTube video about changing trains in Naples. Pompeii was on the Circumvesuviana train that went to Sorrento. All my helpful sites warned against confusing Pompeii, *the archeological site* with the other Pompeii, the separate and unrelated *town* in Italy.

A few days in advance of our Pompeii trip, I went online and bought our one-way tickets to Naples on the government-run train company called Trenitalia. The prices were similar to Italia Rail (also government-run) and were a little pricey for a one-hour high-speed train trip. I didn't buy return tickets because I didn't know when we would return and didn't want to pay for tickets we couldn't use. This was *mistake #1*. We didn't leave until the 10:12 a.m. train because it was a little cheaper than the earlier commuter trains. I went to the trouble of finding an internet café to print our Trenitalia tickets, although I discovered no one looked at them once, no one checked them, and there were no reserved seats on this particular train.

The day before we left, I looked again at train details and descriptions and stumbled on Italo train lines. Italo is a privately owned railway company, and its ticket prices were much cheaper than government-run Trenitalia and Italia. Fearing the cheap tickets would sell out, I went ahead and bought return tickets on Italo for a 6:55 p.m. return. I couldn't return our nonrefundable Trenitalia tickets. *Mistake #2.* Look at all the train lines available. Italo doesn't go everywhere, but if you can use it, you can save some money.

The day of our Pompeii trip arrived, and we caught the train to Naples. At Napoli Centrale train station, we followed signs down to the lower level to the Circumvesuviana train station called Station Garibaldi. Both train stations were in the same building and location—just on different levels. *I'll bet that confuses a few tourists.* Roundtrip tickets on the Circumvesuviana train line were only €2.80.

Circumvesuviana was clearly a low budget operation—very low budget. It was grimy and dark, and it didn't have the usual big main screens showing train times, routes, and platform numbers. Here there was a separate screen on each platform and most were blank. Dave and I stood together at the top of the stairs leading to the different platforms trying to decide where to catch our train.

"The screen on Platform 3—does it say Sorrento?" I asked Dave, squinting at the small screen about halfway down the platform, which was impossible to read from a distance. Dave didn't hear me as he wandered down to look at other platforms.

"The screen on Platform 4 is blank. That can't be the one we want," Dave said, back from his scouting expedition around the station.

"I can't see anything from here. This is crap. Can you walk down to Platform 3 and see what the screen says?" I looked around the station again but there was no information about what trains ran on what platforms. Dave ambled down the stairs to get closer to the tiny screen of Platform 3. As I waited for him to return, a local man eating a sandwich at the mini café nearby spoke to me in English.

"You want Pompeii?"

"Yes."

He pointed at Platform 3 and repeated "Pompeii."

So I walked down to Platform 3 to catch the train.

Once on Platform 3, I immediately had doubts. Looking at the small screen, I saw the final destination on this route was not Sorrento, but all of the websites I had researched agreed we needed to get on the train line ending in Sorrento. I pulled up a route map for Circumvesuviana on my phone. The train we were waiting for included a stop for Pompeii, so I relaxed a little. The train arrived shortly afterward, and with no time to keep double-checking, we jumped on.

As we neared our destination, I kept searching the map and noticed that of the various Circumvesuviana train routes, another route had a stop called Pompeii Scavi. My handy phone translator told me scavi translated to "archeological," and I could see the route that included Pompeii Scavi ended in—Sorrento. My heart sank. We were on the wrong train, going to the *town* of Pompeii. This was *Mistake #3*—jumping on a train without proper consideration and thought. (Remember the helpful local guy who pointed to Platform 3 as the route to Pompeii? I was standing in the train station speaking English with Dave, so clearly I was a foreigner. Did this local guy honestly think I needed to go to the *town* of Pompeii? Do locals sometimes deliberately point silly tourists in the wrong direction? I will never know.)

I hated to tell Dave. "Bad news," I whispered, like whispering would make the mistake better. "We are headed to the town of Pompeii, not the ruins." He blinked and looked out the window. He didn't know where we were or where we were going. I was the family navigator.

We stayed on the train for one more stop until we arrived at the wrong Pompeii. Having seen pictures of the "real" Pompeii station, I knew this wasn't it, and we jumped off the wrong train and ran to the other side of the train station to board a train going in the opposite direction. Luckily we only needed to backtrack three stops to a station where we could change trains to the correct (Sorrento) route. We didn't need to go all the way back to Naples. Still, all this back and forthing and train changing meant we lost an hour and, instead of arriving in Pompeii at 1 p.m., we arrived at 2 p.m.

Then we made *mistake #4*. We didn't join a tour. Since we left late and got on the wrong train, there wasn't much time left to see Pompeii. As we waited in line to see the ruins, edging toward the ticket windows, we talked about the different prices.

"Just to get in is €19 each," Dave said, standing on his toes and peering at a sign near the cashier.

"Plus audio guide? What about a tour?" I wasn't as tall and couldn't read the sign.

"It all starts to add up for two people. A tour just left. We would have to wait for another one."

I grimaced. "I don't want to wait, do you?"

We almost always hesitate when it comes to spending money. *Budget, budget, budget* is the drumbeat in our heads. Even though we did a double pinkie swear[2] before leaving the U.S., promising each other not to "be

---

[2] To pinky swear, or to make a pinky promise, is the locking of the pinkies of two people to signify that a promise has been made. In the United States, it is most common among school-age children and close friends. The pinky swear signifies a promise that can never be broken.

cheap" on this long trip around Europe, we still did go cheap in Pompeii and just bought tickets to get in.

"I'll get a guidebook," Dave said, going to a display to pick up one for each of us.

We slowly wandered off to explore on our own. Dave led the way with the map in hand, and I followed behind him. Pompeii was still and quiet and peaceful and haunting and *huge*. Off in the distance, I saw Mount Vesuvius. It wasn't close to Pompeii at all, and I realized how far the volcanic ash and toxic fumes had traveled to reach the people of Pompeii. *Why didn't they run?* I wondered, imagining the panic of the thousands who didn't escape and simply huddled in their homes.

We wandered, hopelessly lost, and saw a lot of falling down walls. We ran into two other tourists and complained to each other about the useless map. Time was running out, and we did not see anything remotely interesting. Finally, we latched onto a tour group and started following it. We didn't listen to the actual tours themselves since we hadn't paid for them. Still, we followed different tour groups until we saw several significant spots: the well-preserved Villa of the Mysteries, the amazing mosaics of the House of the Faun, and the Temple of Apollo. The tours didn't waste time on the side roads full of falling down walls that we had been exploring.

Finally, it was time to leave. Dave would have stayed much longer. I felt guilty for wasting an hour and getting us lost, but still, we wouldn't see much more in Pompeii without a tour. Neither of us knew what we were looking at most of the time. I didn't even have our Italy guidebook with us. It included a section on Pompeii. I felt like a failure in my self-appointed role as the family navigator/tour guide. Dave kindly did not give me a hard time.

"I propose another double pinkie swear," I said as we walked toward the exit. "From now on, we will pay for tours or pay for audio guides, or we will buy real guidebooks. It is pointless to travel thousands of miles to Europe and then go look at things we don't understand." Dave held out his pinkie, and we made it official.

We returned to Naples without incident and hurried to a pizza place close to the train station. Naples is the birthplace of pizza, and it would be utterly crazy to go to Naples and not eat pizza. The waiter took our order for a Napoli pizza and a bottle of wine. The cook rushed our pizza to give us time to catch our train, and in the meantime, Dave poured the wine. The pizza was fantastic, thin-crust, with tasty ingredients full of flavor. I know everyone says this, I *know* it is a cliché, but there is much more flavor to the food in Italy. That pizza was full of ripe tomatoes tasting like warm sunshine, fresh herbs, and there was the lightest splash of salt on the crispy crust.

The waiter gave us the cork for the unfinished wine, and Dave tucked the bottle into his backpack for the trip back to Rome. Then we made our final *mistake #5*—not getting another pizza in Naples. I wasn't hungry but could have eaten another one just to have that wonderful flavor in my mouth.

TIP: My son and daughter both visited Rome, and each booked a bus tour from Rome to Pompeii. Their tours weren't cheap, but they were easy to join, and they both loved the tour they got at Pompeii. Sometimes being cheap backfires.

• MUNICH OKTOBERFEST •

If there was one thing in our entire year I wished I could live over again, it would be Oktoberfest in Germany. Our trip to Munich for Oktoberfest was one of the earliest trips we planned. Even before leaving the U.S. and before buying our tickets to Rome, we bought tickets to Oktoberfest for September 2017 and booked a room in a hostel. Six million people typically attend the festival each year, and we needed to move fast. Since Dave is part German and loves beer, this promised to be a highlight.

By the time Oktoberfest came around, we had been living in Rome for three weeks and had settled in. The trip to Munich was our first trip by plane within Europe, sort of as locals. I wanted to confirm a lot of things about European air travel, things I took for granted in the U.S. I knew U.S. airline rules on bringing fluids on flights, how early to get boarding passes, when the flight would start boarding, and about how long security would take. I didn't know the rules of flying in Europe and didn't want to make a mistake.

As I searched the internet, I learned that luggage and liquids' rules varied between different European airlines. Still, most online sources agreed that we should get to the airport two hours before our flight, not one hour for a domestic flight like in the U.S. On the day of our Oktoberfest trip, I made sure we woke up crazy early. We got to the train for the airport and arrived at Rome's Fiumicino airport extra early, only to find that we buzzed through security and were left with more than enough time to make our flight. It drove Dave a little nuts that I was so nervous about traveling and always insisted on being at the airport extra early. The idea of missing a plane worried me more than the boredom of sitting at the airport. Besides, in airports, I could buy English magazines. Everything about the airline travel process at Fiumicino was similar to what I was used to in the US. *Maybe I shouldn't have worried,* I thought.

Then we got on the plane. I had just started reading one of my magazines as the flight attendant began announcements in Italian and then repeated them in German and English. I clearly heard her announce we would be landing in "Monaco." Monaco? The country on the Mediterranean? The land of Princess Grace?

"Did you hear that?" I hissed to Dave. "She said we will be landing in Monaco." The flight attendant started through the announcements again, and this time Dave and I both listened.

"Yeah, she did say Monaco," Dave confirmed.

"How did we get on the wrong plane? Were our boarding passes wrong? We aren't moving yet. You have to go talk to the flight attendant." I jabbed Dave in the ribs with my elbow. He was on the aisle, just steps away from her.

"Hold on a minute. Let's see what else she says," Dave said.

"If the plane backs from the gate, it will be too late to get off." I pushed harder. Dave hated conflict or confrontation and would go out of his way to avoid asking for help or information. He would rather fly to the wrong country and sort out problems later. But after more nudging from me, he took off his seat belt and approached the flight attendant. I couldn't hear what they were saying, but Dave's face was serious. I started gathering my jacket and purse. He came back and sat down.

"We are going to Munich, Germany," he said. "Italians call Munich the 'Monaco of Bavaria.'" *I wonder how many people in Italy ended up in*

Monaco (the country) when they intended to go to Munich or vice versa. There was still a lot to learn about flying in Europe, and maybe I couldn't let my guard down just yet.

After arriving and taking the train to central Munich, we found our hostel near the downtown train station. It was within walking distance to Theresienwiese, the large park where Oktoberfest was held. We checked in, dumped our bags, and left the hostel to wander the neighborhood. Groups of people of all ages filled the streets wearing lederhosen and fluffy "frauline" dresses.

"I can see you wearing some of those." I laughed, pointing discreetly at a man wearing a pair of thick leather lederhosen. "Verrry sexy." (We looked at lederhosen in a store before leaving Munich—also very expensive.) It was early afternoon on a sunny day and the party was already started. We followed the crowds to Oktoberfest, where the neon-lighted carnival rides were full of screaming kids, and the beer tents were full of singing and drinking adults.

There were large beer tents and small beer tents. Both of us wanted food, so we wandered until we found an enormous beer tent where an usher-type guy led us to seats in the center "non-reserved" area. This tent was full of older people and families, and everyone was eating, drinking, and singing. A big loud band up on a center dais kept everything lively. After eating some German sausages and drinking a beer, we continued to wander. Another beer tent looked fun, but it was full and was reservation only.

The next beer tent was the best—Paulaner. Dave led the way into the tent, which was overloaded with people singing boisterously.

"Do you see a seat?" I asked Dave.

"Oh yeah, there are a few there in the middle."

Edging our way to the center of the tent, we stopped underneath a tall platform. We grabbed empty seats on a bench at a communal table, right below the loud ten-piece brass band, complete with a singer. Everyone in the tent seemed to know the songs by heart, and they were belting them out. Women in traditional German dress somehow nudged through the crowds carrying overflowing trays of food and drink. The outer edge was reservation only, but here in the center, right beneath the brass band, was non-reserved seating.

"Do you want a beer?" Dave asked as he scanned the room, looking for a waiter.

"In Germany? Yes, I think I'll give up wine while we are in Germany." I laughed and imagined my chances of finding wine in a giant beer hall.

Dave ordered two beers and started chatting with the couple sitting next to us who were from Denver. We talked, compared travels, drank more beer, and danced on the benches. No one was sitting anymore, and we noisily sang at the top of OUR lungs. People came and went steadily. The band played German songs and a lot of American songs, and everybody in the place knew all the words. It was hours later before both of us called it a night and walked to our hostel, thankful we didn't have to maneuver buses or subways to get to our beds.

The next day no doubt there were people who started in on Oktoberfest early in the morning, but I felt a little sluggish/hungover, and it was a picture-perfect crisp, sunny day—a nice break from the heat of Rome. Dave grabbed some supplies for his backpack, and we caught a bus to the English Gardens (Englischer Garten), where we found a stall of bike rentals and rented two E-bikes with an electronic assist.

"You must go to see the surfers in the park. It is here." The attendant circled a spot on our park map.

"Surfers? Is there a water park here?" I tried to imagine surfers in this green, heavily wooded park.

"You will see," he said, smiling.

After wandering the park for several hours and eating lunch at an enormous beer garden in the center (where Dave dithered between a dark Hofbrauhaus Dunkel beer and a Warsteiner Dunkel, before choosing one of each) I led the way toward the spot the attendant marked on our map, in search of the surfers. We found them on the narrow, manmade Eisbach River that ran through the park. Leaning my bike up against a tree, I waded into the crowd of onlookers for a closer look. In this one small section of the river, the water roiled up into waves, and surfers took turns jumping onto their surfboards from the sides of the river. One surfer after another plunged in for the mostly short wave ride.

"That looks pretty intense," I commented to a lady standing next to me.

"They are crazy. I would never try such a thing," she said. I agreed. It looked challenging and exhausting. The narrow river made it even more dangerous. There wasn't a lot of room to maneuver. This was not something for the unskilled or inexperienced surfer.

We left the park and went back to our hostel briefly before heading out for another night of Oktoberfest. This time we wasted no time and went straight to the Paulaner tent. We were calling it "the party tent." Again, the tent was filled to the brim with people, and this time we landed next to three Italians who were friendly and charming if a little incomprehensible. Between the noise in the tent, their Italian accents, and the beer we all kept drinking, I did a lot of smiling and nodding.

Everyone was standing on the benches dancing, singing, and talking. It was impossible to sit on a bench. Dancing on the bench was the best place to watch people, what they wore, how they danced. It was a spectacle of constant music, singing, and movement. This was not like any scene from my daily Denver life. After more than an hour of dancing, I began to feel light-headed and knew I should check my blood sugar. Dancing is great exercise, but exercise often made my blood sugar drop. I went to the bathroom for privacy and tested—69. Not a bad number, but anything below 70 was too low. On my way back to the benches, I bought a pretzel to load up on carbs. I wanted to keep dancing.

Back at the benches, there was chaos. "You missed it," Dave said. "There were two guys behind us, both trying to hit on the same woman. They started punching each other, and security hauled them out." Dave and the Italians were soaked in beer, but no one was hurt. The waiters were trying to clean up the broken mugs quickly but weren't bothering with the spilled beer on the floor. Tables were turned at wrong angles and people stared, pointed, and chattered. Now we couldn't sit if we wanted to. The benches were sticky with spilled beer.

So we stood on the benches and danced and sang and talked for another two hours. The time flew by. The Italians came and went. The music was amazing. This hall full of people knew the words to more American songs than I did, and you haven't lived if you haven't heard 3000 drunken Germans singing Neil Diamond's "Sweet Caroline" at the top of their drunken voices, and if you weren't lucky enough to be there yourself singing at the top of your drunken voice. It was absolutely the most fun I had had in years.

It was very late when the night ended, and the next day I was wiped out. Every bone in my legs hurt, and my leg muscles twitched with random spasms. I didn't want to complain, so we went ahead to the Alte

Pinakothek Museum of Art and wandered for a few hours. Every time I passed a bench inside the museum, I sat. Finally, I spoke up.

"I'm wiped out. Maybe I overdid it a little."

"Yeah, me too. I can't do another night like last night."

"I need aspirin—lots of aspirin."

When traveling, there is this urge to do everything quickly and keep going and going, but on this day, both of us sore and miserable, we gave in. The next day we were going back to Rome. One more night of dancing on the benches would be so much fun, but maybe I just needed to admit my 20's were over. We skipped the rest of the museum and caught a bus back to the hostel to rest. In the evening, we strolled around the square in the old town called Marienplatz and ate dinner. This crazy side trip was over, and it was time to return to life in Rome.

TIP: Don't put your phone in your back pocket. The one catastrophe on the trip to Munich was the loss of my phone. On the last night of dancing on benches, I put my phone in my back pocket so I could get to it and take pictures. On a trip to the bathroom, it flipped out of my pocket into the toilet. I was crushed to lose my video recording of the entire beer hall drunkenly pounding out American songs. When we returned to Rome, I began using the cheap €90 Italian phone we bought on our first day in Rome, and it became "my" phone for the rest of our year of traveling.

• VATICAN CITY—MORE THAN JUST THE POPE •

One of my biggest worries about living in Europe for a year was managing my diabetes. Most people don't understand how tricky Type 1 diabetes can be. The goal was to keep my blood sugar in a safe range—not too high and not too low. But estimating carbs, especially in unfamiliar food, is just a guessing game. Try googling "how many carbs in a potato" and look at how many different answers you get. Also, lots of variables affect blood sugar. Exercise could lower my blood sugar, but stress and lack of sleep could raise it. Consistently high blood sugars would kill me slowly by damaging my heart, nerves, blood vessels, kidneys, and other organs. But low blood sugar was worse. Extremely low blood sugar could lead to a diabetic coma and kill me quickly. I rode the ups and downs of blood sugar numbers every day.

As I researched our trip, I found almost nothing online about long-term travel with diabetes. Many blogs or online articles say, "take double the supplies you will need," which was good advice for the typical traveler who would be traveling a few weeks and then returning home. It was impossible to carry a year's supply of insulin and I was uneasy about finding it in Europe. Online comments from people who bought insulin in Germany or Italy from a local pharmacy for only €40 or €50, without insurance, were encouraging. *But does that really work? Could it be true that an Italian pharmacy would take an English prescription from my American doctor for insulin and just give it to me for a very affordable price?* I wondered. It was risky to rely on advice—sometimes years old advice—from strangers commenting on a blog. I wanted a trustworthy source with up-to-date information and actual on-the-ground experience. A few months before leaving the U.S., the people on the Expats Living In Rome Facebook group filled in an important blank for me.

> Me: Hello, all. I am posting again to get your help. I am diabetic and will be living in Italy for a year. Can I get insulin from Italian pharmacies? Can I use my American prescription?
>
> Luca: Pharmacies in Italy will not accept American prescriptions, but they all have insulin. It is easy to find.
>
> Giulia: Where will you be living?
>
> Me: Rome to start with—then probably Venice.
>
> Giulia: The Vatican Pharmacy in Rome will fill your English prescriptions. It is in Vatican City.
>
> Me: I've never heard of the Vatican Pharmacy. Where is it?
>
> Giulia: Somewhere in the Vatican City. I do not know. My roommate once used it. The Vatican, they do not charge Italian taxes. The cost will be not so much.

This was good news. In all my research, I had never even heard of the Vatican City pharmacy. After more research, I finally found one website mentioning it, but the site was very vague about using it or even finding it. After only a few weeks in Rome, I began planning a trip to the Vatican City pharmacy to add to my insulin stockpiles and figure out how it worked. Dave tagged along too since he also had to get prescriptions refilled for his stockpiles.

We woke up earlier than usual on the appointed day and hopped on a bus to Vatican City. I knew the approximate location of the pharmacy. We sat, trapped on the bus in heavy morning rush hour traffic, but it wasn't hot yet, and there was a breeze coming in the windows.

We arrived, passports and prescriptions in hand, before 8:30. Walking toward St. Anna's Gate, Dave commented on the long lines of people standing on the sidewalk. "What day is today?" I asked, "Wednesday?" Bad luck. Wednesday was the day of the Pope's weekly outdoor audience in St. Peter's Square. It was crowded. We edged down the sidewalk between the lines of people waiting for the Pope on one side and the lines of beggars and people with twisted limbs and open wounds on the other side. People begged all over Rome, but the Vatican beggars seemed to be the most desperate in the city.

St. Anna's gate was at the intersection of Borgo Pio and Via di Porta Angelica, a little bit north of St. Peter's Square, where the Pope would give his audience. The large iron gate for vehicles was closed. I watched the different types of guards standing at attention behind the gates—the Swiss Guards in their funny-looking bright yellow, blue, and red uniforms with wide bloomer pants, and the more plain civilian police service. In the afternoons, when the temperatures soared, I wondered how the Swiss Guards coped with the long sleeves and bloomer pants.

I walked through the side gate for pedestrians and handed the guard my passport and prescriptions. He slowly and carefully examined them and then gave them back to me.

"You must leave. It is not yet the time to open." I glanced at my watch. It wasn't 8:30 yet. Dave and I grabbed an espresso down the street and, at exactly 8:30, walked back and the same guard slowly and carefully reviewed my paperwork again—as if it might have changed in the 10 minutes since he had last seen me. These guys were not messing around.

"You must get a pass from the office," he said, waving vaguely over his shoulder. We walked until we saw the Vatican Post Office. *Maybe the post office issues passes?* I walked inside and asked, "Passes? For the pharmacy?" They waved me back the way we had come, "alla sinistra" (on the left). Backtracking, we came to a building surrounded by wooden scaffolding. No wonder we didn't see the office. Ducking under the scaffolding, we entered through a door marked "Ufficio Permessi" (Office of Permission). A man sitting behind thick bullet-proof glass took our passports and handed us both a temporary clip-on pass. We left the office and turned right at the first road and followed the green signs to the pharmacy.

At the top of the pharmacy steps, I glanced at the cosmetics store on the right-hand side—*something to explore after my pharmacy trip*. On the left, we entered the pharmacy and saw a machine giving out tickets with numbers. On a screen near the ceiling, digital displays flashed red numbers. This was a familiar set-up—like the deli counter at the grocery store back home. We needed numbers. People filled every inch of the room, and we squeezed past bodies toward the machine issuing numbers. Already there was the faint smell of sweat, and the room wasn't air-conditioned.

Even though I wasn't fluent in spoken Italian and sure couldn't understand it when Italians spoke rapidly, I could figure out a fair amount of written Italian. In this situation, my smattering of Italian came in handy. On the ticketing machine, I saw Category A for "Dipendenti Vaticana" (employees of the Vatican). That wasn't what we wanted. Category C was for "Acquisitare I Produtti" (people acquiring products). That was our category, and we each pulled a numbered ticket from the machine. The final category, F, was marked "Ritouro Prescrizioni" and was for people who had to return to pick up products not in stock on their first visit to the pharmacy.

Using my prescriptions as a fan, I walked around the room looking at the shelves of cold medicines, lotions, and soaps for sale. I also kept an eye on the overhead screens showing ticket categories, numbers, and which window to go to. The numbers seemed to flick by quickly, and more than once, I saw two people scurry to the same window.

When my turn came, I hurried to my assigned window and handed my prescriptions to the pharmacist in the white coat. He disappeared into the back room and returned with insulin *pens* (used for daily insulin injections) instead of the insulin *vials* I used to fill my insulin pump.

"Do you have insulin vials?" I asked. I opened my purse and pulled out my small bag of diabetes supplies. Grabbing the vial of insulin I carried, I handed it to the pharmacist. He turned it over in his hand and read the label, frowning, disappeared again into the back room. He came out talking to another man in a white coat, and I saw them shaking their heads. He returned to me and said, "There is no vials here."

I knew I could use insulin pens to fill my insulin pump, and so I accepted pens in place of vials. I got everything I needed, paid and was ready to leave. (Cost: One box of NovoRapid insulin pens (five pens per box for a total of 1500 units of insulin) were €46 or $56.)

Dave and I had been separated in the crush of people in the room, but after I finished with the pharmacist, I saw him in the crowd and made my way over to him.

"Ready to go?" I asked. He was grumpy. "I haven't even talked to a pharmacist yet. My number came up on the display, but some other lady grabbed my spot by the time I got there. I got another number." He showed me the number he was holding. It would be awhile. I left to explore.

Wandering over to the cosmetics side of the building, I saw that everything was high-end and a little expensive. Still, when would I have another chance to buy a Pope lipstick?

I went across the road to the Vatican grocery store, which was larger than my regular Roman grocery store. Inside, priests and nuns were pushing shopping carts loaded with wine and cigarettes up and down the aisles. I wanted to buy some wine, especially since the Vatican didn't charge taxes. Since we were far from home and traveling by bus, I picked only two bottles. The checkout clerk said something to me in Italian. My blank face told her I was clueless. She motioned to the clip-on pass on my shirt, and I handed it over. She glanced at it. "This pass is not for here." I gave her the two bottles of wine and left. At the Vatican Post Office, I bought a €3 stamp of the Pope to use on a postcard for our Catholic neighbors. Their son was named Peter, and they would appreciate a postage stamp from St. Peter's Church in Rome.

When Dave caught up with me, we walked to the office door marked "Restituzione Documenti," and retrieved our passports. As we left the Vatican and began walking to our bus stop, I felt relieved that we had both been able to get more medicine and add to our stockpiles. Even better, the Vatican City Pharmacy was easy to use, and the price of insulin very reasonable. I didn't know if I would be able to get medicine in Croatia, London, or Venice, but now I knew that, in an emergency, it was possible to hop on a plane and come back to Rome to use the Vatican City pharmacy.

• FINDING TIME ALONE •

All my life, I have been an avid reader, but I am an old-school reader. I love paper books. I like the heft of holding them in my hand, and I like dog-earing the pages to mark things I want to re-read later. I stroke the pages as I read. The smell of a new book is soothing and familiar; the smell of new ideas and possibilities. Bookstores feel like home, relaxed and unhurried, and my pulse slows down when I am browsing in one. In my old life in the U.S., I read an occasional book on Kindle, but whenever there was a choice, I read real books made of actual paper.

There wasn't room for real books in our overcrowded suitcases when we made our leap to Europe. We loaded my Kindle and Dave's E-reader with a few books for the plane and set up library links to stock up on more books after we arrived. After being in Rome for about six weeks, I adapted to reading on Kindle, but it wasn't the same when I couldn't stroke the pages. I declared a "day of bookstores," and one sunny Tuesday, I set out alone to visit English language bookstores in Rome.

I left the apartment and walked quickly, almost running to the Ponte Sisto Bridge, where I paused to look at the Tiber River. *God, the air feels good.* The bridge was full of the usual buskers selling knockoff purses and cheap souvenirs, and today their voices sounded upbeat and soothing. I stared at the water and slowly felt the muscles in my shoulders relax. Glancing down at my hands, I loosened the tight grip I had on the railing and flexed my fingers. This was about more than books. I really needed to get out of the apartment—alone. Being constantly together with Dave in a small space had been more challenging than I expected. Little habits became irritating—was it really necessary for him to jiggle his leg constantly while we sat together watching a movie, or did he need to walk around the apartment brushing his teeth? I felt crowded and hemmed in. At home in the U.S., we had more space, a yard, and friends and hobbies. As the days passed here in Rome, my voice began to get sharper and shorter with Dave. He began to tiptoe around me to avoid conflict. I hated how I was acting, but day by day, the pressure I felt ticked up. The small box we were living in got smaller every day.

I kept walking and thinking about the "togetherness" problem, but at the Fahrenheit 451 bookstore in Campo di Fiori, I put problems out of my mind and began browsing. I bought an old favorite by Jane Austen and then started walking to another nearby bookstore I found online. But the Libreria del Viaggiatore on Via del Pellegrino wasn't there. It was still alive on the internet, but the brick and mortar was closed and out of business. I walked around the corner to catch a bus to the Anglo American bookstore.

Sadly, my day of bookstores happened to coincide with a new influx of tourists. *When does it end here?* I wondered. *Maybe there is no "off" season for tourists in Rome.* I fought my way onto a crowded bus and felt sorry for the people getting on the bus trying to buy tickets from the bus driver. Drivers don't sell bus tickets in Rome. Also, it was hot. Again. Sweat trickled down my back in a small stream into the waistband of my shorts.

I jumped off the bus near the Via Delle Vite and walked to the Anglo American bookstore. There I browsed slowly, picking up and putting down different possibilities, reading covers, trying to decide what to buy. "Where is your travel section?" I asked a store clerk. She led me over to a corner of the store. Many of the books were familiar. After years of dreaming about living in Italy, I'd bought a lot of books about travel. Finally, I chose a book written by a man who traveled on a Vespa, a little motor scooter, up the entire length of Italy. *Not my idea of travel*, I thought, but it included recipes, and I can't resist recipes in books.

There was one more bookstore to try, in Trastevere near our apartment, called the Almost Corner bookstore on Via del Moro. I walked in, looked at the crowded shelves, and took a deep breath of the sweetly musty "book" air. An older gentleman was sitting at a desk near the cash register, but he just glanced up at me and smiled without saying anything. *Good,* I thought, *someone who just lets you look.* I ran my fingers along the spines of a shelf of books before pausing and choosing one to flip through. It was an hour before I paid for my selections and left.

On the way home, I stopped and sat on the steps of the Piazza Trilussa. Stretching out my legs, grateful for the shade, I leaned back on a step to think. We lived just around the corner, but I wasn't ready to go back yet to our small apartment. The pressure and tension that had filled my mind when I left the apartment came flooding back. This slow and relaxing day alone with books and bookstores had been a revelation. I wanted, *needed,* to carve out at least a little time every week to be alone—personal time to settle down from the city's chaotic busyness; time to pause and reflect and think about everything going on; time to just turn "off" and be still.

Getting time alone for myself had never been an issue before. Until this trip, I'd always been able to carve out some separate space without even really thinking about it much. When I was working, the commute was my quiet time to unwind, watch the scenery pass by and daydream. I could stretch Saturday errands to an entire day. Our home had elbow room to spread out and I often went to bed early with a book. Here in Italy, there was no alone time and no alone space. Navigating the city every day was stressful; it was busy, loud, and crowded, and old ladies shoved their way onto buses in front of me. Just moving around the city every day left me feeling pushed, poked, prodded, and jabbed.

Gathering up my books, I started toward home. There wasn't room in our suitcases to bring my new books along with us, but just for a little while, I could re-create a bit of home as I sniffed, stroked, and dog-eared my new books. And next week, I would find a new place to explore, alone and on my own, just for a little while.

TIP: Bus drivers in Rome do not sell bus tickets. You must find a tabacchi shop, usually marked with a large "T" on the outside sign, and buy bus tickets. Bus tickets can also be purchased from ticket machines, but don't rely on this as the machines are hard to find and often broken when you find them. Just go to a tabacchi shop. I never found a tabacchi selling monthly passes (or one that renewed them), so we went back every month to Termini train station to top ours off. Rome does not make transportation easy, which is probably why so many people just don't bother with tickets. We followed the rules and bought monthly bus passes even though we only once saw someone checking tickets on a bus in Rome.

TIP: Amazon has Kindle Unlimited e-book subscription service, and for a fee of $9.99 per month, you have access to over one million e-books. We often used the free e-book services of our Colorado public library to get books too.

• OSTIA ANTICA •

The alarm went off early one Monday morning so we could make the trip to Ostia Antica—called the poor man's Pompeii. It was a short commuter train ride from Rome, included as part of our monthly transportation pass, so travel was free. As we were leaving the apartment, I looked at the guidebook one last time to double-check how to get there, and then noticed it was "closed on Monday." Change of plans.

"How do you feel about window shopping on the Via Del Corso instead?" I asked. Dave was not interested in shopping but agreed to tag along if the day included lunch and a glass of wine. I didn't like sudden changes to my carefully laid plans, but there were many things to do in Rome, and we had time. Ostia Antica could wait.

As I planned and scheduled our daily excursions around town, I always tried to check which days places were closed, which was often Monday, but sometimes it wasn't. For example, a few weeks after arriving in Rome, we chatted with a fellow American one night at dinner. His voice quivered with excitement as he raved about a restaurant in Testaccio. I was intrigued and we had to go. Dave and I found the restaurant, but all three times we stopped by, it was never open.

The third time we passed it, I peered in through the windows. "I see white tablecloths and glassware and a small bar. It looks like it is still in business." Dave walked down the street, double-checking the address of the restaurant against the numbers on the building. I backed up and squinted in the sun, looking at the restaurant name, the number, trying to

decipher the problem. Then I noticed the small sign near the entrance—
"chiuso miercoledi"—closed on Wednesday. It just happened that all of
our attempts to visit this restaurant had occurred on Wednesdays. No
problem, though. Since we were now settled in and living in Rome, we
could just keep going back—not like a vacation where you have to move
forward constantly. Having extra time took a lot of stress out of traveling.
We went back a fourth time and finally got to eat a meal at this new
restaurant and it was fabulous as promised.

Ostia Antica was also well worth our time when we finally managed
to get there. It was a lot like Pompeii but on a more human scale. On one
slightly cooler fall day, we arrived there, paid the small entrance fee,
picked up a guidebook, and started down the main road. Our first stop was
a well-preserved stone amphitheater where concerts still take place even
today. Next we walked to a nearby shady courtyard. The guidebook called
it a shopping arcade. Dave and I walked back and forth over the mosaic
tile signs on the ground outside each shop, which depicted the shop's
wares.

"Look at this." I called Dave over to the shop in front of me. "A mosaic
of grapes. This must have been a wine shop."

"This one looks like fruit to me," Dave said, gesturing to the next shop.
"And this one over here is clearly a fish." He kept walking. "Is this an
elephant? Did they eat elephants?"

"No, that was the clothing store for big and tall men," I joked. I could
imagine the large square bustling with chubby shoppers wearing togas.

Off on a side street, there was the community public latrine. It was a
very open place, and more than a dozen people could sit and chat, if they
wanted to, as they simultaneously did their business. Not my idea of
privacy, but privacy is a more modern notion. Our guidebook said back in

the day, there would have been water running underneath the toilets providing an old-fashioned flush.

The 80 acres of Ostia Antica included public bathhouses, apartments, taverns, restaurants, bakeries, fire and police departments. It was a large city for its time, before the nearby river filled with silt and people left. Ostia Antica didn't have the crowds of Pompeii and it was just an easy train ride from Rome—nothing like our crazy, rushed, and chaotic train trip to Pompeii. We relaxed and rambled in the lovely cool shade, and I could imagine life here some 2000 years ago—a little bit of Russell Crowe in *Gladiator* mixed with Kirk Douglas in *Spartacus*. Somehow I couldn't see Russell sharing the public latrines.

• YES, PICKPOCKETS ARE REAL •

Only six weeks into our trip and I had an up-close and personal encounter with a pickpocket.

We had just arrived at the subway station, and from upstairs, I could hear a train arriving on the lower level. "Let's go. We can make it." I urged Dave forward as I rushed ahead of him down the steps to the train. At the bottom of the steps, I quickly glanced at a group of four or five girls standing there, ages about twelve? Thirteen? They were young, clumped in a group, blocking the narrow hall leading to the train platform itself, which was something people tended to do in Rome all the time. They just stood there, not getting on the train or going to the train doors. I paused slightly and they divided into two sides around me as I rushed toward the open train door. *Is Dave going to make it?* I wondered, and half-turned to look back to make sure he was there as I jumped on the train. Over my shoulder, I caught a glimpse of Dave, and also one of the young girls caught in the door as it started to close.

Suddenly an older woman on the train began hitting the girl with her hand and yelling at her angrily. *Is the girl trying to get on the train without paying? Is that why the woman is angry?* Everything was happening so fast and nothing made sense. My heart was pounding, and then the girl disappeared out the train door, and the train started moving. I looked at Dave, who was clearly as confused as I was, and then stared at the woman in shock. She explained something in Italian while I continued to stare at her, eyes wide, and then she said in English, "the girl, she take your purse," and she mimed a hand going down into my purse. I looked down and saw that my purse was wide open, not zipped, not secured at all. The others sitting on the train shook their heads mournfully.

"Grazie." I thanked the woman and looked through my purse in panic. I saw my wallet and my phone, but most importantly, my pouch of diabetes supplies was still there. I carried that pouch everywhere I went. If I lost it or if it was stolen, I wouldn't have the PDM that operated my insulin pumps. My backup plan, the only backup plan for a diabetic like me, involved giving myself multiple daily shots, and it wasn't my favorite option. I squeezed the pouch of diabetes supplies and thanked the woman again. Nothing was missing. This short little five foot nothing older Italian woman with gray hair had saved me.

If they had stolen my purse, those girls would have been very disappointed. The cheap LG phone I carried replaced the phone that had fallen into the toilet at Oktoberfest. I didn't carry the cash, which was Dave's job. I did, however, learn my lesson. I never walked inside another subway station without my purse zipped and in front of my body.

• SICKNESS IN PARADISE •

Ugh. I dragged myself upright on the couch. This was day five of a scorching sore throat. I was sleeping on the couch so I could toss and turn and get up to refill my water glass without waking Dave.

When it started, I ignored it—my standard operating procedure with any medical problem. *It will go away.* Finally, I went into a farmacia and the pharmacist gave me some throat lozenges. The next day my throat was worse, so I tried a different farmacia, and the kind English-speaking pharmacist gave me a throat spray. At first, the new throat spray gave me hope, but this morning my throat was even more swollen, and swallowing hurt. Dave came into the room and looked at me with sympathy.

"The throat spray didn't work?" he asked.

"It did last night. Today it hurts worse." My voice was unrecognizable. "Can you bring me some coffee?" I alternated drinking gallons of warm teas and coffee, gargling with salt water, and using lozenges and throat sprays. Nothing was helping.

"We go to Barcelona Monday," Dave reminded me.

"I know. I don't want to cancel the trip. Maybe it is time to find a doctor."

Being a plan-ahead list-making sort of person, I had already put together a list of the doctors in Rome who were supported by our insurance, but since it was Sunday, they wouldn't be open. I did some Googling and found an Emergency Medical Unit for Tourists near our apartment. Dave and I walked there and Dave found a seat while I walked up to the reception desk. The receptionist spoke a little English. After I explained the problem, she handed me a clipboard with a short form to fill out. They only wanted my name and address. *I would have pages and pages of medical history to fill out in the U.S.*, I thought.

After a short wait, the receptionist pointed me to an exam room. A white-coated doctor began speaking to me in Italian. "English?" I asked. My Italian was not prepared for a medical problem. *I really should have looked up some Italian words for "sore throat" before I came here.* The two of us worked it out with a little pantomime, and it was clear the doctor could understand English even if he couldn't speak much of it.

He picked up a notebook and wrote "burns?" on the paper and then showed it to me. "Yes. Burns," I said, thankful to be understood. He picked up a wooden tongue depressor and motioned for me to open my mouth. He looked at my throat for about one second before tossing the tongue depressor in the trash and reaching for his notebook.

"Pharyngitis," he wrote. He handed me a prescription for an antibiotic, and I was out of there in less than 10 minutes. He didn't take a medical history, he didn't ask about allergies, he didn't prod my throat or listen to my breathing.

"That was quick," Dave said when I came out of the exam room. I went to the receptionist to find out what I owed for the visit. *I hope it isn't hundreds of euros. We don't have medical emergencies in the budget.*

"Do I pay you?" I asked. She put down her paperwork and looked at me, her eyes scrunched up and one eyebrow raised. *Well, obviously, I didn't ask that correctly.* She spoke some English, but she didn't understand me. I remembered how I asked the waiter for our check after a meal in a restaurant.

"Il conto?" I asked. She laughed slightly and shook her head.

"There is no account. There is no fee." Now I was puzzled, but she knew my name and address, so if there was a bill, it would arrive in the mail.

On the way home, we stopped at a farmacia near the clinic, and my prescription cost €10 or $12. In the U.S., I would have gone to a Minute Clinic at Walgreens, paid my $30 co-pay and my $50 prescription co-pay, for a total of $80. The clinic never sent a bill, and the entire throat episode cost me just €10. Italian medical care was working just fine.

· TURMOIL IN BARCELONA ·

When planning our trip to Barcelona, Spain, I was looking forward to escaping the heat of Rome; instead, we landed in the middle of the political heat engulfing Barcelona.

I only vaguely realized it was a turbulent period for the region. Articles I had read just weeks before our arrival reported on the fighting between police and protestors. Barcelona is in Catalonia, one of Spain's 17 semi-autonomous regions, and Catalonia wanted to withdraw from Spain and become an independent republic. On October 1st, not long before we arrived, when people went to vote on the referendum for independence, hundreds were injured in the fighting that broke out. Protestors accused the police of brutality. The independence referendum passed overwhelmingly, but both sides contested the results. Everything in Barcelona was in flux.

On the first day we arrived late, so it was the next morning before we got out and walked to a nearby park to meet up with a free walking tour group. Our guide, a Barcelona local, led our group of 15 around town, pointing out places of historical interest, including two buildings designed by the famous architect Antoni Gaudi. Gaudi was a big deal in Barcelona. The buildings he designed in the late 19th and early 20th century were modern then and even today have a crazy, twisted, whimsical uniqueness. His designs look like something from the mind of someone under the influence of hallucinogenic drugs, but Gaudi was a very religious Catholic and a strict vegetarian. Today seven of his buildings have been designated World Heritage Sites by UNESCO.

As we walked around the city on our tour, I noticed that Catalan's red, yellow, and blue flag was everywhere. I wanted to understand what was going on.

"I see there are a lot of groups of people with flags and lots of Catalan flags hanging from balconies. What is going on here in Barcelona?" I asked the tour guide.

She raised her chin and spoke confidently. "For Catalans, independence from Spain is a very passionate matter. Our culture has been ignored—suppressed. We pay taxes to Spain and get very little from the government. Young people today do not wish to live as their parents have."

"Will Spain let Catalonia have independence?" I asked. Wrong question!

"It is not the right of Spain to give Catalonia anything. We will take independence."

The situation was much more volatile than I realized. After thanking her, we set out for our next stop. I planned to hit most of the major sites in Barcelona during our short trip, but as we walked to the Sagrada Familia Basilica, I noticed even more flags and more groups of people milling about and talking urgently.

"What do you think about all of the people and flags around?" I asked Dave. "People seem tense."

"No, I think everything is fine. You let the tour guide freak you out." Dave—always the calm one.

We spent the afternoon at the Sagrada Familia Basilica, filled with tourists and not a single Catalan flag in sight. Gaudi took over the design of the Sagrada Familia and worked on it for over 40 years until his death in 1926. It still isn't finished today. The massive cranes that surrounded the outside of the church didn't detract from the view of the tall towers or the statuary on the exterior. It is a magical, stunning building, and not one of the dozens of pictures I took inside did justice to the serenity and majesty of the building or the effect of the light streaming through the stained glass. This is one of those places that simply can't be captured in words or pictures. Standing inside the Sagrada Familia, leaning up against a huge pillar near the center, slightly dizzy, I looked around slowly at the arching ceiling, soaring tree-like columns, and soft glowing light. In my mind, I was taking pictures of everything.

After leaving the Sagrada Familia we walked to Gaudi's Casa Batlló, once a family home, now a fully restored example of Gaudi's weird designs. There simply wasn't time to go to the other Gaudi sites in Barcelona like Casa Vicens, La Pedrera, Parc Güell, and Palau Güell. I made a vow to return to Barcelona, maybe in 2026, when they say the Sagrada Familia will finally be completed.

At dinner that night, I forgot about the tensions of the day. Our hostel was in a touristy part of town, near Las Ramblas, and I saw well-dressed tourists and few Catalan flags.

For our second day in Barcelona, I planned a visit to the Picasso Museum in the morning and then a trip to the beach in the afternoon. When we woke in the morning, the sunny, breezy day dispelled any lingering thoughts about Barcelona's conflicts. After the museum, we jumped on a bus to the beach. We were enjoying the views of the city from the bus window when the bus stopped dead in the middle of the street.

I stood to look at the road. "Is that a blockade in the street?" The bus driver made an announcement in Spanish, and everyone around us began gathering their bags and purses and leaving the bus. "What is going on?" I asked Dave. The other people on the bus were chattering among themselves and seemed as mystified as we were. This wasn't an everyday occurrence.

Once on the street, I couldn't tell exactly where we were, but I knew the general direction of the beach, so we began walking. The streets were quiet. The few people on the streets were walking quickly and talking softly. Glancing around, I saw many Catalan flags hanging from buildings. "I'm not sure this is where we should be right now," I muttered to Dave. I didn't see any buses, so we had no choice and kept walking. I pulled out my phone to find the road leading to the beach. The sidewalks became more and more crowded, and Dave and I stuck close together as the crowds swept us along. The group we were in stopped when we arrived at a large square churning with people. More people streamed into the square from side streets. I pulled Dave over to the side of one building and looked around. There was no room to move, and people clustered into groups, mostly talking in low voices, but some were loud and excited, gesturing wildly. On the other end of the square, a man was standing above the crowd, chanting into a megaphone. There was a jittery, tense excitement in the air. Catalan flags were everywhere, on clothing or face masks, some flags tossed over shoulders. On the building in front of us, there was a large Catalan flag. Military-looking people stood at attention in front of the building and I didn't see anyone entering or leaving. I remembered the tour guide of the day before telling us, "We will take independence." That is what this crowd was prepared to do.

"Let's go," Dave said. "I don't think there is a problem here, but I don't like the crowds.

I looked again at my phone and motioned to Dave the direction we needed to go. He started gently pushing through the crowds, and I followed until we were on a wide side street that was virtually empty. At the beach, we found a restaurant for food and a glass of wine. The scene we had come from seemed surreal. Here on the beach, the sun was shining and people were lying in the sunshine with all the time in the world to relax.

"What was that all about?" I wondered aloud to Dave. "I know there was an independence vote. I know it passed weeks ago, so why is everyone so…edgy." We ordered food and began drinking our wine. I opened my phone to find out more about the situation in Barcelona. When the waiter brought our food, I decided to ask her about the turmoil.

"On our way here, we were caught up in large crowds. The people looked very tense. There were a lot of Catalan flags. What is happening? Is there another vote?" I asked her. She was an older woman, probably around 50, and black curly hair surrounded her face. Her eyes shifted back and forth, and she lowered her head before speaking.

"The young people today, many of them feel like they are only Catalan—not Spanish. My parents came here from Andalusia. Spain has many different regions. We can all work together. Many people feel as I do."

"So, you voted against independence?"

"Bah. I did not vote. Many people did not vote. That is why the independence vote won easily. The vote meant nothing."

Dave and I finished lunch and walked out to the beach. We didn't have swimsuits or towels, but I took off my shoes and rolled up my pants. Being a born and raised Midwesterner, just the word "beach" is unique and magical to me. I don't care how cold the water is or how crowded the beach is; just sitting and watching the water and the sun shining on the waves is soothing. That day the rhythmic sounds of the waves on the beach were endlessly mesmerizing. The knots in my tense shoulders slowly relaxed as we walked along the water.

Our plane back to Rome left the next day. On our final evening in Barcelona, we stayed near our hostel for dinner and afterward took a long stroll along the Las Ramblas. "It feels weird to be here trying to have fun, to be a tourist, in the middle of this situation. People are emotional, some angry, and if there are more protests, the police and protestors will get hurt," I told Dave. I didn't know what answer Catalonia would arrive at or what answer was best. Independence. No independence. I didn't live here and couldn't fully understand the issues. I selfishly wanted to make it to the airport to get back to Rome before a transportation strike or a rally shut down the city.

The next day our plane wasn't scheduled to leave until late afternoon, but the Parliament of Catalonia was meeting at noon to vote on independence from Spain. There would certainly be a big city-wide rally and the roads would be full of people. We packed that night, and the next day we headed to the airport early.

I followed the events as they unfolded on the news after we returned to Rome. The Catalonia Parliament met on the day we left Barcelona and declared independence from Spain. Then the Spanish Senate dissolved the Parliament of Catalonia. Long after we returned to the U.S., the situation was still unresolved, and so are my dreams of returning to Barcelona.

TIP: Several groups are offering free walking tours around the U.S. and Europe: www.freetoursbyfoot.com and www.freetour.com. Although the tours are free, it is customary to tip the guide.

• TURNING ON THE HEAT •

Finally, finally, finally, the weather in Rome began to turn from hot and humid to cool. We wore jackets every day. The people around us, real Romans, had begun wearing coats and scarves at least a month earlier. I read how Italians worried about getting a draft or wind on their necks (the "colpo d' aria") and blamed it for most illnesses. The minute the temperature dropped below 70 degrees, the coats and scarves came out. Romans were taking no chances.

Our apartment wasn't particularly cold; those thick stone walls kept in the heat from the sun, but when November arrived, I began touching the radiators in the apartment and looking for a thermostat. The radiators were cold and we didn't have a thermostat. After some online research, I learned the Italian government controls the date when radiators and heaters are turned on in Italy. Rome was in Climate Zone "D," which was allowed heat from November 1st to April 15th for 12 hours a day. In the far south, Climate Zone "A" was allowed six hours of daily heat from December 1st to March 15th. This was a foreign concept to me, but also, it was November 5th, so why were my radiators still cold? Was there something we needed to do?

Claudio, our apartment manager, came by a few days later to collect the rent, and I asked about the heat. "Claudio, we need the heat," I said, touching the cold radiator. Claudio was a big burly guy who always wore an extra-large American-style belt buckle. I wanted to ask him if he'd bought it in America, but his English was not much better than my Italian.

113

"The heat, it comes on soon," he said. I showed him an Italian newspaper article I had found saying Rome furnaces were supposed to go on after November 1st. He frowned as he read the article and then looked at me. "Donata, she say heat, it comes on il quindicesimo…uh uh," he was searching for the English word, "the fiftieth." I was pretty sure he meant the fifteenth. Donata, our landlord, obviously didn't follow the government rules about turning on the heat.

Claudio motioned us to follow him into our kitchen, where he began fiddling with the controls on the big water tank on our kitchen wall. Those controls in our kitchen controlled the heat for all the radiators in the building, and Claudio decided just to go ahead and turn on the heat since he was there. Our radiators quickly warmed up, so much so that after a few days I turned all the radiators down to low except for one. Our apartment building's three-foot thick walls were very good at keeping out and diluting our Wi-Fi signal, but the walls also kept the apartment warm. We barely used any heat for our final month in Rome.

• THANKSGIVING •

Thanksgiving is absolutely my favorite holiday of the year. Dave and I had our traditions. Every year Dave was in charge of the turkey while I cooked the old favorites and maybe tried a new dish or two. We spent the morning cooking, the afternoon eating, and usually ended up at a movie late in the day. Our usual goal was to cram as many people as possible into the house.

This year would be different. For the first time since leaving the U.S., I began having pangs of homesickness. I daydreamed about flying home just for a short holiday where, miraculously, our entire family would be all together in one place, and we could see everyone. In reality, our family was scattered around the U.S., and the cost of airline tickets home would blow our budget. I spent a few days with a nearly constant lump in my throat, looking for anything "American" to give me a feeling of home, but there was no choice. We would have to settle in and make our own Thanksgiving in Italy.

Even though Europeans don't celebrate Thanksgiving, the online expat community spent weeks looking for turkeys. They all shared tips about which butcher offered turkey for sale and about the availability of cranberries. Without an oven in our apartment, cooking dinner on our own wasn't an option. The expat group offered tips for people like us, without ovens, and a few weeks before Thanksgiving, I bought tickets for the full turkey experience (plus football) at a local pub.

All in all, our Italian Thanksgiving pub experience was really good in a skewed sort of way. The entire meal was an Italian version of an American Thanksgiving. The turkey was spot on, beautiful, brown, moist. It was even salted. The rest of the food was a little off. Mashed potatoes but no gravy. Green beans but no sweet potatoes. What looked like cranberry sauce tasted a lot like cherry Jell-O. There were some thin slices of Italian bread instead of rolls with butter. No pie, no pumpkin pie or pecan pie, but there was a smooth, luscious cheesecake for dessert with a crunchy sweet crust. Since this was Italy, there was plenty of wine and we took our share of some dark Tuscan wines.

Best of all, there was football, in English, with English commercials. All the people in the bar spoke English. Dave and I chatted and compared notes with our table mates about travel. As Dave kept talking, I sat at our large crowded table and looked around the room at the dozens of people eating, drinking, and cheering the football players. Being surrounded by an understandable language was as comforting as the turkey. It was isolating to go each day and not understand what was being said around me and not being understood. I missed jokes and humor. After taking Italian language classes off and on for several years, I had a lot of words memorized in my head, but stringing those words together into sentences was much harder than I anticipated. I was afraid of making mistakes and looking like a fool. *No one knows me here. Mistakes are okay.* I reassured myself. But it wasn't easy to put my toddler-level Italian on display. At least on this one night, we could chat and laugh and joke with our fellow travelers, all of us far from home.

As our Italian Thanksgiving Day ended, we got on the phone and called home. We spoke to most of our family and compared notes on our Thanksgiving feasts and upcoming Christmas plans.

"Everyone at home seems fine." I took a sip of my wine. "I wish we could click our heels together and somehow, magically, be home."

"Yeah. But you know we will be there next year." Dave, as usual, was taking things as they came while I wished for more.

"I know. I love being here. But next year, I want to cook a big turkey and have everyone visit us."

I felt left out and missed our family and the fun happening at home but Dave was right. This was a trip we spent years planning. We had researched it, booked it, and were living the sort of everyday life many people envied. It would be over so fast. I was a little tearful, but next year, I promised myself we would cook a big meal, complete with gravy, sweet potatoes, and rolls, and pull out our photos and souvenirs of our trip. Next year we could have both our familiar family life and our memories of living in Italy. And next year would be here before we knew it.

• TRASTEVERE •

It is impossible to write about Rome and not rave about the neighborhood we lived in for three months—Trastevere. When I began looking for an apartment to rent in Rome, I knew we wanted to be close to the real city center and not out in the suburbs. After reading dozens of articles extolling the virtues of Rome's different neighborhoods, I agonized over the choices. Dave, of course, would be happy with whatever apartment I preferred. He was a big believer in the "happy wife, happy life" saying. That put extra pressure on me to not make a mistake and get us stuck in a bad neighborhood. It was luck, not my research that led us to our small apartment steps from the Ponte Sisto Bridge near the Piazza Trilussa.

The streets in Trastevere looked exactly like an Italian movie or a postcard. The entire area was cobblestone roads, narrow alleys, laundry hanging on clothes-lines over the street, crumbly old buildings, shops, restaurants, piazzas, ivy-covered walls, churches, markets, craft beer pubs, gelato stores, and tabacchi shops. At night the nearby Piazza Trilussa became a party zone, and there were always people sitting on the steps of the Piazza talking and sipping drinks. Nearly every night, a variety of ever-changing magicians and street performers entertained the crowd, or musicians played really good music. We could hear the music from our apartment when our windows were open, and we would wander over some evenings to sit and listen. The music played until the early hours of the morning, and afterward, people stumbled home down our small alley.

It was a young, vibrant, lively neighborhood, and we lived there. It was hard not to feel smug when the tour buses stopped and led tours through our neighborhood.

The Villa Farnesina was a short walk from our apartment, and we explored the glittering villa with its 16th-century frescoes by Raphael. Across the street from the Villa was the Palazzo Corsini with art by Caravaggio and other Italian artists of the 17th and 18th centuries. We packed a lunch and spent an entire afternoon relaxing at the botanic gardens. One Sunday, we went to check out the enormous Porta Portese flea market, and another Sunday took a bus to the top of the Gianicolo hill for the breathtaking view over the city. There are almost 1,000 churches in the city of Rome, and Trastevere has one of the oldest, the glittering Santa Maria in Trastevere.

And the restaurants, oh the restaurants. We tried traditional Roman tripe at Ristorante Da Massi (well, *I* tried the tripe), and we ate some of the best "by the slice" pizza at Dar Poeta alla Scala. A photo of Dave and me is taped to the wall at Dar Poeta along with dozens of other tourist snapshots. We went back multiple times to Romolo, nel Giardino della Fornarina, where one night Newt Gingrich (former Speaker of the U.S. House of Representatives) and his wife sat for dinner at a table across the room. And why not? Trastevere was the place to be.

In Trastevere, a casual comment inspired us to begin a city-wide spaghetti carbonara fact-finding mission. At a restaurant near our apartment, we sat examining the lunch menus and waiting to order. We couldn't help overhearing an English-speaking couple a few tables away, and when the woman said to her companion, "When we leave Rome, I dream of their carbonara," Dave and I exchanged glances. Both of us ordered the carbonara, and it was good, but we weren't overly impressed.

Spaghetti carbonara is spaghetti covered in a creamy egg and guanciale (pork cheek) deliciousness. People may argue over the ingredients of an authentic carbonara, and they may argue about whether carbonara was invented in Rome, but it was on nearly every menu in the city.

"Were they talking about this restaurant or some other one?" I wondered out loud to Dave. They had left before I could strike up a conversation. "I think we can do better." Lunch was over and I was planning our next meal.

"I'll eat more carbonara," Dave said. He loved eating pasta and I loved trying new restaurants. Our carbonara mission was the perfect activity for both of us.

We tried carbonara at a dozen restaurants in Rome, but the very best carbonara was at a tiny restaurant in Trastevere called Eggs. There was only room for ten customers, and as we waited one evening for our dinner, I watched the cooks move around the minuscule kitchen with well-executed precision. They offered five to six variations on carbonara, and we returned many times to try them all. Carbonara may or may not have been invented in Rome, but both of us agreed Trastevere produced the best carbonara in the city. Trastevere was our small piece of delight in the crazy, crowded, hot, pushing and shoving city of Rome.

TIP: *After months in Rome, eating high carb pizza and pasta nearly every day, I expected my blood sugar to skyrocket and anticipated using twice as much daily insulin. That didn't happen and I only saw a small increase. There are dozens of factors that affect blood sugar levels, like exercise, stress, time of day, illness, and lack of sleep. I can count carbs and estimate insulin doses, but it is impossible to completely factor in all of the unexplained things happening in my body throughout the day. Diabetes management is not an exact science. I finally concluded that the miles and miles of daily walking in Rome (exercise) offset the high carbs in my daily meals of pasta and pizza. My daily intake of wine also increased and I am pretty sure that lowered my stress levels.*

TIP: True Roman Spaghetti alla Carbonara only has four ingredients:

8 ounces guanciale, diced
1 pound spaghetti
2 large eggs
1 cup Pecorino Romano, freshly grated

Directions:

In a large pan, fry the guanciale over medium-high heat until rendered and crisp, about 10 minutes.

Beat eggs and pecorino together in a small bowl with a fork and set aside.

Cook the spaghetti to al dente, then drain, return to pot, toss with guanciale and rendered fat over low heat, and immediately transfer to shallow bowls.

Pour egg/cheese mixture over each of the four bowls, add black pepper to taste, and quickly mix with a fork to slightly cook the eggs with the hot pasta. The result should be creamy, not dry.

Serve immediately.

• LEAVING ROME •

November 2017 at the Museo Nazionale Romano-Palazzo Altemps:

Me: "The lighting in this museum is better than others. More subtle and less glare."

Dave: "You are comparing museum lighting?"

Me: "Yeah. We may have been in Rome long enough."

Being in Rome wasn't the experience I expected. We didn't become true locals in the dreamy way I had imagined. I tried to speak Italian and all the Italians wanted to speak English. Despite the language barrier, we did settle into the city. The seasons changed and the piazzas became slippery with wet fall leaves. Restaurants fired up their outside patio heaters. Summer fruits and vegetables disappeared from grocery stores. The buses and trams became familiar to us and I could navigate the city easily. We explored out-of-the-way corners of the city and returned to our favorite restaurants over and over. The Christmas lights and decorations began to appear as we finally put on our jackets and scarves.

The things I worried about, the things that had woken me up at 3 a.m. while we planned this journey, hadn't been a problem so far. Our phones and computers worked. We didn't have any health emergencies or accidents. I went to a Roman medical clinic only twice, once for a sore throat and once for an eye infection. Our money was holding out, and we weren't going over budget. Our Roman landlord returned our deposit money. Homesickness had overwhelmed me at Thanksgiving, but I faced it down. Since we avoided catastrophe, I relaxed a little. It was easier for me to let go of fixed schedules and to go with the flow, but I was still alert and on guard for unseen pitfalls, just in case.

I established new diabetes routines in Rome. When we first began traveling, all of my carb/insulin decisions were instantly harder. It was impossible to avoid high-carb pizza and pasta. As we traveled, we ate out a lot more, and I didn't know all the ingredients going into the food I ate. In Rome, I quickly got into the habit of estimating carbs conservatively and letting my blood sugar go higher than usual. High blood sugar wasn't good, but low blood sugar was dangerous. It was safer to deliberately underestimate carbs, let my blood sugar go a little high, and then take a correction dose of insulin to bring it down. Still, I was thankful I had found insulin at a reasonable price in Rome, and I wasn't running out of diabetes supplies or insulin pumps.

Three months in Rome had radically shifted our lives and our relationship. Every day we were bombarded with sights, smells, and tastes that were new and unique. Our lives together in Rome mirrored my life back home—busy, mobile, and active. Dave, the homebody, didn't seem to mind the drastic change to his routines. He was on board with everything I planned and began taking his large camera everywhere we went. He spent his spare time at our apartment editing and cropping pictures. I was happy to see him planning and engaged in something that interested *him*.

We shifted roles and took on new jobs. When we first arrived, Dave offered to take over the family cooking and grocery shopping because I was spending a lot of time planning all of our sightseeing and figuring out the buses/train/subway around the city. We worked together to navigate the challenges of traveling. Things happened, things went wrong, and we could never predict what those things would be, but we worked it out.

Sometimes that meant throwing money at the problem and grabbing a cab during a transportation strike. Sometimes that meant adjusting the schedule and staying home on a sick day and hitting the museum the next week.

In this new foreign post-retirement life, we began learning how to juggle time together and time alone. It was stressful for both of us, but especially me, to be together constantly, day and night. After I finally found the words to explain to Dave how hemmed in I felt, we made some changes. Dave spent more time on his grocery shopping runs and sometimes took the camera and made an afternoon of it. I planned time alone with a book at a piazza or went alone to explore new areas of the city. We were making it up as we went along.

By the time we left Rome, the tourists had finally thinned out and the streets were less crowded. If we had it to do over again, we would still come to this beautiful, crazy, ancient, dirty, stunning, crowded, mesmerizing city. In the end, Rome finally became "ours." But now we were leaving. Our 90 days in Rome had ended and it was time to go to Croatia.

TIP: Never eat near a tourist site. The food is almost universally bad, generally more expensive, tourist food. Get at least three blocks, or more, away from any and all tourist sites before you even think about sitting to eat.

TIP: Go online and find a local newspaper for the city you are staying in and keep up with local news. In Rome, this will likely include information about the dates and times of the frequent transportation strikes. In Croatia, I found times of local concerts and events. I felt more like a local when I kept track of the local city and national news.

PART III: CROATIA

• AN UP AND COMING DESTINATION •

Before deciding to live in Croatia for three months, I couldn't have found it on a map. When we learned we couldn't get the visa necessary to stay in Italy for our entire year-long trip, we looked for an inexpensive country, outside the Schengen area, with mild winter weather. We debated spending three months in Bulgaria or Romania. Both would be inexpensive and both were outside the Schengen area at the time. But then I saw pictures of the sunny beaches of Croatia on the Adriatic Sea. Even though we planned to be in Croatia from December to February, and it wouldn't be beach season, the pictures of sparkling water had me hooked.

In Croatia, I wanted a larger city with more English speakers, better pharmacies, and medical care. The capital city of Zagreb was large and full of restaurants and museums, but it was further north and not on the coast. Dubrovnik on Croatia's southern coast looked beautiful, but it was hilly and full of stairs. That left the coastal city of Split, a population of 178,000 and home to Diocletian's Palace.

When we told our friends and family we would be spending the winter of our year-long trip in Split, Croatia, everyone had a blank look. "Where is that?" they asked. We educated many of our friends and family about this beautiful, little-known country, but Croatia was becoming well-known without our help. In 2017 it was on Trip Advisor's must-visit list of "up and coming destinations" around the globe. Fodor's travel guide listed Split, Croatia, as number four on its 2018 "Go" list. Maybe we were at the forefront of the herds of people coming to Croatia in the future.

In Croatia, the plan was to save money to help pay for the remainder of the year. The spring portion of our trip to London would be expensive. The final three months in Venice would be even more expensive. In Croatia, we vowed to be frugal. Frugal meant I needed to find an inexpensive apartment. It also meant we wouldn't be traveling around Europe like we did when we lived in Rome. We planned to hunker down for the winter and stay put.

When we were still in the U.S., picking places to live and making plans about our unknown futures months in advance, all we could do was pencil in a plan and hope it worked. As we left Rome for Croatia to live our penciled-in lives, it felt like starting over again, and the idea of new things, people, food, languages, and customs had me feeling both eager and anxious.

• ARRIVAL •

I found our apartment in Split, Croatia, thanks to Facebook.

Before leaving Rome, I began searching for apartments in Split with Airbnb and found a few that would work. It was confusing, though. The prices varied wildly from €400 to €1,500 (or more) for identical-looking apartments. Since the expat's group in Rome had been so helpful, I joined a Facebook page for Expats in Split and posted a question.

> ME: Hello to all you, Expats in Split. My husband and I are looking at apartments in Split for a three-month stay beginning December 1st. We want to live near the old city. How much should I expect to pay for a one-bedroom apartment near the old city? Thanks for your help!
>
> Marija: I pay €350 for a one-bedroom, but I am not close to the city center.
>
> Me: Does your apartment have a washing machine for clothes? Do you pay utilities?
>
> Marija: No washing machine and I pay utilities. The apartment belongs to my boyfriend's family.
>
> Željko: My family has an apartment to rent close to the city. It has two bedrooms and the rent is €1,100. Contact me if you are interested in renting it.
>
> Ana: Pam, I have an apartment near the old city. It is listed on Airbnb at this link [..]. I can rent to you for €500.

The link Ana sent me through https://www.airbnb.com was for a small, nicely decorated apartment near the old town, and as a bonus, we would be renting it through Airbnb. I still couldn't bring myself to send money directly to people on Facebook.

Our rent had been €1,200 a month in Rome, so Ana's apartment was a significant savings. There was a washing machine in the bathroom and the rent included Wi-Fi and utilities. Ana and I traded emails, and she gave me the address of the apartment building so I could look at the neighborhood on Google Maps. The apartment was close to the sea-front and the old part of Split. Dave and I quickly agreed to take it and it was a huge relief to know where we would be living for the winter. Of course, I wondered what the apartment would actually feel like or what it would be like to live there. *What if the neighbors next door like loud music, and the neighbor above paces around in heels?* I thought to myself. Pictures on the internet of an apartment can't tell you all the details.

There was only one flight per day from Rome to Split, and on December 1st, we were on it. The airport in Split was tiny, and getting our checked bags and going through customs took less than 20 minutes. We arrived in the evening, and outside the airport terminal we quickly spotted the car Ana helped us find to take us from Trogir to Split. Choosing a car instead of a bus was a little splurge, but we each hauled two suitcases and full backpacks plus my insulated beer cooler of cold insulin. We were loaded down, and the car cost slightly less than a taxi, a bargain.

Ana met us at the apartment. She was a petite woman with large dark eyes and a friendly smile. She led us to the building elevator and helped us wrangle our suitcases up to the fourth floor. Inside the apartment, she showed us around.

"Here is the main room." She gestured around the narrow room, which contained a warm red couch, TV, and round wooden dining table. "I lived here with my daughter for many years, but she grew up. Teenagers need more space from their Mama." Ana laughed and I nodded in understanding. *Teenage daughters should come equipped with a separate apartment.* We peeked through a door into a small bedroom with a full-sized bed, the only bedroom, and went to explore the kitchen.

"The kitchen, you see, there is a stove, dishwasher, microwave, toaster, and machine for coffee." Ana opened a cupboard to show us dishes and a drawer with silverware and, *exciting*, some kitchen knives. We had left behind the kitchen knives bought in Rome; they didn't seem worth the airport security questions.

"On the counter, is that an oven?" It was separate from the microwave and larger.

"Yes. If you do not want it, I can remove it," Ana said. We definitely wanted it and I looked forward to doing some cooking, and entertained visions of roast chicken.

"The things, the oven, toaster, dishwasher, microwave, and coffee, you cannot use them all the same time. The electricity cannot do it," she warned.

In the bathroom was a clothes washer, but no bidet, and the shower was larger than the one in Rome. Of course, the apartment didn't have a clothes dryer, but outside the door overlooking the large interior courtyard, there was our own personal clothes-line. Ana gave us a quick final lesson on the Wi-Fi, the heater, and the trash system. "I would like to meet you for coffee. Maybe next week?" she offered. I agreed and promised to email her after we settled in.

Locking the door behind Ana as she left, I turned to look at the apartment a little more. It was every bit as cute and charming as the pictures on Airbnb. Although it wasn't large, it wasn't as scratched and scruffy as our Rome apartment, and the décor was welcoming. There were pictures on the walls and a thick rug on the floor. We even had a balcony.

Dave pulled out the bottle of wine he had packed in his suitcase and poured a glass for each of us before following me out onto the balcony. I leaned over the railing and looked to the right. There was just enough sun left for me to see the light sparkling on water—the sea. The fresh air gave me a little burst of energy.

"What a long day," I said. Of course, I had made sure we woke up extra early in Rome to get to the airport.

"We need two extra people to haul all of our luggage around."

"Well, we get to stay in one place for three months. No dragging the suitcases anywhere for a while." I stretched and rolled my head around to work the kinks out of my neck. "First stop tomorrow—the grocery store." Dave agreed and we went inside to warm up and pull pajamas out of our suitcases.

In the morning, the apartment was barely warmer than the air outside. I took a turn pushing buttons on the remote that controlled the heater on the wall then handed it over to Dave. After grabbing a blanket from the bed, I sat on the couch, leafing through the binder Ana left us with information about the apartment. The instructions for the heater were in Croatian.

"We have to call Ana. I am freezing!" I said. Dave didn't disagree, but as I went to find my phone, he worked out that it was necessary to press and *hold* the "Start" button before the heater would start. Dave made coffee using his suitcase stash while I pulled on clothes. As we drank coffee, we played with the heater and quickly discovered 18° Celsius was still pretty chilly, and 24° Celsius made the apartment very hot. Even though the rent included utilities, I didn't want to run up a big bill for Ana. Utilities cost a lot more in Europe than they do in the U.S. Before leaving for the grocery store, I turned the heat to low and pulled on an extra sweater. After melting in Rome's heat for months, I promised myself not to complain about the cold in Croatia.

TIP: CONVERTING CELSIUS TO FAHRENHEIT:
Take the Celsius temperature and double it, then add 30.
The result is very close to the temperature in Fahrenheit.

TIP: Make contact with expat groups, usually on Facebook, in the city or cities where you will be traveling. Expats are on the ground and they can give valuable insider tips. Remember, though, that Expats are not tour guides, so use them sparingly and wisely.

• LEARNING THE LANGUAGE •

How should I pronounce "gdje"? It was immediately apparent that the Croatian language was far outside anything I had seen before. Italian is a Latin-based language, and in Rome, I could generally read signs, menus, and papers and figure out what was being communicated. Italian is similar to English in many ways. On the other hand, in Croatia, there are a lot more "J," "Z," and "V's" in their words. Street names on signs looked like code words. To say "where is the bathroom" in Croatian would be "gdje je kupaonica." On the plus side, we found many people spoke English, so when a waiter came up to us and said, "Zdravo, što mogu vam donijeti" (Hello, what can I bring you?), we smiled and said "Hello," and the waiter shifted smoothly into English.

Hearing this new language made me curious about its roots. The Foreign Service Institute, which trains U.S. diplomats for their overseas jobs, created a ranking for languages according to difficulty. They say Italian is similar to English and is a Category One language. On the other hand, Croatian is a Category Four language or a "language with significant linguistic and/or cultural differences from English." This wasn't good news, especially after my struggles with Italian in Rome. *Maybe I could learn some basics—please, thank you and hello—keep it simple.*

At the grocery store the day after we arrived, Google Translate saved us. Some of the food looked familiar, but many of the food items were utterly new. There were baskets of two-foot-long slabs of what appeared to be dried fish. Although the canned and jarred food had pictures, the pictures could be anything—salsa, or pureed tomatoes, or tomato sauce. It was hard to tell. Sometimes Google Translate couldn't even translate the words on the containers of food.

The grocery store was small, but we were used to that from Rome. We stocked up on some basics—eggs and fruit for my breakfast and cereal and milk for Dave—more coffee for both of us. Pasta and pasta sauce for quick dinners at home. Fruit and vegetables needed to be weighed and a price label attached, but no one picked up the produce with gloved hands. As in Rome, the first shopping trip took a long time as we took turns pondering the labels and pictures on the food containers.

I stood in the checkout line behind Dave and watched the people ahead of us as they paid for their food. Everyone was using a scannable shopping discount card like those used in the U.S. I went ahead of Dave to help put our food on the conveyer belt and to find out about the cards.

"Excuse me. Can we get a grocery store card?" I mimed scanning a card like I had seen other people do. The cashier smiled at me but didn't answer and her face was blank. She said something in Croatian and I shrugged helplessly. The older couple who checked out ahead of us and who were about to leave the store, turned back to help.

"You need a card?" they asked. *English.*

"Yes. I think so. Do we get discounts with the card?"

"You get sale prices. Without the card, you pay full price." They spoke to the cashier, in quick Croatian, and she smiled again and reached into a drawer and handed me a discount card. The people in line behind us seemed interested in our exchange and stared at us curiously. Although Split was a reasonably large city, I began to wonder if we would find as many English speakers as I expected. What about pharmacists, doctors, bus drivers, and people outside the hospitality and tourist sectors? The common Croatian words and phrases I hoped to learn wouldn't get us very far in everyday life.

• CHRISTMAS •

After only a few days in Split, I could tell Split and Rome "felt" completely different. Maybe it was the season because when we arrived on December 1st, Advent was just beginning in Split. Maybe it was just us. When we left Rome, both of us were a little grumpy and ready for a change. We were tired of the city's pushy, crowded, busyness—tired of the grime, graffiti, and litter. Split felt young, energetic, and fresh. The light bounced off of the Adriatic Sea. It was clean, bustling, and brightly lit, full of people drinking beer and mulled wine and walking along The Riva— the waterfront section of shops and restaurants. Christmas was just around the corner and a sense of excitement and celebration was in the air.

Advent was huge in Split, and I followed the events as best I could by looking at *Croatia Week*, the local online newspaper. Nearly every day, there was a concert, choral group, or children's activity going on in the city. On the Riva, a bandstand held daily concerts, and it became our favorite place to savor a glass of mulled wine and watch the parades of people. We went after dark to the brightly lit "Children's" Park near the Golden Gate of Diocletian's Palace and wandered for more than an hour through the Christmas light displays showing dozens of Christmas characters and scenes.

One night we found a concert by the Splitski Guadacki Kvartet with two violins, a viola, and a cello. They played traditional Croatian songs but also several American Christmas songs. When they started playing "O Holy Night" with slow, haunting loveliness, my throat began to hurt, and

I couldn't swallow. I wiped my eyes on my sleeve. This familiar song was Christmas, comfort, family, connection, love, all wrapped in one song. *We are so far from home.*

Afterward, walking back through the cold darkness to our apartment, the sudden burst of pain subsided—*that song.* My tears had caught me off guard and I didn't want to talk about it. We were here. It was Christmas. We would be fine. Dave wrapped his arm around mine in silent comfort. My mind wandered to last year's Christmas. I could picture it. Everyone had a stocking hanging over the fireplace. It took me weeks to find stocking-sized gifts for everyone. The air smelled of ham, and the pies, made yesterday, sat on a side table. The fire would be lit. There wasn't room to set up a Christmas tree with our small house full of people, so I had given Dave the job of tacking Christmas lights up around one window.

I needed to pull my mind away from the past and think of how we could bring our normal life to Croatia. "What should we have for our Christmas dinner?" I asked Dave. Food always made both of us happier.

"Something different. Lamb"

"And mashed potatoes."

"And pie."

"You know I won't eat the pie." I laughed. "Or maybe just a little taste."

"Peanut butter cookies." Dave knew my favorites.

"Don't tease me. You won't find peanut butter." He just smiled and I knew I had issued a challenge. If there were peanut butter in the city, Dave would find it.

As the days passed, the city filled with more decorations, lights, and people. Bakeries overflowed with baked goods, and Christmas huts along the Riva sold traditional Croatian foods and gifts. On the road near our apartment, a Christmas tree lot popped up around the 15th of the month, and they were doing a brisk business. Near the Christmas tree lot, old ladies sold plastic dishes filled with bright green grass, while another nearby vendor was selling bags of moss.

We settled in quickly and I texted Ana about getting together for coffee. She had been helpful, sending me links about Christmas activities around town, and I knew she could answer some of my questions about Christmas traditions in Croatia. When we walked into the small coffee shop to meet Ana, a wall of cigarette smoke hit me in the face. Restaurants didn't seem to allow smoking indoors, but all of the coffee shops we passed were full of smokers. We ordered coffee and I walked outside to find a table on the patio. There were still smokers there, but the air was fresher. Ana found us and brought her coffee to our table.

We exchanged bits of news about the apartment and our impressions of Split. She was surprised to learn that we thought the city was young and vibrant. I saw lots of strollers and small children in Split. In Rome, the average age seemed to be about 60.

"Ana, Christmas in Croatia is so bright and cheerful, but I don't understand the customs. What is the grass I see ladies selling?" I began.

"Oh, that is not grass. It is wheat. It is sown on St. Lucia's Day and then put on the table on Christmas day. If your wheat is healthy, it means you would have success and good luck in the New Year." I made a note to buy some wheat. Who didn' t need good luck?

Articles I read said straw was placed underneath the Christmas Eve table cloth but didn't say why. Other articles said the straw was a symbol of good future crops or, alternatively, a fertility symbol. Maybe the straw tradition had lapsed because I didn't see any straw for sale in Split. I moved on to moss.

"The bags of moss? Are they for good luck too?" I asked.

"The moss is for the family Nativity Scene. Every family has one under the Christmas tree. I have many different sets. My daughter sets up one and I choose another." That made sense. On one trip to the Mall of Split, I had seen dozens of Nativity sets for sale in every shape, style, and size.

Ana explained more of the customs. She told us kids in Croatia might receive Christmas gifts on several occasions. In some parts of Croatia, Santa Claus (called Djed Mraz) put treats in shoes Croatian children left on the windowsill. In other areas, St. Lucy was the traditional bringer of gifts, and baby Jesus got some credit for bringing gifts on Christmas Eve. Naughty kids didn't get coal in their stockings, but a giant monster with horns called Krampus might leave them golden twigs so they would remember to behave. Ana laughed at the idea that naughty kids received coal in America.

Dave and I waved goodbye to Ana and left the coffee shop to do some Christmas shopping. We wanted to find a Christmas ornament from Croatia to go with the ornament we had picked up in Rome. We planned our Christmas carefully. Because we were far from home and alone, it was important to make the day special and not focus on what we were missing. I had picked up an elegant leather Italian wallet for Dave in Rome. Dave bought me the pair of handmade Croatian earrings I admired at a local shop. Our gifts needed to be small, light, and had to travel well for another six months.

The butcher at the nearby butcher shop sold lamb for our Christmas dinner, but he didn't speak any English. Pointing at what we wanted, we struggled to avoid brushing up against the enormous body of a whole dead pig hanging in the window at our backs. Early in December, I sent Amazon gift cards to our family so they could pick their own Christmas gifts. I thought about sending gifts from our travels, but Dave convinced me the shipping costs would cost more than the gifts.

Our neighbor was a tiny, tiny elderly Croatian lady named Lucia who didn't speak a word of English, and yet whenever she saw us in the hallway or hanging laundry, she smiled broadly and went out of her way to speak and pantomime words. A few days before Christmas, Lucia brought over a plate of home-baked Croatian treats for us, and we gave her a small plate of American-style cookies, including peanut butter, baked by Dave.

The friendliness in Split was heartening. Often when we were in a crowd, say at the grocery store, the person standing next to us would start chatting in Croatian. We would smile and reply in English and they would chuckle and smile back or speak English if they could. Random public friendliness was much appreciated, especially at Christmas. We were making small connections here.

On Christmas Eve, we called everyone in our family and caught up on the news. It was sweet to hear their voices. Finished with calls, Dave and I sat on our cheerful red sofa with a glass of wine and talked about how the lights, food, decorations, and friendliness of Croatians had comforted us both during our quiet Christmas season.

Sretan Božić. (Merry Christmas.)

• GETTING OUT OF TOWN •

"Maybe it is time to get out of town?" I said, looking at a calendar. Dave was immediately on board with my idea.

Once Christmas and New Years were over, Split slowed down quickly. I knew things would be quiet, but I hadn't anticipated how many restaurants and shops would close for the offseason. Our daily routines changed dramatically. In Rome, there was something and somewhere new to go every single day. There were only a dozen or so real "tourist" sites and museums in Split, and I planned to spread them out over our three-month stay, not go to all of them the first few weeks.

Opening the computer, I sat at the dining table and looked at my budget sheets before starting to move numbers around. Our rent in Croatia was lower than in Rome. We didn't buy monthly transportation passes here. Our Rome budget had included €1000 per month for traveling, but we weren't spending that now. We were eating out less but buying more groceries. How much extra money was leftover each month? Could we go somewhere with our extra money? Dave sat down beside me as I worked.

"I know Croatia is our chance to save money for the months ahead, but…if we adjusted a little here and there, if we planned only ONE trip from Croatia, if we ate at home a little more…" Muttering to myself, I liked the numbers I was seeing on the budget. Dave knew I was thinking about a trip to Egypt. I had been tracking prices with an Egyptian tour company for weeks.

143

"A trip to Egypt would be amazing," Dave said. It was true. Every time we traveled, every time we navigated a new city, we somehow found our way to whatever Egyptian exhibit was nearby. Egypt fascinated both of us. After seeing so many Egyptian re-creations, maybe it was time to see the real thing.

"You know Egypt isn't Europe. It will be harder. Different." Now I was the one hesitating. Going to Egypt had always been our "crazy, off the wall, wouldn't it be wonderful, what if we could make it work," back of the envelope idea. Still, Egypt wasn't Europe.

If we went, it would be a guided tour—which made me feel less nervous. The company I was looking at received good reviews from customers. The airfare from Split was only a few hundred euros each, *much cheaper than if we flew from the U.S. to Egypt.* I was talking myself into this, defying my fear and hesitation. My thoughts were racing. *If we went in January or February, it will be the offseason for tourists, and the trip will be a little less expensive. Dave wants to go if I want to go.*

Toggling over to my email, I saw a new email from Memphis Tours, the company offering guided Egyptian tours. If we booked the tour quickly, we could get a 15% discount. The discussion was over. We jumped on it. Christmas was over and we would have most of January to settle into Split before setting off for Cairo.

• NAVIGATING THE CITY •

Google Maps totally spoiled me. In Rome, I simply put the name of our destination into the Google Maps app on my phone, and the app displayed directions to walk, drive, or use public transportation to get to the destination. *Voilà!* I didn't even need an address. In Split, the Google Maps app only gave me walking and driving directions and didn't seem to realize buses existed. Most of the time, we stuck to the center of town and walked everywhere. In the city center, the small alleys were only for pedestrians. Three small grocery stores were nearby. The Riva and the sea were less than a mile away and we could walk to dozens of restaurants. But for those times when we went out into the surrounding city, we needed the bus.

I began to piece together a way to get around the city. Step one, I looked on Google Maps to see, generally, how to get to our destination, i.e., where was Ulica Kavanjinova? Step two, I opened a website I found for Split buses (www.promet-split.hr) and looked at each bus route, one by one, to see which routes were in the general section of the city where we wanted to go. Finally, I toggled back and forth between the Google Maps app and the Promet bus website until I could guesstimate and narrow down the bus that would get us closest to our destination. It was not a perfect system, but it did work, more or less, and we could get to the mall and the doctor's office. The bus stop in the large square in front of the Croatian National Theater became our starting point for trips to the outer parts of the city we routinely used.

Dave had heard all of my complaints about the inadequacies of Google Maps, but he was the one who pointed out the problems with the bus stops in Split. He stopped abruptly one morning as we walked by the bus stop outside of our apartment building.

"Do you see a bus number?" he asked, pointing. I looked at the small bus shelter. I hadn't paid attention to it as it wasn't one we used. Circling the bus shelter, both of us examined it carefully for the first time. "There is no bus stop number or name," he said.

Dave was right. I walked inside the shelter and started trying to decipher the signs, but they were clearly just advertisements. Nothing in the shelter gave a route, name, number or bus schedule. What buses stopped here? Where did they go after they left? As we inspected the shelter, a bus stopped in front, and two people hopped off. Well, now I knew at least one bus, the number eight, used this stop. When we got home, I found the bus stop on the Promet website and figured out that the number eight was the only bus using that particular stop. It really should not have been so difficult.

Split had a really good, extensive bus system. The tickets were cheap, they ran on time and were clean and not crowded. I just wish they were easier to use. If Split really becomes the hot, go-to destination of 2018 and beyond, Google Maps will have to incorporate the Split bus routes and schedules in its app, and the Promet bus system will need to invest in signs.

TIP: In both Rome and Split, we often used Uber to go somewhere early or late in the day when we didn't want to struggle with buses. Dave downloaded the Uber app to his phone, and it worked perfectly in every city we traveled to (although there was talk in London about banning Uber).

TIP: In Split, unlike Rome, you can buy bus tickets from the driver. There are also working kiosks where you can buy tickets. If you purchase a ticket from a kiosk, you need to show it to the driver when you get on the bus. Also, unlike Rome, in Split we often saw ticket-checkers going up and down bus aisles to make sure people bought tickets. People without tickets were sent to the bus driver to buy tickets, and there didn't seem to be any penalty for being ticketless.

• COOKING CLASS •

Our landlord Ana was friendly and helped us settle in, finding concerts and events for us and recommending restaurants. She told us about the Skmer Cooking School, and just after the New Year, I went online to book a cooking class.

The class I picked included a tour of the local markets, so early one morning we met the instructor, Chef Petar, near the large outdoor Green Market to select vegetables for the meal the three of us would be cooking together. The sky was threatening snow, but still, the Green Market was busy with dozens of vendors selling vegetables, meats, baked goods, flowers, eggs, clothes, and handmade items. Everyone was bundled up against the cold, and the air smelt of smoked meats and spicy greens.

Chef Petar was a young man, probably around 35, and like many Croatians, very tall. He led us past several vendors, seeking out the back corner of the market. "Some vendors here buy vegetables from the grocery store and re-sell them," Petar said. He led us to a vegetable vendor where he bought some onions and Brussel sprouts. "At this stall, vegetables are from the farm." Petar pointed out a few other trustworthy vendors. Dave still did most of the grocery shopping and took note of the vendors to deal with in the future.

Next, we followed Petar through the winding alleys to the fish market. Even before arriving at the market, I could smell the salty, fishy aroma. Petar had already bought the fish we would need for our day of cooking but wanted to show us where to find the market. Dave and I walked by the fish market nearly every day but never bought anything. Fish at the market were fresh out of the sea, and neither Dave nor I had experience buying or cooking fresh fish.

"How do you know which fish is the best?" I asked

"Look at this fish," Petar said, pointing. "The eyes are clear, not cloudy." Petar bent over slightly and moved his face closer to the fish on the table and sniffed, showing us how to check for freshness. "It does not smell like fish. A fresh fish should never smell like fish," he said.

With all of our supplies in hand, we began walking to the cooking school. The Skmer Cooking School was on the ground floor of an apartment building, and the facilities were top-notch and professional. The sizeable main cooking station was for large cooking demonstrations, and there were four other separate smaller cooking stations, each complete with a five-burner stove, oven, pots, pans, and ample chopping space. Petar set up in one of the smaller cooking spots, and Dave and I watched while he made a red mullet ceviche, cooked a fish and prawn soup, and the main dish of grilled fish and Brussel sprouts (which Petar called little cabbages). This wasn't a hands-on class, but we helped fillet the red mullet just to get a feel for it.

The kitchen began to smell delicious, and even though I'd eaten breakfast only two hours earlier, I got hungry. Time flew by quickly as we chatted with Petar about Croatia, his family, traveling, life in our country and his, and food.

"How long have you been a chef?" I asked Petar.

He smiled and shook his head. "A long time. I studied at a school in Italy. I would like to go back."

"How did you get to Split? Didn't you say you own a restaurant here?"

"My wife is from Split. When my daughter was born, we moved here for the family. My restaurant, yes, is called Mazzgoon, in the city center."

"We just ate there a few days ago," Dave said.

"Yes, it was great. Will you stay open in the winter?" I asked. Whole blocks of the city center were dark and shut down. Finding an open restaurant was becoming harder.

"The restaurant will be open, but I am taking my wife to Italy for a month to visit a restaurant I hope to buy. Croatia is changing. Everything costs more—butter, eggs, meat. Wages, they do not go higher. The tourists come and they only want cheap fast food."

I knew Croatia had entered the European Union several years earlier, but it was not yet part of the Schengen Zone and didn't use the euro. It still used its own currency, the kuna. One U.S. dollar bought around seven kunas, which was great for travelers like us but not so great for residents. When Croatia started using the euro, would their kunas be worth 1/7th of a euro? *That would wipe out a lot of savings.*

"So, you want to move to Italy?" I asked.

"Yes, if my wife will go. The family is everything in Croatia and now we have a child." He sounded glum, like he was stuck. There was a lot to think about, and we were all quiet as Petar finished cooking.

When the food was ready, Dave and I started with the fish ceviche, served over a bed of rucola lettuces with a light dressing of olive oil, lemon, and orange. We ate every bite of the ceviche and sopped up the sauce with bread. The next course was grilled fish and Brussel sprouts, and after that, a third course, a light, flavorful fish soup. As we ate, Dave poured from a bottle of red wine Petar opened. For dessert, Petar brought out a crème brulee he had made ahead of time. The crunchy topping looked delicious, but I shook my head regretfully. I just couldn't do it, so Dave ate both servings. After thanking Petar and wishing him luck with his visit to Italy, we started the walk home. I was longing for a nap, but I also began thinking about a trip to the fish market.

TIP: Croatians eat a lot of fish and seafood. After our cooking class I was determined to try to cook a whole fish. I bought a fish from the fish market (after carefully checking the eyes). The book of Croatian recipes that I had bought was short on details so I had to wing it a little. The following recipe is for cooked trout (kuhana pastrva)

> 1 kg whole trout (2.2 pounds)
>
> 1.5-liter water (about 6 cups)
>
> Parsley (I used about one-quarter cup.)
>
> 3 garlic cloves
>
> 2 onions (medium)
>
> Salt
>
> Pepper
>
> One-third of a lemon
>
> 3 tablespoons oil
>
> 3 tablespoons vinegar
>
> Bay leaf

Bring all ingredients to a boil and add trout. Simmer for 10-15 minutes. Remove from heat and let sit for 10 minutes.

TIP: The best Croatian website, www.frankaboutcroatia.com has a mouthwatering section on Croatian food.

• THE VACATION IS OVER •

In one word—what is the real difference between a vacation and a real, long-term trip? Haircuts. When you are going on vacation, you get a haircut before you leave. On a long-term trip, you have to find someone to cut your hair. Hopefully, this "someone" knows what they are doing, and, as an added bonus when you travel, you hope they speak your language. Just getting a haircut in your home country can cause a lot of anxiety and dread in women. Trying to explain how you want your hair cut using pantomime is a recipe for disaster.

Bad haircuts happen and they'd happened to me more than once. In middle school, my mother started trimming my hair and just didn't stop. I ended up with a haircut only slightly longer than my two brothers. Worse, she did this right before school picture day, and I have the pictures to prove it. Once as an adult, I went to a stylist for a trim. When I left, my bangs were far north of my eyebrows and would take months to grow out. I should have refused to pay and walked out, but I meekly paid up and went to my car to cry. Haircuts can be traumatic.

I sought advice on the Expats in Split Facebook page and got a recommendation for a stylist named Angela at Frame Habitat Salon. They said she spoke English and gave great haircuts. I called ahead to make an appointment and check prices. Angela charged 180 kunas for a basic haircut, which sounded expensive, but with one dollar equal to seven kunas, a haircut for 180 kunas translated to only about $25.00.

When in Rome, I found a stylist to do a little trim, and she just basically followed the bob hairstyle I always get. Angela did something different. My hair had movement. There were new layers and they all worked together. She cut the hair shorter in the back and longer around my face in front. As she snipped my hair, we chatted, and she told me she was leaving for New York in a few weeks to compete in a hair-cutting contest. When I was ready to go, I calculated a really good tip and assured Angela she would do great. I had gotten very lucky. At home, it was easy to stick to one stylist forever, even when their haircuts weren't exciting. Here I was forced to try something new and, to my surprise, it worked. Angela was proof I needed to let go a little more and experiment with change.

• FAMOUS CROATS •

Although it was winter, the weather was beautiful in Split. Most days were sunny and the temperatures were routinely in the 50's. We spent a lot of time walking around the city, sitting on benches along the Riva, sipping wine, reading, people watching, and looking at the quiet, still, sparkling Adriatic Sea. Walking along the seafront looking at the boats of all shapes and sizes, we took turns picking the ones we would buy after winning the lottery.

At least once a week, we took the number 12 bus miles out to Marjan Park—a rugged public green space on the tip of a peninsula jutting out into the Adriatic Sea. Once inside the park, we would hike through the luscious, pine-smelling woods to a sunny flat rock on the water, perfect for lounging. I couldn't believe no one else ever grabbed this rock. The Adriatic waves splashed against the bottom of the rock and lulled us into a deep, sleepy, calmness. We generally took a lunch and some books and would relax on "our" rock until the sun passed behind the trees and left us in the shade.

Our bus to the park passed right by the Meštrović Gallery. One cloudy, chilly day, we detoured from a trip to our rock and stopped to explore the gallery of Croatia's famous sculptor.

The Gallery had started out as Meštrović's home, studio, and exhibit space, but he and his family didn't live there very long before donating the property to the state. The grounds were beautiful and the view from the terrace over the Adriatic Sea was stunning. We lingered over the exterior sculptures before going inside. I liked the sculptures well enough but was more impressed with his painting of the Last Supper. The painting was huge and colorful, but I really liked its odd composition, showing several disciples' backs instead of their faces.

We left the gallery and walked to the gift shop to buy postcards. I recognized the image in one as that of a sculpture we passed nearly every day in Split. It was a large sculpture by Meštrović of Gregory of Nin outside Diocletian's Palace. The shopkeeper told us about Gregory.

"He was a bishop in the Church, but he always defended Croatia and insisted on services in Croatian, not Latin." She laughed slightly and her blue eyes twinkled. Her handsome face had the strong, square chin I saw on many Croatian men and women. "If you rub his toe, you will get good luck." Croatians have a lot of good luck charms, I thought, wheat at Christmas and now Gregory's toe.

The next day, we made our way back to the Diocletian's Palace in the center of the old city to look at the statue again. I thought Gregory looked intimidating, one arm raised in the air menacingly, a scowl on his face and full bushy beard, the other arm clutching a large book. He looked more like a wizard from Harry Potter than a bishop.

"Is it just me, or do his hands look strangely larger than normal?" I asked Dave.

"Look at his toe." Dave pointed at Gregory's big toe. It was a shiny gold where all of the dark color of the statue had rubbed off. Dave and I looked at each other and shrugged before rubbing the toe. Why not?

Probably most people who come to Split don't make it to the Meštrović Gallery, but everyone makes it to Diocletian's Palace. The Palace was Split's number one tourist attraction, and even in the dead of winter, tour groups wandered through the Palace. It was built around A.D.

294 by Roman Emperor Diocletian as his retirement palace. History remembers Diocletian as the last Roman Emperor who tried to wipe out Christianity. He failed in the attempt, but it was a bloody time in Rome's history. Now Diocletian's Palace and the entire center of Split was a UNESCO World Heritage site. Diocletian made Split famous. The outer walls of the Palace are still basically intact. Still, over the centuries, buildings grew up around the outside, and the center of Split was a charming maze of tiny alleys, old stone buildings, shops, restaurants, and markets.

Split ran the gamut from old to new—from Diocletian to Nicola Tesla. I noticed Tesla's name and picture all around Split, maybe because January 2018 was the 75th anniversary of his death. The TV shows were in Croatian, but they piqued my interest and I began researching him. He was handsome with dark, brooding eyes. One article I read said Tesla had a "complicated relationship with women." He never married and had some strange phobias, like an aversion to pearls. He wouldn't speak to any woman wearing them. Still, the man was a genius, held hundreds of patents, spoke eight languages, and won the Nobel Prize in 1909 for the development of the radio. He didn't create an electric car, but his experiments with electricity paved the way for the development of today's electric vehicle. Sadly Nikola Tesla died in New York City in 1943, in poverty, after some of his early investors stole many of his patents.

The slower pace of our life in Croatia left time to think about, explore, and examine the history all around us. There was a lot more to Split than beaches and cruise ships, and I felt a little sorry for the cruise ship tourists who would spend five hours in Split and then leave with a few dozen pictures they thought made up the "real" Split. They thought they could sum up the city with a few selfies on their phones. They were barely scratching the surface.

• DAILY LIFE IN CROATIA •

When we arrived in Croatia, it was December 1st, and the city was full of Christmas lights and decorations. The bars, restaurants, bakeries, and shops were overflowing. We went to free concerts, pushed through the busy crowds on The Riva, and admired the bright Christmas decorations throughout the city. I made mental notes of places to return to when there was more time. The commotion and festivities lasted until just after the New Year in January, and then the city went dark. Many shops and restaurants closed completely while others began renovations. This was the offseason in Croatia. It was a quiet time.

Of course every minute of our travels would not be full of fun and restaurants and museums, especially in Split. This was our chance to save money and relax. In Rome, we were in non-stop motion. In Croatia, once everything shut down, time slowed to a crawl. The days were long, and I woke up every morning with nowhere to go and nothing to do. This was a completely new situation for me. For decades, between working, raising kids, and taking care of a house, free time had always been a luxury. Now that I had free time, I didn't want to waste it. It didn't feel normal to have hours every day with nothing useful to do.

Wait a minute, I thought. *Even the way I think about time is messed up—"waste it" and "useful."*

It was tough for me to shake off my automatic American mindset that busy was better. For me, it was satisfying to have projects, objectives, and targets, and I liked checking things off my to-do list. Now I was list-free, plan-free, and schedule-free for maybe the first time ever in my life.

All of this kept rolling around in my head for days. Finally, I convinced myself to look at this time as a gift. This was a chance, maybe a first for me, to find out what I *wanted* to do, not what I should do. Soon enough, there would be projects and lists. Just for this little time in Croatia, free time was a bonus, a reward for decades of work, and I reminded myself every day to try and savor it.

So daily life in Croatia expanded on its own, with no rhyme or reason, with no two days alike. Our everyday life included a lot of reading. There were several books in my Amazon queue I planned to read and in Croatia, I almost got caught up. Having hours of free time for reading was my book lover's dream. There was a bookstore near our apartment, and I often walked there to browse and get some time alone.

We saw a lot of movies. Even before the announcement of the Oscar nominees in January, we watched Oscar contenders when possible. In Rome, it was hard to watch movies at the theater since films in the "original" English language were dubbed into Italian and came with English subtitles. In Croatia, it was easy, and all movies were shown in the original language. We went to the Mall of Split in the suburbs on the number 18 bus and spent afternoons there going to movies, eating American-style fast food, and walking around the mall for exercise. By the time we left Split, we had watched all of the Oscar-nominated movies and many others. With the strong Wi-Fi signal in our apartment, we could stream movies on Netflix or Amazon Prime. Not like in Rome, where the thick stone walls blocked all streaming. Every weekend we spent hours watching mini-marathons of old black and white films of the fifties, Hitchcock films, and other old favorites.

Besides movies, we cooked a lot more. With our countertop oven, we made dishes neither of us had eaten in months. I bought a Croatian cookbook and tried a few of the recipes, using Croatian seasonings and spices. I discovered a spice blend called Vegeta and brought back enough for all the cooks in my family. The grocery store was an almost daily destination. Dave made cookies and baked goods several times after he finally found baking soda, and shared them with our neighbor Lucia. We found the L.A.B. Craft Brewery and spent an afternoon taste-testing a variety of beers. The Imperial Stout made by L.A.B, Dave's favorite, won best craft beer of 2018. At the neighborhood liquor store, we worked our way through local wines—plavac, babić, and dingač were the Croatian equivalents of merlot, cabernet, and pinot noirs. The winter weather was unusually warm, so we could get outside most days, often to Marjan Park, where we lounged in the sun or rented bikes. Dave carried his camera and took pictures. I bought a sketchbook and some pencils and took them with us on our walks or used them as we sat on The Riva. When the darkness descended at 5:00 p.m., we would make dinner and settle into the warm apartment for an evening of reading, playing cards, doing puzzles, or watching movies.

It was tight quarters in our apartment, so I made a point of going into the bedroom some evenings for an hour or so and would close the door to read or journal in private. Dave tried to stretch out his grocery store runs to give me time alone in the apartment, and occasionally I wandered the alleys of the city by myself or sat in a coffee shop with my journal. It had become clear in Rome that I needed time alone to de-stress, but our quiet and simple Croatian life was so peaceful, I didn't need nearly as much of that here. I wasn't getting crowded, crushed, and run over by people in the streets of Split like I had in the streets of Rome. I didn't have to plan our daily schedule (there was no schedule) or cross things off of my to-do list (there was no list). For now, living in a small space together was easier.

One Sunday, after Dave made breakfast and I was cleaning up the dishes in the kitchen, he came in to get more coffee.

"It looks sunny out there," he said, looking over my shoulder out the kitchen window. "Let's go out and walk off breakfast and then find someplace for lunch." I finished wiping down counters and considered our options. It was ridiculous to waste a sunny day, and we had quickly adopted the Croatian custom of taking long Sunday lunches.

"I'm in, as long as we try the Villa Spiza. If they have truffle pasta, I have to go there." The Villa Spiza was a tiny restaurant deep in a narrow passageway near the Palace that we had stumbled upon one afternoon as we followed our noses down the alleys. It was barely large enough for a dozen customers, and every day the menu changed depending on what food was available and what the cook felt like cooking. I always ordered the truffle pasta when it was on the menu while Dave rotated through every dish they offered. I especially loved watching the cooks in the open kitchen area bob and weave their way around each other as they worked.

We bundled up and left the apartment, walking past the empty fish market and continuing until we reached the end of the pier where large ships docked. The wind was a little fierce, and we ducked into a coffee shop to warm up and linger, relaxing, drinking coffee, and checking our phones for emails and news from home.

Dave glanced at his watch. "It's almost 1 p.m."

"We should go to get a table before all the big families take over the restaurants." I looked out the coffee shop window. "The Villa Spiza isn't near here. We're closer to Konobo Fetivi. How do you feel about fish?"

"If you're willing to give up truffle pasta, I can go with fish instead."

162

For fresh fish, we always went to Konoba Fetivi. Konoba means tavern in Croatian, but the konobas we frequented were mainly about food. At Konoba Fetivi we would get the platter of whatever fish was fresh that day, and the waiter would bring it to the table surrounded by roasted seasonal vegetables. He would deftly debone the fish, making it look easy, and slide large slices of perfectly grilled fish onto our plates. We tried the Croatian carafes of cheap house wine and fell in love with one wine called Bogdanusa, translated as "gift from God." Savoring long two-hour Sunday lunches became the highlight of our week and something we promised each other we would make a permanent part of our future routine when we returned to the U.S.

When we ate out in Croatia, it was easier to calculate my daily insulin doses than it had been in Rome. Fish and other seafood were staples on every menu and seafood has no carbs. There were many familiar potatoes, soups, and roasted vegetables on menus, so I felt like I understood what I was eating. Even though figuring carbs was easier, my daily blood sugar numbers went up in Croatia, and I had to increase my daily insulin doses. I guessed this was because I wasn't walking as much as I had in Rome. Diabetes isn't a disease where you can "set-it-and-forget-it." It doesn't march along in a straight line—it zigs and zags, goes up and then down, sometimes all in one hour. I have to tweak and adjust what I do *all* the time.

An ordinary day in Croatia wasn't so different from an ordinary day at home in the U.S. There were still the daily, ordinary chores like laundry, cleaning, and paying bills. But to get to the grocery store, we walked down narrow alleys lined with stone buildings that were hundreds of years old. Standing at the main bus stop, we could examine the Croatian National Theater building that opened in 1893. Walking to dinner, we cut through the middle of Diocletian's Palace. Nothing was *ordinary* in our ordinary daily life and that is the beauty and allure of travel.

TIP: *There is no free ketchup in Croatia. When ordering your burger and fries at McDonald's in the Mall, also order, and pay extra for, your ketchup.*

• CROATIAN DRUGS •

One of the first things I did after arriving in Croatia was to go to a nearby pharmacy to refill prescriptions. I didn't need more medicine yet but keeping my stockpiles topped off felt safer. Dave was with me as I walked into a small pharmacy near our apartment and took a place in line. When it was my turn, I handed over my paper prescriptions and the pharmacist studied them for a long time. Becoming nervous, I exchanged glances with Dave. What was going on? The pharmacist finally smiled at me and spoke. "Can you wait? This will take a few minutes." I agreed and wandered around the pharmacy looking at the unidentifiable products. *Funny how the urge to shop ends when you can't understand labels and don't know what anything is.*

When she called my name, I handed over my credit card to pay, but the cashier came back from running the card with a frown. "This card is not accepted," she said softly. I motioned Dave over. He carried a different credit card, which he pulled out and handed over. Luckily his card worked. We left the pharmacy, and Dave jumped on the phone to call our credit card company in the U.S. about the rejection.

"The card was flagged. It was being used in Croatia," said the account representative.

"Um. That is because we are in Croatia. We've been here two weeks using the credit card. Why was it rejected today?" he asked. He was irritated because he had spent a lot of time notifying all our credit card companies about our travel plans before leaving the U.S. Still, it was good to have two problems solved in one day. The company cleared the credit card for use, and the Croatian pharmacy accepted my paper prescriptions.

A few weeks later, I pulled out an inhaler I used. *Hmm, this will be empty in a week*, I noticed. I kept our surplus medications and supplies in a box in the only closet in the apartment. Pulling out the box, I sat on the bed with it on my lap. One by one, I pulled out and set aside each extra container of test strips and each extra bottle of medicine. I didn't see a back-up inhaler. One by one, I put each container and bottle back in the storage box. I still had the empty box my inhaler came in, complete with the prescription label on the outside, but I didn't have another inhaler. Mentally I thought through all of the doctor appointments we had gone to before leaving the U.S. We got shots. We got our teeth cleaned. We got prescriptions. We bought supplies. Then I realized what had happened. I had been hyper-focused on working with my endocrinologist and getting all of my diabetes medications and supplies organized. I completely forgot to ask my general physician for a written prescription for an inhaler. I emailed my doctor and asked if she could email me a prescription for the inhaler, but this apparently broke U.S. drug laws, and she refused.

The next day I walked back to the pharmacy I liked to use, and the same smiling pharmacist was behind the counter. I explained the problem and showed her both my inhaler and the empty prescription box. She disappeared behind the wall of drugs to consult with another pharmacist. When she returned, she was carrying a box.

"This is the medication used in Croatia for breathing problems." She showed me a box with a Croatian prescription. "Your medication is different. The formulation is not what we use. I cannot change your medication."

"How can I get that Croatian medication?" I thought I knew the answer that was coming, and sure enough, she wrote down the name and address of a Croatian doctor I could go see to get a prescription for a Croatian inhaler.

When I returned to the apartment, I called and got an appointment with the doctor. On the day of my appointment, I took an Uber to the office in the outskirts of Split. It took 20 seconds for the doctor to listen to my chest before giving me a prescription. The appointment was a pricey 350 kunas ($50), and the inhaler was even pricier at 409 kunas ($58), but at least it would last 60 days. When we arrived in London, I hoped refills of the inhaler would be cheaper.

Even though I didn't need insulin yet, I checked availability and price at a pharmacy. One box of rapid-acting NovoRapid insulin pens—containing a total of 1,500 units of insulin—would cost 330 kunas or $47. One box of slow-acting basal insulin called Levemir would cost more at $73 per box. Just like in Rome, vials of insulin were not available in Croatia.

The cost of prescriptions, other than the inhaler, wasn't too bad. Even though it required a trip to the doctor, it was a relief to know I could get all of my medications in Croatia.

TIP: In Europe, the NovoLog brand insulin I usually bought in the U.S. was called NovoRapid. It was the exact same insulin with a different name. After my inhaler experience, I realized it might have been a good idea for me to check the formulation of my U.S. drugs with the formulation of the same medications available in Europe so my doctors could have given me prescriptions for the European brand formulas.

• DON'T DRINK THE WATER •

"I'd long had a strong sense of history, but here (in Egypt), I was being exposed to civilizations and beliefs far more ancient than any I'd known." One Soufflé at a Time Anne Willan

"Don't drink the water" was the first piece of advice our tour manager gave us. It was late January and we had arrived for our guided tour of Egypt. We would be on a strict bottled water diet until leaving Egypt. The tour manager also reminded us to rinse our toothbrushes with bottled water and avoid letting water from the shower go in our mouths. It was an immediate, huge culture shock to leave quiet Croatia for a seven day guided tour of Egypt.

"Don't make eye contact," was the second piece of advice the tour manager gave us, and that made no sense to me. Why not look at people? I didn't know it when we first arrived, but our foreign clothes and faces would make us magnets for everyone and anyone selling anything and everything.

Final advice: "This is a tipping culture." The baksheesh (pronounced with a silent "k" as "bah sheesh") means "tip or gratuity" and anyone who provided any service, no matter how slight, expected to receive one. On our tour in Egypt, many people told us, more than once, that the Egyptian currency, the Egyptian Pound (EGP), had been beaten up badly after the 2011 Arab Spring revolution. Tourists simply stopped coming to Egypt.

Before the crash, tourism was the second-largest source of income for the country, after fees for the Suez Canal, so many people in the tourism industry lost their jobs, and the ones left struggled.

Tipping dilemmas would be only one of the many cultural differences we would encounter during our seven days in Egypt.

• CAIRO •

Circling over Cairo preparing to land, the city looked like a vast sprawling expanse of identical beige and brown buildings with one very noticeable, very large, salmon pink building in the center. Our tour manager with Memphis Tours, Anas, collected us inside the airport terminal and whisked us through customs. A car and driver waited outside the terminal to take us to the hotel where we would stay while we explored Cairo before leaving to begin the Nile cruise part of our trip.

The traffic on the highway was bumper to bumper, stop-and-go traffic. No lines marked the lanes. Young boys stood in the middle of the highway selling snacks and trinkets. It was loud, crowded, chaotic, complicated insanity. A thick mass of cars, trucks, and buses swerved and curved like a school of fish on the road, and the entire time car horns blared and blasted.

"Car horns are the universal music of Cairo," Anas said.

From the ground, the buildings we had flown over looked empty. Most were dark. It was evening, and I expected the lights inside apartment buildings to be on as families returned home for the evening. The drive to our hotel took more than an hour, and I noticed that, up close, nearly all the buildings looked half-finished. The upper floors were open, there were no ceilings, and there were no windows in the window slots. Rebar was clearly visible, sticking up into the air at the top of the buildings.

"There is a lot of building and construction in Cairo?" I began questioning Anas as the driver focused on the traffic.

Anas shifted sideways in the front seat to look back at me. His brown eyes looked wary. "What do you mean? Construction?"

"The buildings are not finished yet. They are being built."

Anas laughed and said something in rapid Egyptian to the driver, who chuckled.

"The building is not finished now; this is because it is maybe not legal. No permit. The family that lives in these buildings do not pay taxes if the building is not finished. Now the Papa and Mama live on the bottom. The sons who marry live above. The building gets bigger if the family gets bigger."

So the family finished the living areas of a building on an "as needed" basis. That explained all of the unfinished buildings.

"The buildings are mostly dark. Is there electricity?" I asked. I didn't want to offend Anas with my questions.

He wasn't at all taken aback. "Yeesss. Sometimes there is electricity. If the family can pay or if the family has friends with the electricity company. It is the custom to pay people who help."

I didn't want to call it bribery and offend Anas, but it sounded like you needed to know someone or pay someone to get utilities. Later another guide told me that many of the millions of people living in Cairo lived on the outskirts of the city because not many "finished" apartments were available in the city.

Finally, we arrived at our hotel, Le Mèridien, near the Giza pyramids, and joined a line of cars waiting to enter the parking lot, which was blocked by a dusty steel barrier. When our car arrived at the front of the line, a bomb-sniffing dog was led slowly around it. We were allowed to enter the hotel courtyard, and inside the lobby, we walked through a metal detector while our suitcases and backpacks went through an x-ray scanning machine. Security was tight. We ate dinner at one of the hotel restaurants, too apprehensive from all the security precautions to leave. Besides, there was nothing within walking distance of the hotel. That night, sitting by the pool, we stared at the darkness where the Giza pyramids were waiting. We were ready for our guided tour of Egypt to begin.

• THE TOUR BEGINS •

The next morning our guide Kadria picked us up at the hotel. She was lively, passionate, knowledgeable, and friendly as she led us to the Giza Pyramids and the Great Sphinx. She told us the history of all the sites in an engaging, easy to understand way, and afterward, she liked to quiz us. "So, I ask you. How old is the Sphinx?" Then she praised whichever of us got the answer. It became a mini-competition where Dave and I tried to be the first to answer as she gently tested us on Egyptian history.

Leaving the sphinx and Giza pyramids, Kadria and our driver took us out into the surrounding dry brown desert where many groups of camels and owners waited. Kadria turned us over to one man surrounded by eight or ten camels, and the owner helped us onto two giant, smelly beasts. Without warning, I was pitched forward onto my camel's neck as he started to rise, back legs first, into the air. I gripped the horn of the saddle and struggled not to fall off, and when I looked around, Dave was next to me on his camel. "Did you almost fall off?" I asked. He nodded.

A young boy in bright white robes began leading our camels across the desert back toward the pyramids, constantly chattering in English: "How are you?" "Where are you from?" "Do you like Cairo? Egypt?" "Have you seen the pyramids?" "How long will you stay?" He chattered on and on. He was very good at his job and offered to take our phones to get pictures of us on the camels. In the photos he took, the pyramids are in the background, surrounded by hazy air, and the camels are touching noses like they are exchanging a kiss. Those are some of my favorite pictures of our year of travel.

Next, Kadria took us to the old Egyptian Museum, which I recognized as the large salmon pink building that had been so noticeable when we flew over Cairo. The old museum was half empty, and many of its exhibits were in the process of being packed up and moved to the new, partially opened Grand Egyptian Museum. Still, there were hundreds of exhibits to see in the older museum. We saw items from King Tut's burial chamber and a dozen mummies from different periods in Egyptian history. All through the museum Kadria kept giving us information and calling our attention to specific pieces of influential art or jewelry. It began to feel overwhelming and this was only the first real day of our tour.

After the museum, there was time for a visit to the old, mosaic-filled Hanging Church (built on the orders of the same Emperor Diocletian who built the palace in Split) and the Ben Ezra Synagogue before going to a grand, expansive market called the Khan al-Khalili. For the first time, we ran the gauntlet of vendors we would come to know so well. The market was a labyrinth of small, narrow alleys lined with shops, some as tiny as office cubicles, and all crowded with people chatting, talking on their cell phones, sipping tea, smoking, and shopping. Kadria was taking us to a specific shop and led the way quickly through the maze. I was afraid of getting left behind and could only catch glimpses of the different things for sale—copper and colored lanterns, bright fabrics with sequins, metal teapots, dishes, hookahs in every size and style imaginable, carved wooden boxes, leather goods, and so much more. It was cramped and chaotic. I fell a little behind Dave and Kadria, and different vendors began pestering me to buy things, repeatedly, over and over, without stopping:

"Come on, lady."

"I have nice silver, lady."

"Two dollars only for this shirt."

"Do you need a necklace? A hat?"

"These dishes for 100 Egyptian, 50 Egyptian, 5 U.S. dollars."

"Buy my spices."

"This teapot is very good quality."

Now I understood why the tour guide warned us not to make eye contact. I couldn't look at anything for more than a second without getting surrounded by vendors putting their wares, and their faces, in my face. One man put a shirt over my shoulder as I walked by. I backtracked quickly and handed it back to him. Putting my head down, I hurried to catch up with Dave and Kadria.

It was a relief to leave the small alleys and enter a wide-open space near a mosque where there was room to regroup and just watch people. One young girl came up to ask if she could take a picture with me. I agreed, and then her sister came up, and I did another picture with the sister and then yet another picture with me and the two of them together. As we wandered in the open space, more and more people approached us, asking to be in a picture with Dave and me. We began to feel quite famous.

"Where are you from?" they asked.

"The U.S."

"AMERICA!" they shouted.

They were very excited about America. It was great fun and everyone was smiling and friendly. Groups of mostly women sang and danced in the open courtyard, and it felt like we had stumbled into an Egyptian party.

That night we said goodbye to Kadria, and another guide took us to the Giza train station to board an overnight sleeper train for our 14-hour train ride to the city of Aswan. In the station, people crowded together in every variety of robes and Western clothing, most carrying bags, baskets, or duffels. As we waited, trains came and went regularly. Every time a train arrived, people surged toward the open doors, trying to shove themselves into whatever sliver of space was available. Some people shouted, pushed, and argued while others helped pull passengers onto the train. Women with babies strapped to their bodies and bundles on their heads tried to push onto the trains, and smashed babies cried in the melee. One train pulled in, more packed than most, and somehow, even *more* people shoved their way on. When it left the station, the train doors could not close, and, unbelievably, the train rolled down the track with people hanging off of every doorway, holding on by their fingernails with friends clutching their arms to keep them from falling off. It was impossible to tell where one body ended and another began. Our guide must have seen my unease.

"Do not worry. Those are the trains for Egyptians. They are not trains for foreigners." *Okay, good to know.*

The guide was right, and our overnight train was not crowded. He walked us aboard the train to a cozy compartment with a couch on one side. On the other side of the compartment, there was a small washbasin, a tiny hanging space, and a door leading to the adjoining compartment. The cabin was very simple, a little banged and scratched up, but clean and comfortable. When he extended his arms, Dave could touch both walls of the compartment. We explored a little and found the bathroom we would share with the entire carriage at the end of the hallway.

"The bathroom is clean," Dave said, looking through the doorway.

"For now," I said. "I don't want to see it in the morning." A sign on the door warned us not to use the toilet when the train stopped at a station.

I didn't examine the toilet too carefully and assumed it involved a direct, onto the ground flushing system.

The train didn't have a lounge car or restaurant car. Shortly after leaving the station, our elderly porter brought us trays of dinner containing four small metal boxes with rice, chicken, French fries, and a dessert. Our dinner table was two heavy plastic trays that slid into a slot in the wall.

After eating, the porter came to set up the beds. He carried a large, heavy gold key that unlocked the top bunk which slid down from the ceiling, and then pulled the bottom couch out into a small twin bed. A niche high in the wall held our sheets and pillows. The ladder to get to the top bunk was a very clever telescoping ladder that slid under the couch when not in use. The only real problem was that neither of us wanted the top bunk.

"I know I will roll out," I said. The train was moving now, and it had a distinct swaying and weaving motion.

"The bottom bunk is longer. If I sleep up top, I can't stretch out."

I looked again at the top bunk. It did have a railing at the edge, which would probably keep me from rolling onto the floor. I gave in, and we shuffled from side to side to give each other room to change into pajamas. After the long day exploring Cairo, I fell asleep instantly, and even though the train stopped many times throughout the night, and even though there was the occasional clanking noise from the tracks, the swinging motion of the train was calming, and we both slept well.

In the morning, the porter brought breakfast and then disappeared. He hadn't said a word to us on this whole trip. We were supposed to arrive in Aswan at around 9 a.m., so there was an hour to relax and enjoy the scenery. *How crazy is this? A sleeper train like something out of a movie.*

It wasn't elegant, but it was one of those unforgettable things that not many people got to do.

A little after 9 a.m., the train stopped at a station, and I saw large numbers of tourists getting off. They left in droves, dragging their big suitcases behind them. Dave and I grabbed our stuff and ran down the hall toward an exit door. As we rushed by one compartment full of people, we stopped briefly and asked, "Is this Aswan?" They all began talking at once, but the consensus was that no, this was not Aswan. So we hauled our bags back to our compartment. There on the floor of our compartment was my backpack full of insulin and all my diabetes supplies. *Oh, my God. I almost left everything on the train!* My hands shook as I picked up the backpack and tried not to think what it would be like to try getting insulin in *Egypt* without a prescription.

I hung out in the doorway of our compartment, watching the train continue to empty out, and tried to look down the platform at a sign. *If this isn't Aswan, what station are we?* I couldn't see anything. Within minutes a train worker came down the hallway screaming, "Aswan!!!!" He began talking and gesturing, but I couldn't understand anything. Then our porter, rubbing his sleepy eyes, appeared at a run and unlocked the exit door near our compartment to let us off the train. We were indeed at Aswan station.

The chaos of getting off the train left me a little shaken, and I was thanking the diabetes gods I hadn't left all of my insulin and supplies on the train. Still, a guide and driver waited outside the station, ready to take us to the boat that would be our home for the next three nights for the Nile cruise portion of our tour.

The Nile boat cruise was a revelation. It was a zone of food, wine, sun, and relaxation broken up with daily trips ashore for tours, where we became used to the gauntlet of pushy vendors clamoring to sell us trinkets and souvenirs. There were probably a hundred tourists on board the boat, but our tour group was small—consisting of just me, Dave, a couple from India, and a couple from Ireland. Every morning our small tour group and guide left the boat for tours to mosques, tombs, temples, museums, and historic buildings. We went to the Aswan Dam, Luxor, Valley of the Kings, Karnack, Temple of Hatshepsut, Kom Ombo, Edfu, and Philae. The days passed all too quickly as we walked through thousands of years of Egyptian art, religion, and culture. It was stunning to see, in person, the vast, ancient well-preserved temples, built to impress both allies and enemies. The scale and size were amazing. With his degree in Egyptology, our friendly and outgoing guide knew what each of the tombs and carvings meant, and his excitement and enthusiasm infected us all. This was a crash course in thousands of years of history, and we could only skim the surface.

Every afternoon, when we finished the tour of the day, Dave and I showered and then invariably climbed the stairs to the sun deck at the top of the boat to wait for dinner, relax with a glass of wine, and recap our day.

"I don't think I've figured out tipping yet," I said on our second day on the boat. The local currency was the Egyptian Pound Note (EGP), and we had some bills from the hotel ATM in Cairo.

"You pissed off that guard today, at the Valley of the Kings. Didn't he hand back the tip you gave him?"

"Yes." I groaned and pulled my jacket tighter over my shoulders. "He made a face of disgust and gave me back the money. So I guess 5 EGP is not enough of a tip for taking a picture of us."

"The cash from the hotel ATM was mostly large notes, but should we tip a 20 instead of a five? How much is 5 EGP?"

"I don't know. Not enough. Maybe we should tip more. But we are tipping the tour driver 40 EGP a day, so 20 EGP for taking a picture seems like a lot. The guide did say that the guards at historical sites received pitiful salaries," I said.

We were both quiet. I brushed a bug away from my face and took a sip of wine. I wanted to do the right thing but just couldn't figure out what that meant when it came to tipping. We traveled on our tour with a driver and a tour guide. Did the driver get 20 EGP or 30 EGP? And did the tour guide get more? How much more? I found a relatively recent online article on tipping in Egypt, and it said a driver would get 40 EGP for a whole day of driving. So a half-day of driving would be 20 EGP? But our tour guide told us the recommended tip for our driver, at the end of a half-day tour, was 50 EGP. In the end, we just paid the driver 40 EGP for any driving of any length. If only I could get my hands on a stack of $1.00 bills. Everyone asked for American dollars when giving the price of their souvenirs or food. Dollars made everyone happy.

The boat continued slowly up the Nile toward Cairo and I tried to forget about tipping dilemmas. We sat in the shade, enjoying the breeze and watching light sparkling on the water. Life on the Nile went by. There were small sailboats, called felucca's, filled with people, and on the shore were crops and cattle. It was the time of year for burning the harvested fields and the air was hazy with smoke. I could almost imagine life on these shores hundreds of years ago. Maybe it had not changed so much.

When we arrived back in Cairo, there was one final day of sightseeing before we returned to the airport to return to Croatia. On our last night at the hotel, we sat outside by the pool and looked at the hazy darkness where we knew the pyramids were. Our short time in Egypt was over.

§ § §

Egypt was my first visit to a "third world country," a phrase that I hate because it sounds to me like a back-handed way of saying "third rate country." As a foreigner, a tourist, I had no business criticizing the way of doing things in Egypt, but there is no denying there are challenges. Egypt was less industrialized and developed than the countries we had navigated so far, and it didn't have the usual American/European amenities, toiletries, and creature comforts. Trash was piled along the streets and falling out of overflowing dumpsters. Entire blocks of the city were lined with handmade shelters full of people sitting, eating, washing, talking, staring, cooking, and sleeping. Donkeys and carts used the streets alongside battered cars and buses. Some streets were little more than mud-packed ruts that you could only navigate very, very slowly. There was a lack of electricity, the water was not drinkable, and some parts of the city lacked sewers. Our guides spoke a little about Egypt's political situation but were fearful and nervous and asked us not to share anything they talked about with anyone. Public criticism of Egypt's leadership could be dangerous, and I admired the Egyptian people's tenacity and determination. I tried to imagine living the life of an ordinary Egyptian and just couldn't.

As a tourist, I felt guilty. I could still see the face of the guard who handed back the tip I had given him. Was my job as a tourist to travel and give big tips? But why was his salary so small? Did tourists who came to a country with so many struggles actually help the ordinary person or just help support the government that kept them poor? In Egypt, I dropped into the middle of a situation I couldn't understand, and, like in Barcelona, it felt frivolous to be trying to have "fun" while ignoring more significant issues. Still, if I stayed home and gave up traveling, it wouldn't improve the life of the ordinary Egyptian.

On this trip, I realized that being born in the U.S. was like coming out on top in some random geographical lottery. My mostly small town and suburban neighborhoods had all been safe. I could get clean water and ice from a door on my fridge. My electricity only went out when there was a big weather emergency. I could criticize my government publicly. The value of the items in my purse and small suitcase probably was worth more money than many Egyptians saw in a year. These are things I wasn't accustomed to thinking twice about—but now I would. It was a lesson in appreciation, in gratitude. When our trip to Egypt ended, Dave and I promised each other we would return when the large new archeological museum opened in a few years. In the meantime, hopefully, Egypt, this ancient, exotic, alien, fascinating country, would prosper.

TIP: After we returned to the U.S., a friend heard my stories about Egypt and suggested that we donate to a charity that helped everyday Egyptians. We followed her excellent suggestion and made a donation to **www.savethechildren.org** *to support the work they have been doing in Egypt since 1982.*

• THIS IS NOT ALLOWED IN CROATIA •

"Are you going out today?" Dave asked me one morning as he got ready to leave the apartment for the grocery store.

It was the middle of February, and I had been sitting at home, afraid to leave the apartment for four days. I was waiting for a shipment of insulin pumps.

When I left the U.S., I carried a six-month supply of my Pods/insulin pumps—enough to last until around the end of February. My daughter Vanessa had received a shipment of Pods while we were in Rome, but after hearing so many horror stories about trying to ship anything to Italy, I didn't even ask her to send them to me. The Expats Living in Rome group all agreed on only one thing: the Italian post office and any delivery service in Italy were not to be trusted with anything important. My insulin pumps were important.

As soon as we arrived in Croatia, I gave Vanessa our address and asked her to ship a box of Pods. On January 20th, she got the Pods in the mail, and I could see from USPS tracking that they arrived in New York on January 23rd, where they sat until February 2nd. USPS promises ten-day delivery, even to international addresses, but that clearly wasn't going to happen. I didn't panic yet. We weren't leaving for London until March 1st. But when the Pods didn't arrive in Croatia for processing by Customs until February 13th, panic was clearly the correct response. According to Google, processing by Croatian customs could take from three *weeks* to four *months*. I began obsessively checking the package tracking four or five times a day. I couldn't leave the apartment in case the mailman attempted delivery of my Pods while I was out. I didn't even shower unless Dave was home to answer the door.

Now, I looked at Dave with his coat on and one foot out the door.

"No," I answered. "I'm staying home. Maybe today will be my lucky day. Besides, I can pack and do some things to get ready for London. Did you mark the mailbox downstairs with our names?"

"Yes, both the mailbox and the buzzer for our apartment have our names in big, bold print."

I didn't know what to expect. The box wouldn't fit in our mailbox, but would the mailman leave it on the floor near the mailbox? Would he ring the buzzer, so I knew it was there? Did they have Porch Pirates in Croatia who would sometimes steal unattended boxes?

I was ecstatic when the doorbell rang on February 20th and a mailman was standing at the door. I looked at his hands, but he wasn't holding a box. He handed me an envelope containing a questionnaire. With the help of Google Translate, Dave and I filled it out and took it to the nearby post office, where we waited for the clerk to fax it to the customs office in Zagreb, the capital of Croatia. I put my email address and phone number on the questionnaire, but after two days and no word from the customs office, we made our way back to the post office. The first clerk spoke no English and passed us off to another clerk who spoke very little English. The second clerk examined the fax and then disappeared behind a door. I could hear her in the back office, talking on the phone for what seemed like hours. I paced around the small post office and peeled off my coat in the hot, stuffy space.

"This is not allowed in Croatia," she said, coming back to the counter where Dave and I waited.

"I can't get my box? I am diabetic and I need my insulin pumps!" I could tell she felt sorry for me. I rubbed my head and tried to think. Her mouth opened and closed wordlessly, helplessly. She wanted to help but didn't have enough English words in her vocabulary to explain to me what was wrong. Dave and I left the Post Office and stopped at a nearby restaurant for a glass of wine.

"It will be okay," I said out loud, partially to reassure Dave as well as myself. "I have needles. I have insulin pens. I will just go back to giving myself daily insulin shots." This was not something I was looking forward to. Every morning and evening, I would have to give myself a shot of *long-acting* insulin that would last approximately 12 hours. That was my basic, foundational dose of insulin. Then, all day long, I would give myself additional shots of *fast-acting* insulin when I ate or drank (to cover the carbs I consumed) and more "correction" shots of insulin if my blood sugar stayed high. It was more complicated and more painful than the insulin pumps, but I had no choice other than to suck it up and make it work. When we got to London, I could try shipping Pods again. Maybe in London, my Pods would be "allowed."

Two days later, another envelope was hand-delivered by the postman, confirming my Pods were not allowed in Croatia. Inside the envelope was a slip of paper marked "Interdit: Zabranjeno" (Banned). Google Translate was not always exact, but the letter inside the envelope said that the "import of medicine for personal needs of citizens was only allowed if there was a prescription by a competent medical practitioner." It sounded like I needed a prescription to import my insulin pumps.

A few days later, I was confused when Vanessa received a notification that my package was ready to be picked up in Zagreb. I searched for hours before finding a phone number for Zagreb's customs office. I called and was shuffled from person to person until I got someone with a little English.

"This package is to be picked up this day," the customs official informed me.

"It is in Zagreb? I can't fly to Zagreb. I leave Croatia in two days to go to London," I said. After giving up hope of getting my Pods, knowing they were a short flight away was torture. There wasn't even time to ship them from Zagreb to Split.

"I was told the package was not allowed. Why did I get a letter saying the package was banned?" I was hoping for some answers, so I didn't make the same mistake when I tried to get the Pods shipped to London. The customs guy on the phone didn't know what I was talking about. He just wanted me to pick up my package. It was very frustrating, and I even debated flying to Zagreb, but instead, I told him to ship the package back to the U.S. Three weeks later, my supply of Pods returned to Vanessa.

• MOVING FORWARD AND MOVING ON •

After returning from our trip to Egypt, we were home in Croatia, holding plane tickets to fly to London on March 1st. In our final weeks in Croatia, we met up again with our landlord Ana to get coffee and talk about life, travel, and family. She was eager to get her daughter into a good college, worked at a busy job, and volunteered to save beautiful Marjan Park from private developers. Her New York boyfriend was coming soon for a visit, and she admitted she sometimes imagined herself moving to New York. *Trading Croatia for New York—now that would be an adjustment,* I thought. Overall, Croatia had not been a great adjustment for either of us. (Okay, the language was a shock.) The food and culture were not so different from home. Families got together for Sunday lunch and played with their children in the parks, drank coffee and met up for drinks after work, shopped for groceries, and strolled outside on the short, sunny afternoons.

And yet, even though Croatia wasn't a huge adjustment for us, I still turned our apartment in Croatia into a mini-imitation of our home in the U.S. *Why do I travel and re-create the life I left behind?*

Life pushed and pulled me. I loved comfortable, familiar places and habits. After almost six months of traveling, my comfort zone had become portable, as I stocked our temporary apartments with flowers, books, candles, and kept some routines from home. There was safety and consistency in that. But, at the same time, I loved to travel. I got a strong, distinct, addictive surge of adrenaline when I planned a trip, found a good airline deal or hotel bargain, and pressed "book it." Being surrounded by new things all the time was thrilling. Months of traveling also helped subdue the anxious voices in my head—the voices that said, *what if you get sick, what if there is no insulin, what if you can't do this.* The voices were still there, and I was always going to check and double-check everything and make lists, but so far things had worked out, and by this halfway point in our trip, the voices were quieter.

Dave and I settled into an easy dance through our days in stress-free Croatia. We only occasionally rubbed each other the wrong way, and mostly argued, I noticed, when one or both of us were tired. On those days, communication went sideways, and we would start having circular arguments/conversations: "but you said...." "but I meant...." "no, that's not what you said..." This wasn't a new phenomenon in our relationship. Those days required a reset. One of us would take a long walk, and later we'd start over. A touchy, feely couple would rehash the whole conversation (because that worked so well the first time), but we were different. Dave would bring me a cup of coffee, and I would tell him a funny story from the newspaper that I knew he would like—peace offerings—the ebb and flow of a relationship.

In our final days in Croatia, I had to adapt to the new unsettling reality of giving myself multiple daily insulin injections. I missed my Pods. Dave knew me well, and when he saw me sitting at the table scowling at the array of diabetes supplies in front of me, he stood behind me and rubbed my shoulders. "Too much?" he asked.

Yes, it was too much. I wasn't squeamish about needles—they were small, thin needles. It was the whole process I disliked. I had spent years giving myself multiple daily shots until I finally began using the insulin pump. For daily injections, it was essential to alternate the shots around the stomach area, arms, or legs. In public, I tried to lift my shirt and give myself a shot in the stomach, quickly and privately, but I looked up more than once to find someone staring at me with a curious expression. They had watched me go through all the steps involved in just one simple insulin shot. There were a lot of steps.

I started by pulling out my tester and inserting a test strip in it, pricking my finger and squeezing out a drop of blood. Then I applied the blood to the test strip, took out an insulin pen, attached a needle to the pen, lifted my shirt, swabbed my skin with an alcohol wipe, pinched up a piece of skin, and inserted the needle. I had to slowly push the insulin pen's plunger to give the full dose, and then the needle should stay in place for 10 seconds. Some diabetics who took public shots related having been mistaken for a drug addict injecting drugs. Often I would go into the bathroom and give myself a private shot in the thigh instead of the stomach. Sometimes I put off giving myself a shot that I needed because I didn't want to do it in public.

Still, I wasn't one to sit back and silently let people stare and judge me. The next time we were in a restaurant and someone stared at me while I took a shot, I had a word for them: "droga" (drugs). Then I winked.

• THINKING OF HOME •

As we began to prepare for our move to London, we *both* came face to face with another unsettling reality. Time was going by quickly, and our year of travel was almost halfway over.

"Are you ready to head home in September?" I asked Dave as we sat drinking coffee one morning.

"I guess so. Do you still want to fly home from Paris?"

"I've checked, and it is a lot cheaper than flying to the U.S. from Venice, even adding in the airfare from Venice to Paris," I said. We had saved money in Croatia and planned to spend some of our savings in Paris at the end of our travel year. Thirteen years earlier, Dave and I had spent a chilly week in Paris on our honeymoon.

Dave pulled out the computer and handed it to me. I looked again at the flights I had bookmarked back to the U.S. and we debated the options.

"This one is cheaper, but what is the luggage allowance?" Dave asked, looking over my shoulder.

I skimmed the details and squinted at the screen. "Checked bags are twenty-five euros extra."

"That isn't bad. Still pretty cheap."

"Except that airline has bad reviews. They cancel flights all the time. I don't think it's worth the risk to save money on luggage." Reliability sometimes trumped the budget in my mind.

We made our choice and I booked two tickets, leaving September 3rd from Paris. This time there was no surge of adrenaline. A part of my brain was looking forward to going home. But my heart couldn't fathom living in the same place for the rest of my natural life.

I stood up, stretched, and looked over at Dave with a smile. "Let's go walk on The Riva." We were leaving Croatia soon, but there were still six months of travel to enjoy, and I wasn't going to let thoughts about returning home overshadow the time we had left.

PART IV: LONDON

• ARRIVAL •

"Did you grab the shampoo from the shower?" I asked. Dave and I were packing for London. Again.

Our March 1st flight to London had been canceled at the last minute after a huge blizzard hit London, called the "Beast from the East." It was such a massive storm it got a name. The airline rebooked our flight for March 4th and the delay was hugely frustrating. We were all packed. Each morning we pried things out of our suitcases, carefully, since Dave had wedged everything in. We pulled out shampoo, toothpaste, and clothes. The kitchen was clean, and the refrigerator empty, so we ate out for those three days. It was not great for our budget, but secretly I liked visiting some favorite restaurants one last time.

After we arrived in London and caught an Uber from Heathrow Airport to our apartment, I was in love. This apartment was the largest we had rented so far on our trip. From a central hallway, there were four doors. To the right was the bathroom with our first bathtub for soaking. On the left was the galley kitchen with a large oven, a full-sized fridge with a freezer, and a washing machine. No dryer, so once again, we would use a hanging rack to dry our clothes. There were plenty of pots, pans, and prep knives in the kitchen, another first on this trip. Rentals always claim to provide a "well-equipped kitchen," but our experience so far had proved they were always missing something essential, usually decent knives. Spatulas didn't seem to exist outside of the U.S., but I eventually found one in Rome and carried it with us from place to place.

The other two doors from the central hallway led to the bedroom and the living room/dining room. The living/dining room was large, with one wall of windows, two couches, a dining table for four people, and a big TV. It was very light, bright, and comfortable. The bedroom was also large with a king-sized bed, a closet for clothes, and our suitcases fit into the corner where we didn't trip over them. I loved the light and space in the apartment, and especially liked the doors on each of the rooms, giving us both separate, private space.

This moving around thing was getting easier. There was a routine. For starters, Dave always traveled to a new location with a bottle of wine in his suitcase for the first night in a new place. We started by unpacking suitcases and deciding where to put our clothes, shoes, books, computer, chargers, and miscellaneous stuff. The first full day in a new location, we spent doing essential housekeeping things: money, food, and transportation.

On our first morning in our Greenwich apartment, we left to walk to the neighborhood news agent's shop a few blocks away to get transportation passes. Both of us wore coats and scarves against the chilly, overcast day. At the shop, I took the lead; as the family navigator, I had researched travel passes.

"We need two Oyster Cards," I said to the clerk. He pulled two blue and white plastic cards from underneath the counter. "And we need to load them with monthly travel passes," I continued.

"What zones do you need?" he asked. For this, I needed some help. The price of the monthly pass depended on how many zones you traveled through. We would be going from our apartment into central London (Zone 1). But our apartment looked like it was right on the border of Zone 2 and Zone 3. A Zone 1-3 travel card cost more than a Zone 1-2 travel card. I gave him our address. The clerk pulled out a detailed map that he examined for several minutes before announcing we were in Zone 2, so we would save a little money.

"That will be two hundred eighty-two pounds," said the clerk.

Beside me, Dave gasped. "For one month?" In Rome, monthly travel passes only cost €60 a month for both of us. In Croatia, we'd bought cheap packets of 10 tickets. Our transportation budget would take a hit in London, so we would have to cut somewhere else. I handed over a credit card to make the purchase, and the clerk reminded me to set up an Oyster Card account to register our cards when I got home. "If you do not register your cards, they will not be replaced if they are lost or stolen," he advised.

After leaving the store, we began walking to the bank a few blocks away to get cash from the ATM. I filled Dave in on the details.

"It is a lot of money for these passes, but we can travel on anything— buses, the Tube and trains—unlimited travel. It's cheaper than buying individual tickets like we did in Croatia."

Dave didn't seem convinced.

"Hey, here they don't go on strike every week, like in Rome," I said. "Promise?"

The passes were a bargain overall. London's transportation system is huge, efficient, and well maintained. We used the passes every single day, and it made life much easier to be able to jump on and off buses, trains, and the Tube without counting the cost of each trip. And they never went on strike.

At the bank, Dave pulled out his ATM card to get cash. I stood behind him with my fingers crossed for good luck. Since our first experience using that ATM in Europe at the train station in Rome, I didn't trust ATMs. But there were no problems, and we left the ATM with a wad of English banknotes. We were still sticking to our budget system of using a daily cash spending allowance.

Dave tucked the money into his wallet and we crossed the street carefully. Cars came at us from the "wrong" direction. Looking down, I saw bold, painted letters on the curb, saying, "look right." There were signs on nearly every street crossing to warn people of the direction of oncoming traffic—to borrow a British phrase, "Brilliant!"

At Marks and Spencer (M&S) grocery store, Dave grabbed a grocery cart and I started down the produce aisle. After six months of grocery shopping in Rome and then Croatia, this store reminded me of the grocery stores in America, easily five times as large as a Roman or Croatian grocery store.

"Look at this," I said. "Bins full of cauliflower, broccoli, and leeks— and celery. I haven't seen celery in six months." It was hard to restrain myself in the produce aisle.

"With that large fridge and freezer, we can buy more food than usual. I won't have to go to the grocery store every day." Dave was as delighted as I was. Together we moved to the next aisle.

"Cheddar cheese."

"Irish butter."

"Flavored yogurt."

"Taco shells and salsa."

We moved together down the aisles, pulling things from shelves and pointing out foods to try later. A section of ready-made meals was full of British specialties like Shepherd's Pie, Bangers and Mash, Cornish pasties, Scottish beef, and Irish lamb. We could eat every meal for a month just from the frozen and ready-made food aisles. The choices were staggering and so enticing after months of eating a limited range of food. At the end of the store was the liquor section. Here Dave was in heaven—British beers.

"I'm going back through the store one more time," I said. "You'll be happy here for a while, I think." Dave didn't even look up and I wasn't sure he had heard me.

As I walked the aisles again, I realized I hadn't used my phone to translate a single label. Grocery shopping was easy here. I grabbed a bunch of cut flowers and circled back to the liquor section to round up Dave. He had been busy.

"Do you want all of that?" I said, looking skeptically at the beer in his arms. "We have to take the bus home." He looked down at the two six-packs in his arms and put one back on the shelf. "We'll be back soon. I promise. After dropping off all this food at home, we can go to the pub." Problem solved. We paid for our food and left the store with two big bags overloaded with food, and used our new bus passes to lug everything home and finish unpacking and settling in. Money, food, and transportation—check, check, and check.

• CHLAMYDIA •

After arriving in London, unpacking, and settling in with groceries and transportation passes, I set about finding a clinic so Dave could get a test for chlamydia. That sounds like a punch line from a joke, but there was nothing funny about the situation. And it all began in Rome.

Months earlier, in November, when we were in Rome, my eyes became very red, and in the morning there was a sticky discharge in my eyes. I knew immediately that this was conjunctivitis, also known as pinkeye. Five or six years earlier, I had contracted pinkeye and remembered the drill. I made a trip to my local medical clinic in Rome for medicated eye drops and, since pinkeye is highly contagious, I threw away all of my eye makeup and washed my bath towels and pillowcases. I began washing my hands a lot and tried to remember not to touch my eyes no matter how itchy they felt. The pinkeye disappeared in a week.

Then in December, we moved to Croatia, and the pinkeye came back. I assumed I hadn't been as careful as I thought about washing my hands and maybe re-infected myself. I found an eye clinic near the local mall and the doctor gave me a thick eye gel to use. I threw away the new eye makeup I had bought and washed everything I could put my hands on. Problem solved again, or at least I thought so for a little while. When the symptoms returned about a month later, I had no choice but to return to the eye the doctor again.

My first trip to an eye doctor happened in Rome in November. My second trip to an eye doctor was in Croatia in December. In January, I made a third trip to an eye doctor (also in Croatia). On each trip, I saw a different doctor. I had now been fighting pinkeye for three months. The infection went away just fine and I used the eye medication religiously. The problem was, it kept coming back. My hands were dry and chapped from constant washing and I didn't think I was re-infecting myself.

When the infection returned for the fourth time, it was early February and we were just back from our seven day tour of Egypt. It was time for some answers. In only a few weeks, we would be in London, but I couldn't wait until then to deal with this. Not wanting to struggle through the language barrier on the phone, I stopped by the Croatian eye clinic to get an appointment. The receptionist didn't speak English but pulled aside a colleague who did, and there was an opening in one hour, so I took it. As I sat waiting, I watched the TV attached high on the wall. Usually, at doctor's offices, I read magazines. *No English magazines for me here.*

An assistant with a clipboard came through every few minutes calling names and leading people to offices. When she called my name, I didn't recognize it.

"Pahmahlah?" she called out, looking around the room.

Was that my name? Looking around the room, I saw no one else moving, so I stood and walked over to her. "Pamala," I said, pointing at myself. She looked at the papers in her hand as if they knew how to pronounce my name, then shrugged and led me to an office. I was glad to see the same young woman doctor who had treated me in January. Her English was very good. The doctor glanced at me and began examining the paperwork from the nurse.

"So you have been here already. You still have problems with your eyes." She motioned me to sit in an exam chair and went to a sink in the corner and washed her hands. Her examination of my eyes was brief, and then she went back to the sink and rewashed her hands.

"I don't think I am re-infecting myself," I said. "Right?" I squeezed my jiggling leg to force it still.

She didn't answer and took the paperwork to a small desk where she made some notes and then wrote on a pad of paper and walked back to me. *Another prescription?*

"I think I know what is the...ahh...problem but must be sure what infection is in your eyes," she said. "The medication that you have taken has not...uhm...cured the infection. This paper is for a laboratory to test your eyes."

On the small paper she handed me was some handwriting, her signature, and a name and address. I asked a few questions, and she assured me I could go to the lab immediately and get the test, no appointment necessary. I walked outside and called Dave.

"The doctor wants me to get my eyes tested at a lab," I told him. "I just want to get this over with. Can you arrange an Uber?" The Uber app was on Dave's phone. My basic, cheap Italian phone didn't have the storage space for anything beyond phone calls, texting, Google, and the navigation apps I relied on every day. I gave Dave the lab's address and walked over to stand outside the mall so the driver could find me easily.

The Uber driver wound through the streets and up a hill before stopping in front of an apartment building. *This can't be right.* I handed the driver the piece of paper from the doctor, and he examined the address, then gestured toward the building. I climbed out of the car clutching my paper, and walked to the building. A white sign near the door said "laboratorija," which looked like "laboratory," so I walked inside. The hallway smelled of cooking odors and there was a stroller parked near a doorway. Looking right and left, I saw an open glass door down the hallway. This was the right place. Inside, two white-coated women glanced at the paper from the doctor and motioned for me to sit while they gathered their supplies. One woman brandished a long cotton swab and held my eyelids open to swab my right eye. She placed the swab inside a tube held by the other woman before repeating the process on my left eye. I was finished. My first Uber was gone, so Dave arranged another and I made my way back to the apartment.

In less than a week, the doctor called with my lab results. She didn't sugarcoat it. "The infection in your eyes is chlamydia. You must come to the office and get prescriptions for medication. The receptionist will have what you need."

"Chlamydia?" I was dumbfounded.

"Yes, that is correct."

"I…will come by tomorrow and get the prescription." My mind wasn't taking this in.

"Yes, that is best. Goodbye."

I sat down, hard, on the dining room chair, looked at the phone in my hand, and then over at Dave sitting on the couch reading. "Who was that?" he asked.

"Uh, the eye doctor. She says I have chlamydia in my eyes."

"What? Chlamydia? In your eyes? How is that even possible?"

"She didn't give me details, just said I need to pick up another prescription."

This was utterly incomprehensible to both of us. How did chlamydia get in my eyes? How did chlamydia get anywhere in my body? Dave and I had been married, in a monogamous relationship, for 13 years. We Googled chlamydia and discussed it from every angle, backward and forward, then started over again. So had chlamydia been there, dormant, in one or both of us for 13 years? Was that even medically possible?

"Neither of us has ever had symptoms," Dave said.

I was reading an article on my phone. "This article says there sometimes are no symptoms." He went back to reading articles on his phone

"Remember that time I came down with a respiratory infection a few years ago? The doctor gave me antibiotics. That would have cured any chlamydia infection." I was looking for ways to prove the doctor wrong.

"Yeah, but if I were infected, I would have re-infected you after the antibiotics," said Dave—not what I wanted to hear. Obviously, if one of us was infected, then the other was also infected. Had we been passing it back and forth for 13 years? (Ick.) Nothing made sense.

After spending hours reading every article on the web about chlamydia, we were both exhausted. Dave tried to joke. "Is there something you want to tell me?" I was not in a laughing mood and just glared at him in reply.

The next day I returned to the eye doctor's office to pick up my prescription. I took Dave along for moral support. When we arrived, my prescriptions were waiting at the reception desk. Azithromycin tablets and azithromycin eye drops—a double dose of medication. The doctor was taking no chances. I just couldn't leave without talking to the doctor, although I was also embarrassed (an STD!). Part of me wanted to take my prescriptions and slink away, but I really couldn't understand this. When the doctor was free for a few minutes between patients, the receptionist led me to her office.

"I don't understand how I have chlamydia in my eyes," I began. *Oh lord. That wasn't what I meant. Did the doctor think I didn't know how people got chlamydia, that it was an STD?* "I mean, I understand chlamydia is transmitted by sex, but my husband and I don't have chlamydia." This wasn't a good conversation.

I started over. "I go to the eye doctor every year to get my eyes checked," I told her. The risks of developing retinopathy, cataracts, or glaucoma are higher for diabetics. Diabetes is the primary cause of blindness in adults. I never skipped my annual diabetic eye exam.

She looked at me kindly and asked if I had been in a swimming pool recently.

"Um. Yes. I was in a swimming pool a few weeks ago, in Egypt," I said.

She explained that it was possible to transmit chlamydia through the water in swimming pools and that, after I took the antibiotic she prescribed for me and *my* chlamydia was cured, my husband and I shouldn't have sex until after he received treatment for chlamydia too.

I couldn't take any more. I bolted from the doctor's office and went to get my prescriptions filled. I told Dave about my conversation with the doctor, and as we waited to get my new prescriptions, he began Googling swimming pools and chlamydia. It turned out that the whole "swimming pool transmits chlamydia" idea is a myth. You also can't get chlamydia from a toilet seat, doorknob, or hot tub. Maybe the doctor was as embarrassed as I was and just wanted to get me out of her office. I took my antibiotics, my eyes cleared up, we abstained from sex, and since we were leaving Croatia, I decided to get further testing done in London.

So here we were, our first week in London, looking for an STD clinic, known in London as an STI clinic. Not how I planned our London itinerary. After googling it, I found dozens of free, walk-in STI clinics in London and picked the one promising "conversations are always free of judgment." I wasn't sure how this experience could get worse, but getting the stink eye from an STI clinic worker wouldn't be helpful.

When we arrived, I could see we should have gotten there earlier. The waiting room was wall-to-wall people, mostly women, many of them trying to corral multiple small children as they waited. We each were handed a clipboard with paperwork to fill out and climbed over strollers to empty seats in a corner. After finishing the paperwork, Dave carried both clipboards back to the receptionist, and we sat some more. The room was beginning to clear out before our names were called. Dave went first.

When my turn came and I walked to an exam room, I explained everything to the worker; the repeated eye infections, my 13-year monogamous marriage, the Croatian lab work. I think she hadn't seen a patient like me before.

"We cannot test your eyes here. We do not test eyes. A test for chlamydia now is not necessary for you. You have taken antibiotics. That is how we would treat you if you tested positive." She shrugged. "Your husband must be tested."

"Yes. My husband is seeing a doctor here, now, in another office."

She nodded and wrote something on a piece of paper. "Do you need HIV testing?" she asked. *God, no.* I escaped back to the waiting room to wait for Dave. *What is taking him so long?* When he came back, we gathered our coats and left. The cold air outside felt refreshing.

"How did it go?" I asked.

"Fine, but I don't know anything. First, I saw a doctor. Then I waited for them to take a urine sample. I have a confidential number I am supposed to call in a week to get my results."

A week later, our suspense was over. Dave tested negative and didn't need any treatment. My eye problems cleared up permanently after taking the antibiotic. Nothing about this entire situation made sense. I wondered if the eye doctor's lab order had instructed the lab on what to test for, and the lab obligingly found it. I would never know.

I hesitated about even sharing this story. It is embarrassing. It was so out of left-field, crazy, and inexplicable, but in the end, that is why I included it. If you plan to travel, you need to adapt to the freaky, weird, uncomfortable, unexpected, and twisted—and be ready to roll with the punches. Travel isn't all museums, sightseeing, and restaurants. I was learning a lot about twists and turns on this journey. I still believed in lists and planning, but I could never have planned a response to something like this in a million years. I wished I could ask the Croatian doctor a few more questions, but now we were in London, and I wouldn't get answers from her. It drove me a little crazy, but all I could do was move forward and live with the mystery.

• GREENWICH •

Looking back, I think so much of our trip was a series of lucky breaks. We accidentally found a charming apartment in Trastevere from a new, unknown rental site a friend happened to mention. Croatia's winter weather was unusually warm and sunny, and we could get outside nearly every day. And in London, I stumbled onto an apartment in the suburb of Greenwich and we broke our rule about staying in the center of town. Rentals in the center of London were very expensive and very tiny. By the time we began looking for an apartment in London, I had realized that having some breathing space was essential for my peace of mind. Dave stayed up later and liked to watch TV at night. I liked the quiet of the bedroom for reading or journaling. I think even Dave had come to value his time alone. So faced with tiny apartments and high prices in central London, we reluctantly compromised on Greenwich as an affordable option. This was our lucky break. Greenwich is a bustling city with great neighborhoods, transportation, and full of shops, restaurants, pubs, and museums.

"What is the plan for today?" Dave asked me two weeks into our time in Britain. We were sitting at the dining table, eating breakfast and looking through the wall of windows at the middle school outside. It was another day of heavy drizzle, but the students arriving for school looked underdressed to me, their heads covered with only a hoodie. Of course, teenagers were too cool to carry umbrellas. The sky was overcast and the forecast called for a day of sporadic rain. I shivered slightly. My shoes were still damp from the day before when we braved the rain with our umbrellas to go into London.

"Maybe something closer to home?" I suggested. I didn't want to sit home, but didn't want to travel into the heart of the city and be damp all day. I began leafing through a stack of brochures our landlord had left in our apartment. "We have options. Here." I tossed Dave a brochure. "Right down the road is the National Maritime Museum. Or we could go to the Queen's House." We both began looking at brochures. "I like the price. These places are all free."

Dave went to shower and I got up to put my wet boots on the radiator. If I alternated shoes, I could manage to get one pair dry each day. I didn't plan to sit in the apartment, no matter the weather.

With umbrellas in hand, we made the short hop from our apartment to the Greenwich National Maritime Museum, where we lingered for hours, inspecting the exhibits and learning about British naval history and the creation of the British Empire. After the museum, we crossed the street to the bank of the Thames River for lunch at the Trafalgar Tavern. This pub became our favorite lunch spot in Greenwich, especially if we were lucky enough to snag the seats near the roaring wood fire. We could sit at a table near the fire, relaxing in front of the wall of windows, and watch boats of all sizes navigate the Thames.

In Greenwich, there was the Queen's House, a house built for one Queen, Anne of Denmark (wife of James I), who died before it was finished, so it was lived in by another Queen, Henrietta Maria (wife of Charles I). The house had been converted into a museum and housed art by many famous artists (including those I consider the "Fab Four" of

British art: Gainsborough, Turner, Reynolds, Canaletto[3]), but my favorite picture was the portrait of Queen Elizabeth I called the Armada Portrait. This first Queen Elizabeth, who became Queen in 1558 when she was only 25, had fascinated me for years. She was the daughter of Henry VIII and the second of his six wives, Anne Boleyn. Henry had poor Anne beheaded when he tired of her, but Elizabeth I became the most powerful woman of her time, a time when normally women had no power at all. She managed to keep England from erupting into religious disputes, fought off Spain's huge naval Armada, and passed on stability to her successor. Seeing the Armada Portrait of Queen Elizabeth I in person was a thrill for me.

When the March weather cooperated, we took the train or tube into London. However, on days when the rain and gray skies took over, there was still more to see in Greenwich, like the 18th-century British clipper ship, the Cutty Sark, and the Greenwich Observatory near the Prime Meridian line where the eastern and western hemispheres meet and the official demarcation of time begins (Greenwich Mean Time). We learned about the Old Naval College in Greenwich and climbed the scaffolding there to take a tour of the extraordinary painted ceiling up close as the conservationists restored it to its 300-year-old glory.

The weekends were the best. On weekends we almost always took a trip to the Greenwich Market and made a beeline for the oyster vendor.

"How many do you want today?" Dave asked me as we waited in line to buy oysters.

---

[3] I know Canaletto (Giovanni Antonio Canal) was really Italian but so many of his paintings are in England that I consider him an honorary Brit.

I watched the vendor twist an oyster open with his knife. His hands were thick and strong with many red scars. The display case in front of him was nearly empty.

"What if he runs out?" I muttered to Dave as we both watched the oysters dwindle. When our turn came, the vendor stooped down and brought up a plastic bin filled with oysters and ice, which he dumped into his display case. I relaxed, knowing there was no shortage of oysters. We each ordered a dozen and wandered over to find seats at the communal picnic table.

One day as we were nearing home on the bus, I saw a familiar sign on a building.

"Let's get off," I hissed to Dave as I pushed the stop button on the bus and gathered up my bag. We stood by the door together as the bus began to pull over.

"What is it?" he asked.

"I saw a library."

He didn't ask any questions. Libraries and bookstores were my happy place, just like pubs were his. We crossed the street and shook off our umbrellas near the entrance. I approached the front desk.

"Can I get a library card?" We were sort of residents, for three months, but I wasn't sure our Airbnb rental would be sufficient proof of residency for a library card. The librarian didn't even blink, just handed me a short form to fill out. With library card in hand, I loaded up books, and Dave picked some movies. The shelves were full of dozens of magazines and they put on weekly movie days—another great hangout place for those drizzly, rainy days.

Every week we stumbled on new things in Greenwich. Along the Thames, the pedestrian paths kept going for miles. On some Sunday mornings, we ate brunch at Bill's on the Greenwich main street and hung out reading the newspapers. The Greenwich Picture House was down the street from Bill's, and nearby was a Waterstones bookstore where we could dawdle over a coffee and look at new books. On every block there was a new pub to explore and a variety of grocery stores we could duck into to pick up things before heading home. When the weather warmed up, we took a picnic lunch and explored the enormous Greenwich Park with its deer park, gardens, and massive old trees.

Greenwich was its own small village of delightful things to do and places to relax, and it was all a 10-minute bus ride from our front door. The average tourist on a week-long trip to London may not make it to Greenwich at all, and I felt lucky to have lived there and gotten the chance to know it so well.

• LONDON-MY FAVORITE •

After we returned to the U.S., people asked a lot of questions about our trip, but the most common question we heard over and over was, "What was your favorite part?" Venice will always be my favorite city on earth, but when asked this question, I invariably said, "London."

I've always, always loved all things British—history, art, authors, (I mean you, Jane Austen), culture, the accent, the Beatles, Churchill, grand houses, pubs, red double-decker buses, gardens. There was so much to do in London. Transportation was plentiful, clean, and efficient, and people were friendly. I could read the daily newspaper and understand the evening news, so I felt involved in the country's life and issues. There was a lot of diversity in London and it was easy to mingle and fit in. Even though I struggled with blood sugar numbers that were bouncing around a lot, I still woke up every morning eager to go out into the city to soak up the history and art that were everywhere, literally all around me. There was an energy and zest to every day in London.

For anyone interested in military history, the Imperial War Museum is a must-see place in central London. We bought a membership so we could visit several times and see all the exhibits in the huge building (formerly a mental hospital). The membership also included admission to the Churchill War Rooms and the HMS Belfast, a World War II Navy warship docked on the Thames. We spent hours at the Tower of London. All around the city, we saw statues, memorials, monuments, and plaques commemorating famous soldiers or battles. History was everywhere.

I didn't realize the sheer size of the collection of artifacts held by the British Museum, including the most extensive collection of Egyptian artifacts outside of Cairo. The Egyptian artifacts weren't the reconstructions of ancient tools, relics, art, sarcophagi, and mummies found in most American museums. They were authentic artifacts and included the Rosetta Stone that had been used to decipher ancient hieroglyphics. Even though we had been to Egypt, we were eager to learn more about its ancient culture, so one Friday we arrived there early to spend the day taking free tours of the museum's different Egyptian artifacts, beginning with the Eye-opener Tour of Ancient Egypt. After taking a break, we went to a Spotlight Tour highlighting the Rosetta Stone and ended the day with a talk on Death in Ancient Egypt. We came back one more afternoon to look at Egyptian artifacts not covered by the tours, and even after a third visit, we barely saw a fraction of the other exhibits on display. The British Museum, like many museums in London, is free.

Our experience was the same at the National Gallery museum of art in Trafalgar Square. We returned three or four times to the gallery, each time exploring one section of the museum, and never seemed to finish seeing it all. I especially wanted to see the two paintings at the National Gallery owned by Johannes Vermeer. Vermeer was a Dutch painter of the 1600s, and I loved the light in his paintings and his simple scenes from everyday life. I had never seen one of his paintings in person, and when I finally did, the light was so soft and real I felt like I was sitting in the corner of the room he had painted, just observing.

There weren't many paintings by Vermeer in existence and I turned our time in Europe into a search for them. Besides the two Vermeers at the National Gallery, the Queen owned one called *The Music Lesson,* and when we took a tour of Buckingham Palace, I made sure I saw it. *The*

Guitar Player was another Vermeer painting I was able to see at Kenwood House in the suburbs of London.

Dave was more of a Van Gogh man, but we agreed on one thing; seeing a painting in person is completely different from looking at a picture of it.

"It feels so odd to me to see this painting in person after seeing it dozens of times in picture books or online," I said to Dave, trying to interest him in the Vermeer we were looking at in the National Gallery. "The color of the paint in the original is different than the photo in a book. There are details photographs just couldn't capture—wisps of hair, or bits of embroidery on a dress."

Leaving the Vermeers, we made our way over to see Dave's favorite, Van Gogh's famous *Sunflowers* painting. Dave stood on one side and I stood on the other.

"The paint is thick and bumpy," Dave observed. He was standing very close to the painting and I glanced around quickly to see if a guard was nearby to yell at us.

"I know, right? Van Gogh must have applied the paint with a trowel. If you look at this picture in a book, you don't see all the texture."

We both backed away from the painting.

"From here, the bright yellow sunflowers look more golden, I think," I said.

"And you can see more details from a distance. Up close, everything blurs together," Dave said.

We walked along, stopping at different paintings to look at them up close and then from a distance, playing with the images, changing perspective. I don't think you need to be an expert to enjoy art. From the National Gallery to the Wallace Collection, the Dulwich Picture Gallery, the Royal Academy of Art, the Tate Modern, the Courtauld Institute of Art, the National Portrait Gallery, and the Sir John Soane Museum, there was a lot of art in London.

Besides history and art, there were castles and great houses to tour. Windsor Castle was only a short distance outside of London to the west, and we spent a day there only weeks before it was the site of Prince Harry and Meghan Markle's wedding. We took many tours of fantastic, beautiful old sites: Hampton Court Palace, Kew Palace, Chiswick House, Osterley House, Kenwood House, Leighton House, Kensington Palace (where Queen Victoria was born), Spencer House (the family home of Princess Diana), Apsley House (the family home of the Duke of Wellington) and Buckingham Palace (the family home of the Queen). There was no shortage of old houses to tour and admire.

I thought I'd been to one too many churches during our time in Rome, and debated skipping St. Paul's Cathedral and Westminster Abbey, but we went anyway and I was glad we did. Westminster Abbey especially fascinated me as the burial site of so many kings, queens (including Elizabeth I), poets, soldiers, authors, explorers, politicians, and scientists. Not as famous, St. Martin-in-the-Fields Church looks very ordinary from the outside, but the inside was lovely and light and had ideal acoustics. There was a constant rotation of classical concerts on offer, many of them free. I was happy to catch a Vivaldi candlelight concert one evening at St. Martin's church.

There are the Top 10 lists of London and the things everyone says you "Must See," but there are also parts of London that are small, delightful, and worth looking for. London's Chinatown was only a few blocks in size, the food fantastic. The Horniman Museum and Gardens on the south end of London had detailed and fascinating natural history exhibits. We took an afternoon cooking class at a Waitrose grocery store. We saw two plays in London's East End theater district. Since we are both Harry Potter fans, we waited in line to get pictures of ourselves at Platform 9 ¾ inside Kings Cross Station. Portobello Market is well known, but we returned several times to Borough Market on the south side of the Thames across from the Tower of London. There are bike-sharing stations all over London and miles of bike trails. We stumbled onto the London Drinker Beer Festival, held in a cramped community hall, and learned about the Bermondsey Beer Mile. The "Mile" was a very unofficial collection of breweries, bottle shops, and pubs on a stretch of road under some elevated train tracks in southeast London. Dave was definitely interested in the beer mile. I don't know if there is a beginning or ending to the Mile, so we jumped in at one pub somewhere in the middle and spent an entire Saturday on a self-guided walking tour enjoying many pints of beer we knew we would never taste again.

Just seeing the everyday sights in the city of London would be a month's long job, and what do you do if you, like most people, don't have months? I've listed dozens of things to do, and I'm sure there were many more I missed, wonderful places I walked right by and didn't notice. What to do with only a week in London?

I say, go with the things you love and care about, your passions, and skip the rest. If you love gardens, go to Kew Gardens, Archbishops Park Gardens, Kensington Gardens, the London Garden Museum, the famous Chelsea Flower Show (held in May), Buckingham Palace Gardens, and more. You can skip St. Paul's Cathedral and Westminster Abbey. Sacrilege! I know. But it is *your* trip to London. You won't see it all. If you are passionate about art, you must spend your time lingering over the art and looking slowly, carefully, and closely and if you miss a ride on the

216

London Eye, you won't have lost out on anything you really cared about. If you've always been interested in World War II, dive in. There are plenty of museums, and Free Tours By Foot has a *World War II in London* walking tour. Make your own itinerary, find all the statues, monuments, and plaques in the city.

If you follow what you love, your favorites, and your passions, any place you travel will always be your own private, unique, personal, memorable journey.

• OUTSIDE OF LONDON DOWNTON ABBEY AND STONEHENGE •

Sadly we didn't have much time, or much in the budget, to explore outside of London, but I was determined to see Highclere Castle, the setting of the wildly popular Downton Abbey show on PBS. Like most fans, I've seen every episode multiple times. There was no shortage of tours taking people to Highclere Castle, about an hour and a half outside of London. I hesitated for days before signing up for a tour because of the price, over £250, but after a deep breath, I took the plunge. Dave stayed home because Downton Abbey isn't his thing and £250 is a lot of pounds.

Early one morning in May, I joined my tour group near the Marble Arch. There were 14 of us plus a guide loaded into a large van. We drove an hour to a small farm where shooting took place for the show's farm scenes. Then the van drove us to the small village of Bampton in Oxfordshire where the village scenes were filmed. The quiet green English countryside was a total contrast to the streets of London. After Bampton, we climbed back into the van for the 45-minute drive to Highclere Castle, where the guide turned us loose with our entry tickets to tour the house.

It was raining outside as I waited in line to enter the house. Once inside, I wandered slowly, thinking back to scenes from the TV series. The library was one of the rooms used most often in the series, and as I wandered slowly through the crowds in the room, I could imagine the characters moving around the rooms in front of me. *Lady Mary, drinking tea in the library before Nanny brings in the children.* The rooms felt smaller than I imagined and the bedrooms looked surprisingly plain. Along one passageway, I noticed some chipped paint and worn upholstery, quite unlike the opulent and shining perfection of the show. *Where was Carson the butler to whip things into shape?* Still, it was a beautiful house.

After finishing the house tour, I walked outside to the café, ordered a cup of tea, and looked out at the rain-soaked grounds. I glanced down at my shoes, wet from walking around the farm and village, and wiggled my toes. My feet felt cold and my socks were soggy. I debated going out to walk around the grounds surrounding the house. In the end, even after a cup of tea, I just didn't have the energy left to walk around in the rain in my wet boots to see the garden. Highclere Castle joined the list of other places I would have to come back to—someday.

§   §   §

Dave is a pretty laid-back guy. He will go with the flow no matter what I put on the itinerary. Of course, he voiced some preferences. In Rome, he was happy to go to beer pubs when I found them and he loved Pompeii. In Croatia, we couldn't order food at a restaurant until Dave thoroughly reviewed the beer list to make his selection. In London, he liked the military history museums, and of course, we tried a new pub every week. Dave's other "must-see" while we were in London was Stonehenge.

Like tours to Highclere Castle, there were dozens of tours and tour guides offering trips to see it. Dave was the one who wanted to go to Stonehenge and I thought he should decide which tour to book.

Dave isn't chatty. Sometimes getting words or opinions out of him was hard, almost like tricking a spy into giving up secrets. If I asked the right combination of questions, I could get information. My interrogation began slowly.

"Most of the tours of Stonehenge I have looked at are just walking in a circle around the stones—maybe 15 yards away. We will need binoculars to see anything," I said.

Dave frowned.

"There are a lot of tours. I've bookmarked some. Do you want to look at them?"

He agreed, and I handed over the computer and walked to the kitchen to get another cup of coffee. I puttered around the apartment while he scrutinized tours. Before long, we had to leave, and the next week we were busy, going out and about as usual.

We were running out of time to book our Stonehenge tour and Dave hadn't brought it up. I didn't know which tour he had picked. My interrogation had to continue.

"Did you find a Stonehenge tour that looked good?" I asked.

"No. Not yet."

The words I dreaded the most—"not yet," the most frustrating words to someone like me. I looked. I decided. I planned. Bing. Bam. Boom. Dave didn't do that. He looked and then stopped—putting things aside, where they languished, unfinished and often forgotten. This was a common, recurring conflict in our relationship. Gritting my teeth, I felt the familiar warmth churning inside my stomach and spreading up across my face. *Breathe. This is not worth an argument. This is supposed to be fun—a trip to Stonehenge.*

"Do you want to look at the choices together?" I kept my voice fairly neutral.

He did.

Together on the computer, it was easy to pick a tour that gave us access to the inside of Stonehenge, the middle of the prehistoric stone circle. It cost extra and we would have to go outside of normal business hours—either a sunrise or a sunset tour. Neither Dave nor I are sunrise people, so we booked a sunset tour and a week later met up with our small group plus a guide for the trip to the city of Bath, the old thatched village of Lacock, and for the finale, Stonehenge.

The visitor center was closed when we arrived and sunset was coming. A shuttle bus took us from the visitor center out to the Stonehenge site, where the tour guide broke our group into two smaller groups. Only a limited number of people were allowed inside the Stonehenge inner circle at any one time. Dave and I were part of the first group, and while he took about 200 pictures, I walked from stone to stone and tried to imagine what led people to begin building this massive monument over 5000 years ago (circa 3000 BCE). The experts debate the meaning of Stonehenge. Researchers have found human bones, so maybe it was an ancient burial site. Other experts guess there was a religious or ritualistic use of the site because of the position of the stones. The tour guide kept talking about possible explanations, but Dave jabbed me in the arm to get my attention. "Remember John? From Missouri?"

Of course, I did. When we lived in Missouri, our neighbor was a man who believed that Stonehenge, the Egyptian Pyramids, and the stone faces on Easter Island had been brought to earth by ancient alien astronauts. He could tell you about it for hours. John was the neighbor Dave tried to avoid running into when taking out the trash.

After our turn inside the circle, Dave and I walked around the perimeter and waited for the other half of our tour group to have their turn inside the circle. In the background, I could hear the odd contrast of cars on the nearby highway. The sun was just setting. We'd been to the Egyptian pyramids and now had seen Stonehenge, built only about 500 years apart but in different parts of the world—ancient history on display. I began to think about how complicated life must have been in the ancient world. The "olden days" weren't simple at all. It must have taken a lot of resources, cooperation, communication, organization, and labor to build the pyramids and Stonehenge, much less get through a typical day. How did people do it?

I pictured a stone-age version of Dave and me. I would be in the cave saying, "Did you get that stone up today?" and he would say, "No. Not yet." I smiled at the picture of us wearing animal skins while we replayed our recurring conflict. Dave would laugh when I told him this idea.

I knew, and Dave knew, it wasn't in my DNA to be as laid back as he was. I was the hustle and bustle Type A person and he was the calm and slow Type B. Dave lived in the present and I looked forward. I planned, made decisions, and kept lists and Dave was happy I planned, made decisions, and kept lists. But when he *promised* to do something and then didn't follow through, things fell through the cracks. The pressure ratcheted up on me to remember everything. Sometimes our Type A/B personalities were in conflict and our conversations were loud and heated. Still, at the end of the day, he and I would laugh at the same things, want to do the same things, and we shared the same viewpoints on life, love, money, and family. After 13 years of marriage, we met in the middle of Type A/B land more and more often—and that took a lot of resources, cooperation, communication, organization, labor—and love.

• DRUGS •

Prescriptions and medical care turned out to be a recurring theme of our travels, but anyone who travels, either long term or short term, worries about possible prescription problems. There could be issues with not packing enough medicine, or medication could be lost or stolen, or you could even need a new medication while on the road. Bad things happen when traveling, and getting medication, or finding a doctor, may suddenly become one of the life-saving things a traveler has to deal with.

I thought I had filled all of my prescriptions in Croatia, but after checking my stockpiles, I would not have enough of one medication to last until we returned home. Dave hadn't filled all of his prescriptions in Croatia, so he needed four filled. Online expats told me British pharmacies would not fill our American prescriptions, and we would have to find a British doctor to give us new ones.

I got help from an expat in an online forum. Google "walk-in private medical center in London," they advised. When I did, I got dozens of hits. The prices ranged from £29 up to and beyond £100. Of course, we went cheap and made two appointments with www.doctap.co.uk, which was the equivalent of a Minute Clinic at Walgreens pharmacy in the U.S. I made two appointments and we walked out with prescriptions that we could fill at any London pharmacy.

My insulin supply was holding out just fine, and I probably could get through the rest of our time in London and then three months in Venice with my stockpiles, but just to be sure, I asked the doctor to give me a

223

prescription for insulin pens. At a Boots pharmacy, I was able to buy a box of NovoRapid insulin pens for £41 or $56 (five pens per box for a total of 1500 units). I was able to find lancets, the devices used to prick my fingers to draw blood for testing, for only £11 on Amazon UK, far less than the $35 co-pay I would have paid in the U.S.

When I added my boxes of English insulin to the refrigerator at the apartment, I thought back to when I left the U.S. with my six-month supply of insulin packed into a beer cooler. It seemed like a million years ago. At the time, I worried I wouldn't be able to buy insulin while we traveled, and my carry-on suitcase almost overflowed with diabetes supplies, some of which were easy to find everywhere we went. Why had I packed cotton balls, alcohol swabs, and backup batteries for my testing meter? Did I think there were no batteries in Italy? It was ridiculous, but still, I could look at my old self with sympathy. When you worried about everything like I did, it was hard to sort out which worries were valid and which were excessive. Traveling had taught me a lot, including that batteries are available *everywhere*.

TIP: *There are several expat groups and forums online and one may appeal to you more than another. In London, I regularly looked at www.uk-yankee.com and www.theamericanhour.com for information and tips.*

• AMSTERDAM •

Months earlier, when we were in Croatia, I had created two new lists. One tracked the money we saved by living in Croatia, and the other listed what we wanted to do with our savings. I didn't plan to bring this money home and put it in the bank. Oh no—I planned more travel. Our Croatian savings financed our trip to Egypt. After booking that trip, Dave and I started looking at ways to spend the remainder. It didn't take us long to settle on Edinburgh, Paris, and Amsterdam.

Edinburgh was Dave's choice and he had talked about going to the Fringe Festival in Scotland for years. As an added bonus, Scotland has good beer. The Fringe Festival is a month-long music, theater, comedy, party extravaganza held every August in Edinburgh. Once I put together some firm numbers on my savings list, I booked our plane tickets and a place to stay in Edinburgh with Airbnb.

Paris was also an easy pick since Dave and I spent our honeymoon there. When we returned home at the end of our year-long European journey, we would be flying out of Paris. I earmarked a portion of our savings to spend an extra few days there before we left Europe.

Looking back now, neither of us can remember why we chose Amsterdam as our third trip. It must have been the combination of wonderful art, lots of history, plus airfares to Amsterdam from London were cheap. It was a short hop across the English Channel.

On the morning of our trip to Amsterdam, the alarm went off at 5 a.m. Dave groaned as he rolled over to shut it off. We both lay there silently for a minute.

"Why are we doing this again?" he asked rhetorically.

"Amsterdam?"

"No. Why are we getting up so early?"

There was clearly criticism in the question. Our flight didn't leave until 9 a.m. We needed to be at the airport two hours before our plane left, at least according to Google and my worried, hyper-vigilant mind. Our flight was from Luton airport, in north London, and our apartment in Greenwich was in south London. It took an hour and a half to get to Luton airport from our apartment. I knew this because I insisted we make a trial run to Luton on the train the week before our Amsterdam trip. Over-analyzing things, like airport travel time, was my way of trying to control the unknown.

"It takes a long time to get to Luton airport from here," I said. "Plus, we'll get to Amsterdam early! Extra time to explore!" I was trying to be perky and upbeat, but I hadn't slept well the night before, wondering, *What if we don't hear the alarm or the Uber doesn't show up?*

Dave stumbled into the kitchen to start the coffee and then went to take his shower. I rolled my suitcase to the front door and then pulled insulin out of the refrigerator. I had packed all my other diabetes supplies the night before. On our short trips around Europe, I always followed advice from the travel blogs and took double the diabetes supplies that I thought I would use. For our five-night trip to Amsterdam, I brought out my small FRIO® cooling pouch that could hold a vial of insulin plus a couple of insulin pens. These little pouches could keep the insulin cool for up to 45 hours using evaporation for cooling. I thought they were magical.

I left the pouch immersed in water in the kitchen sink to soak for 10-15 minutes and went to get dressed. When I came back into the kitchen, the pouch had changed from thin and flat to fat and fluffy. Crystals in the pouch wall absorbed the water, and as the water evaporated, the pouch would stay cool. After we got to Amsterdam, I would put my insulin in the refrigerator of our rental, but if I needed to keep using the FRIO®, I could reactivate it by putting it in water again.

When we were both ready to leave, Dave called an Uber to take us to the train station. Even the buses didn't run this early. We arrived at the airport more than two hours before the flight and flew through security. They didn't even announce our gate until 45 minutes before the plane left, so there was more than enough time to eat breakfast and try to drink enough coffee to wake up. It was crazy busy at Luton airport. Around us, even at 7 a.m., large groups of people were laughing, drinking beer, and throwing back shots with their eggs. Luton was the party airport. One man, wandering the airport in a pink tutu and pink wig, seemed to have lost his stag party.

We arrived in Amsterdam, took an Uber to the apartment I found on Airbnb, and after exploring the area around the apartment and grabbing some dinner, we went to bed early. In theory, getting to Amsterdam early in the day would give us hours of extra sightseeing. The reality was that early flights left us both feeling half dead with weariness and we didn't do extra sightseeing. (I made a note to myself: early flights just don't work for us.)

After a good night's sleep, Amsterdam was a blast. The city has more bikes than people, and on the first day there, I planned to rent bikes and explore. I navigated us to a bike rental shop near Vondelpark, and we pointed our bikes hesitantly down a bike path alongside a busy street. When we got to a corner, I stopped.

"This is crazy. There are bikes, cars, and trams coming at us from every direction." I tucked my sunglasses into a pocket. I needed to see clearly.

"It's just like Rome. You have to cross the streets in a group." Dave had a plan and he was right. We had survived Rome.

I pointed in the direction I thought we wanted to go, down a narrow cobblestone street along a canal. Dave joined a clump of bikes going in that direction, and when the light turned green, we followed the crowd of bikes across the street. *This is easy.* At each busy corner, we waited carefully for green lights. As we rode, our progress was slow and halting as we dodged bikes, cars, buses, and pedestrians. More than once, a fellow biker zoomed around us shrilly ringing his bell as a warning. We were too slow. It was overwhelming. *This is not easy.*

"This isn't working," I said to Dave when we stopped at a corner. "I imagined a relaxing bike ride. This bike ride is a white knuckle experience."

"What do you want to do?"

"Let's go back to Vondelpark and bike there." We turned around and backtracked to the park. It was full of joggers, dog walkers, kids, and people lazing in the sunshine. No one was trying to run us over. At lunchtime, we found a restaurant, locked our bikes, and shared a picnic table near a canal with two guys. As we drank our beers and ate, we traded travel stories. They worked together in England and came to Amsterdam every month or so to party. The younger of the two pulled out a bag of weed and began rolling a joint as we talked. When he finished, he lit it up and passed it to his buddy, who took a deep drag.

"Want some?" He offered the joint to Dave, who looked at me, eyebrows raised.

"No, thanks," I said. "We are on bikes." They nodded good-naturedly and finished off their joint while we talked. Eventually, Dave and I said goodbye and left the merry pair as they rolled yet another joint. We had a bike ride to finish.

"It's weird to see people getting high in public," I said to Dave the next time we stopped. "We've passed almost a dozen people lighting up in this park." Colorado legalized marijuana in 2013, and we occasionally bought some, but even Colorado didn't allow public consumption.

"We could get some while we're here," Dave said.

"Maybe." Weed tended to make me anxious and I liked it better at home in familiar surroundings. Being in an unfamiliar city would probably just aggravate the anxiety. I imagined myself being high and getting lost, holding the map upside down, incapable of figuring out directions. "Let's see how it works out."

After two nights of sleeping at the apartment, it was time to move to a canal boat for our final three nights in Amsterdam. Amsterdam began as a fishing village, built around a dam on the Amstel River, but became a trading powerhouse, and the population multiplied rapidly. Today there are three main canals, and our canal boat was on the Keizersgracht canal not far from the train station. After getting the keys from the owner, we went inside. It was a tiny space.

"Watch your head," I warned Dave as I stepped in. The first room was topside with a wall of windows, a steering wheel, and a small seating area. "This looks like the Captain's room." A steep ladder led to a lower level. "I'll go down first and you can hand down the suitcase."

Once downstairs, we both explored the space—a minuscule dining table and two chairs, a coffee pot, microwave, and a small fridge. There was a full-size bed in a side alcove and the smallest bathroom/shower space I've ever seen, only slightly larger than an airplane bathroom.

"I can't stand up." Poor Dave was hunched over.

"You'll be fine. We're leaving for the museum anyway."

We edged our way out of the boat and began the trek to the Rijksmuseum carrying umbrellas. The weather forecast was for intermittent rain and the clouds in the gray sky looked ready to dump a monsoon. Once inside the museum, I took our coats and umbrellas to drop at the coat check and Dave found the desk to rent audio guides. We had been keeping our promise to each other, made on the day of our trip to Pompeii, always to spend money to take tours or rent audio guides or read guidebooks. It was money well spent, usually, but I kept battling the audio guide as we walked through this museum.

"Does your audio guide work?" I asked, sidling up to Dave as he looked at a painting.

"I haven't tried it yet," he said.

"Here. Try mine."

He took my audio guide and began pushing buttons. He frowned and pushed more buttons as I looked on.

"I want to know how to get to the Vermeer paintings," I said. "Is there a search feature? I can't find it." Defective electronics happened to me all the time, and I thought some part of my body gave off a magnetic force that caused electronic devices to malfunction as soon as I touched them. Usually, Dave would push a few buttons and everything began to work. As he struggled with the audio guide, I walked over to a rack of paper maps of the museum and took one. I quickly found the Vermeer paintings on the map and went back to Dave.

"Never mind. I found the Vermeers."

He looked at the paper map in my hand. "These audio guides are not very user-friendly. I don't see a search feature. I can only enter a picture number and get information about that picture."

"No map of the museum?"

"I can't find it." This was the first electronic device I had seen that had beaten Dave.

Well, let's just wander."

The art at the museum more than made up for the useless audio guide. The Rijksmuseum owned four Vermeer paintings I was excited to see. I lingered over his *Woman in Blue Reading a Letter, The Milkmaid, The Love Letter,* and one of his few street scene paintings, *The Little Street.* The lustrous, clear, soft light in the paintings was perfect. Dave preferred looking at *The Night Watch*, an enormous painting by Rembrandt. It was by far the largest painting I'd ever seen.

"Do you think he used a ladder to paint it?" I asked Dave.

"I don't know, but the audio guide says it took three years to finish." Dave had wrestled with his audio guide long enough to get at least a little information about individual pictures.

"Poor guy. I'll bet he was sick of it by the time he finished."

The rain held off as we left the museum and finished our day with a boat cruise around Amsterdam's canals, admiring the boats and the tall narrow houses crammed together along the canals.

The next day we took a tram to the most widely visited site in Amsterdam—the Anne Frank house. As I stepped through the revolving bookcase that hid Anne, her family, and four other people from the Nazis for over two years, there was silence as everyone began listening intently to their audio guides. The only sound was the creaking stairway I walked up. Slowly we made our way through the sparsely furnished rooms, listening soberly. This hiding spot, the Secret Annex, was haunting and sad. It felt like a sacred space.

After the tour, Dave and I found a café nearby and tried to shake the gloom of the experience.

"She was only 15 when she died," I said. My throat was full and it was hard to talk.

"Did you notice no one was talking inside there? It felt like a church."

For a few minutes, I sat silently. "I've read Anne Frank's diary, but seeing the spot where they lived makes it more real. But at the same time, somehow, I can't absorb it—the brutal, cruel world that would send a young girl to a death camp."

After finishing a quiet lunch, we grabbed a bus to the Van Gogh museum. But if we hoped to escape the gloom, this was the wrong place. It was not an uplifting museum. I have always liked Van Gogh's bright colors and dreamy style but knew nothing about him personally. The poor man was very talented, but he suffered from so many mental health issues he ended up killing himself. He was never financially successful in his lifetime, though in 2017 one of his paintings was sold by Christie's Auction House for $81.3 million. Ironically that painting was one Van Gogh painted from the window of a French asylum where he had committed himself.

I wished there was some way Anne Frank and Van Gogh could know how their lives affected the world. It wouldn't erase the hardships they faced in their lives, Anne's death in a Nazi concentration camp, Van

Gogh's poverty and mental illness, but I have to think they would take some comfort if they could see the influence they had on the world.

Our time was short and we kept moving. The Iamsterdam Card for tourists that we picked up at the airport included entry to over 50 different sites, which was how I found the Museum Van Loon and the Willet-Holthuysen museum canal houses. On our final day in Amsterdam, we toured both.

Houses fascinate me. Even when I was in grade school, I noticed houses, and I used to pretend I lived in one particular house just because I loved its wrought-iron fence and big front porch. I'm always curious about how people decorate their houses. If you leave your blinds open, I'm going to look in. My Pinterest is full of color combinations and furniture ideas. I've renovated several houses and flipped houses for about a decade simply because once I finished one and began living in it, I got bored. In older houses, there was the added interest, for me, of imagining the life of the family that lived there back in the "olden" days. How many servants did they have and what did they eat? These houses hold history in their walls.

The Van Loon canal house didn't disappoint. It was the home of the Willem Van Loon family. Willem was the founder of the Dutch East India Company, an early mega-corporation. I imagined him as the Bill Gates of 17th century Amsterdam. The rooms were beautiful, full of art and antiques, and I left with a good sense of how a wealthy Dutch family lived. After finishing that tour, it was only a few blocks walk to the even more stunning Willet-Holthuysen house museum—chandeliers, lavish furniture, mirrors, art, dishes, rugs, stained glass windows, and a gorgeous garden. Servants? Yes, they had dozens. *What would it be like to never, ever, cook a meal, sweep a floor, or wash a blouse?* Nope. I couldn't imagine, but it was fun to look at old houses and fantasize about being filthy rich.

On our last night in Amsterdam, we sat outside on the deck of our boat with glasses of wine and waved at people on the canal cruises that navigated up and down the canal. More than a few people looked envious. Our boat swayed side to side in the wake from the canal cruisers. Light from the sky, the boats, and the street lamps sparkled across the water. The canal boat had been a unique experience and well worth pushing the budget. True, poor Dave couldn't stand upright when he was downstairs, but drinking coffee every morning in the Captain's room full of windows, and drinking wine on the boat deck in the evenings plucked us out of our usual, safe, bland apartment space. Amsterdam had been an ideal place to spend some of our Croatian savings.

TIP: The Iamsterdam City Card is a bargain even if you have time only to visit a few of the over 60 museums and attractions offered with the card. It includes free unlimited public transportation, one free canal cruise, and other discounts. Prices range from €60 to €105 depending on whether you pick a 24, 48, 72, or 96-hour card. It's activated whenever you first use it. (Admission to the Anne Frank House is not included with the card.) After buying the Iamsterdam City Card, you should book your time slot to go to the Van Gogh museum (other museums and sites on the City Card do not require booking in advance). I ordered the card online and picked it up at the Schiphol Airport (Iamsterdam Visitor Information Center, Arrivals Hall 2. Open daily from 07:00 to 22:00).

Canal boat rentals are on Airbnb and other mainstream rental agencies. I chose a small company (www.houseboathotel.com) and was pleasantly surprised by how easy it was to book and pay for the rental.

• A NIGHT ON THE TOWN •

After Amsterdam, we settled back into London/Greenwich and spent every day exploring new places. One morning, earlier than usual, we left the apartment and took the train into central London to visit the National Gallery. It was one of those rare sunny days in London, and after leaving the National Gallery, we made the most of it and began wandering the streets, looking at shops for hours, until we finally sat to rest at a table outside a pub. I felt the sun on my face as I sipped my glass of wine and was doubly glad. Besides the rare, warm sunshine, this was the first day in weeks I had been able to use an insulin pump. The daily insulin shots I'd been giving myself for weeks took more time, more calculations, more equipment, and were more painful, so I was thrilled when a box of pumps arrived at our London apartment from my daughter in the U.S.

The previous night, I had given myself a final shot of long-acting insulin. That morning before leaving the apartment, I poked my finger to check my blood sugar, and it was a nice, safe, middle-range number. I filled a pump with insulin and attached it to my arm. It immediately began giving me low doses of insulin. All day long, I checked my blood sugar repeatedly. Every number, all day, was fine. It was a great day.

Late in the afternoon we got home, and I collapsed on the couch, exhausted from the long day and hours of walking. I was hogging the couch, so Dave went to the bedroom to read.

"Wait," I called after him. He stuck his head back in the door.

"I don't feel like cooking dinner tonight. Let's go somewhere—have a night on the town." It was Friday night and I didn't want the feeling of the great day to end.

"How about the pub down the street," he said.

I made a face. We had already been to the local pub several times. Still, getting out for the night sounded good. "Okay. Let's do it. We can grab dinner at the pub." I flipped on the TV as Dave took his book to the bedroom.

When I opened my eyes, the afternoon was gone and there was darkness outside the windows. I must have been sleeping. Across the room, a pair of shoes was lying in the corner, but they looked wrong somehow—blurry and dim. My eyes were fuzzy and cloudy. I blinked. The shoes moved toward me and then away—then closer again before receding. The walls wobbled and looked like they were melting. My brain couldn't think of the word "shoes." I was cold, and my head swung to the right. Dave, pale and wide-eyed, was sitting next to me on the couch. I was groggy, and single words floated without meaning through my head. Dark. Table. TV.

"Here, take this." Dave handed me a soda, and I drank some of it, but my stomach churned. "I'm cold," I said and Dave left the room to get a blanket from the bedroom. My arms and legs wouldn't move, and Dave wrapped the blanket around my frozen body and urged me to drink more soda. "The sugar will help you," he said. I sat sipping the soda as slowly, gradually, the pieces of the room settled down and quit moving. I saw the red plastic emergency glucagon kit open on the couch beside me.

"I was reading in the bedroom until it got dark," Dave spoke softly. "I came out to ask you about going to the pub, but I couldn't wake you up.

You were still breathing. Your purse was on the table and I found your test strips. When I tested your blood sugar, it was only 20."

He knew what to do. We had looked at the emergency glucagon kit every year after I bought a new one, and then every year we put it aside, unused. The bright red plastic kit held a tiny vial of glucagon, a hormone that raises blood sugar, and a syringe with a half-inch long needle. When he found me unconscious on the couch, Dave knew the glucagon was the only thing that could save me. He filled the syringe and plunged the long needle into my thigh.

"You didn't move after the shot. I paced around the room and found the number for an ambulance, but I kept checking your blood sugar, and it kept going up, so I waited." Dave's voice was shaking.

"I don't know what happened," I said.

"We should go to the hospital. We can't just sit here," Dave said.

I didn't want to go. Just sitting quietly on the couch felt like the only thing I wanted to do for a long time. Talking took too much effort. Thinking took too much effort. My arms and legs each weighed 100 pounds.

"I'm going to call an Uber," Dave said, handing me another soda and leaving the room to make the call. When the Uber came, we climbed in, and Dave wrapped his arm around me as we sat in silence for the short ride to the hospital. At the hospital, I talked to the triage nurse briefly and she waved us to empty seats to wait for an available doctor.

I sat on the hard plastic chair, my head on Dave's shoulder, my eyes closed. My head felt empty, groggy, light, and my thoughts were slow. I kept sipping sugary soda. Behind me, I heard the glass sliding doors opening and closing, and each time they opened, a wave of cold air moved across my back. Voices all around me murmured in a slow ebb and flow, loud and soft. *It sounds like the ocean*, I thought, but the smell was wrong. The air smelled like cleanser, antiseptic, not the fresh, salty smell of the beach.

I opened my eyes, but the lights were bright, florescent, and painful. Better to keep my eyes closed. I must have dozed off because then Dave was shaking me awake. A heavy-set woman with oily brown hair and a clipboard was standing in front of us.

"Pamala?" she asked.

"Yes."

"The doctor is ready for you."

I stood, blinking, taking a moment to look around while Dave gathered up my purse and the paperwork the nurse had handed us after we arrived. To my right, a woman was rocking a crying baby. Beside her, a man held his arm tightly to his body, slumped shoulders, head down on his chest. A line of people stood waiting to talk to the triage nurse, who sat behind thick glass to my left. There wasn't an empty seat in the drab beige room. The glass door slid open, and another person walked in and joined the line of waiting people.

We followed the nurse to a small room where a man in a white coat sat waiting. He took the papers from Dave and examined them. As I waited for him to speak, my eyes moved around the room. The doctor's arms stuck out past the sleeves of his white medical coat. There was a coffee stain on the front. Maybe the coat wasn't his. Maybe it was borrowed like the room—there were no pictures, no plants, no books or diplomas in the small space.

"So you have diabetes," the doctor began.

"Yes, for five years now."

"Did you eat today?" He led me through the usual questions. When had I eaten? What had I eaten? What were my blood sugar numbers when I woke up? When did I take insulin and how much? From my purse, I pulled out the PDM that operated my insulin pump and answered all of his questions. The PDM recorded everything, the entire day and all my movements on display. If I answered all of his questions, he could figure out what had happened. But my hands shook as I searched the PDM. I had questions too.

How did this happen? What did I do wrong?

The doctor paused and I looked at him. His eyes were tired.

"Do you have a history of heart problems?" he asked.

"No."

I could tell he didn't have any answers to give me. Like a lot of doctors and nurses, he didn't understand diabetes very well. I wanted some explanation. I needed help. But after hours of waiting, it was past midnight, and I just wanted to go home. He sent me next door to another generic office and I lay on a bed while a nurse attached electrodes to my chest. When she finished with the test, Dave and I sat until another nurse brought over more paperwork and, more importantly, a prescription so I could get another emergency glucagon kit to replace the one Dave had used earlier in the evening.

Dave and I took an Uber back to the apartment and sat together on the couch. Both of us were exhausted and, I think, a little in shock. Again I pulled the PDM out of my purse and checked my blood sugar. It was a little high.

"A high number feels safer," Dave said.

"I'm so tired, but don't want to sleep." I slumped on the couch, hesitating.

That night, I didn't take insulin to lower my high blood sugar, and I changed my insulin pump settings to decrease the overnight dose of insulin I would receive from the pump as I slept. I didn't know what else to do. I was too tired to talk anymore, and I don't know which of us was more wary and nervous when we went to bed.

The next day we went back to the hospital pharmacy to get another glucagon kit. Once, they had been seemingly unimportant. Now, these emergency kits took on a new meaning—without them, I could die. I'd carelessly tossed them onto my bedside table for years, but they could be all that stood between me and death.

Neither of us spoke on the ride to the hospital. In the pharmacy waiting room, I sat next to Dave and silently leaned my head against the wall. My mind kept replaying an endless circular loop—waking up in the dark, the wobbly walls, the shoes receding into the corner, the doctor's coffee-stained white coat, the nurse holding paperwork. Then again—dark, walls, shoes, doctor, nurse—and again.

Dave squeezed my arm but didn't speak. Immediately my throat swelled until I could barely breathe and tears began rolling down my face. I shifted my head to lean on Dave's shoulder and he squeezed my arm again. My hands were shaking as I wiped my eyes with the neck of my t-shirt. I swallowed, and the lump in my throat lessened. I still couldn't speak, but some dam had broken, and I could pull my mind away from the images circling my brain.

Slowly I thought of a word with meaning—thankful. I was so thankful. Thankful Dave was there and knew what to do. Thankful there had been no real damage. Thankful we had the daring and determination to push ahead through all the challenges and go on this year-long trip.

Whatever came next for me and my diabetes, from this point forward, we would have our year-long adventure and the experiences and memories.

All my life, I had avoided risks—on this whole journey, I had tried to plan everything, control everything, and avoid the unknown—but this experience showed me all that was nonsense. Risks were all around me, despite my best-laid plans and my carefully drafted lists. If we hadn't made this trip, if we had clung to the safety and security of home, I would have regretted it. My lists weren't so important after all.

§ § §

"If you lapse into a diabetic coma, you're alive—but you can't awaken or respond purposefully to sights, sounds, or other types of stimulation. Left untreated, a diabetic coma can be fatal."
Mayo Clinic

After the emergency room visit, I realized that when I switched from giving myself multiple daily insulin shots back to using my insulin pump, I had accidentally given myself an insulin overdose. When we returned to the U.S. and I talked to my endocrinologist about my emergency experience, she told me I should have done things a little differently. When I re-attached the insulin pump the first day, I should have decreased my basal (basic) insulin rate to 50% of normal for at least 12 hours. Then, for the next 12 hours, I should have decreased my basal rate to 80% of normal. After 24 hours, all pump settings could return to normal. Nothing in this chapter is meant as medical advice for all people with diabetes; this is my advice from my doctor, the doctor I should have contacted for help before

I changed from taking daily shots back to the pump. Always consult your own medical professional on managing your health while traveling.

> TIP: We never paid a penny for the emergency room visit or my glucagon prescription refill. As an American from the land of expensive health care, this amazed me. With money shortages plaguing the British National Health Service, there is some talk of changing the rules to begin charging foreigners when they receive medical care in Britain. That seems only fair since tourists don't pay the same taxes as residents.

• LEAVING LONDON •

"What else do you have to go in here?" Dave asked, looking at my suitcase on the bed, calculating how much more stuff would need to fit inside.

Here I was again, agonizing over what to bring and what to leave behind as we got ready to move on to Venice.

Even after nine months of traveling, packing was still not something I had figured out. When we were packing to leave London at the end of May, I was confident we would have an empty suitcase after donating four large bags of winter clothes to a thrift shop. But I wasn't thinking about the sizeable inflatable mattress that took up over half of one suitcase. The mattress was for three different sets of family and friends who would be staying with us in Venice. Finding even general household items in Italy had proven difficult, and I knew we didn't stand a chance of finding an inflatable mattress there, so we bought one in London to haul with us to Venice. Our suitcases were jammed to the max, and it would take all of Dave's concentrated Tetris skills to make everything fit. The weight of the suitcases didn't worry me because….what could I do? Throw money at the problem. If the bags were overweight, we would just pay up.

One thing I knew I wanted to leave behind as we left London was worry, planning, arranging, and organizing. After everything we had slogged through the last nine months, the scares, the ups and downs, the *hospital emergency room*—what did I really have to worry about? The small notebook I usually carried in my purse—full of lists, ideas, schedules, plans, and places to go—was not coming with me to Venice. It was time to put down my lists and guidebooks and look around me a little more.

More than two decades earlier, on my first solo visit to Europe, I had gone to Venice alone, and for me, it was unlike any other city on earth. It spoke to me—special, magical, unique. Venice would be swarming with tourists, and I wanted to get away from them. I wanted to wander and explore the side streets and back alleys. I wanted to get lost. I wanted to start the day not knowing where it would lead or where it would end.

When I thought of Venice, there was no room in my head for worry. Bits and pieces of the city lived in my mind and in my heart—the sun and sky reflected in the canals, boats gliding on the water, and the quiet, cool, shady alleys. Living in Venice, being a resident, a local, was something I had been longing for and dreaming about since Dave and I began planning our year-long journey. As we were packing to leave London, visions of Venice were dancing through my head.

Leaving was harder for Dave. "We can't leave without another night at our neighborhood pub," he said as we walked through Greenwich Park toward our apartment. I looked at him. He didn't often try to arrange our time. He left that up to me.

"Yeah, I'm going to miss the pub too," I said. "What's not to like?" Pubs were places where we could go with newspapers or a book and sit and sip a drink and relax. There was no rush or hurry. The only purpose of a pub was to relax and drink, with no guilt. Dave and I both excelled at relaxing and drinking. "Life is easier here, isn't it? We can talk to people and understand the TV."

"I have your favorite newspaper here." Dave waved it in his hand. "We should go to the pub now." He was carrying the daily Metro newspaper and knew I looked forward to reading its "Good Deeds" column. People wrote in to the Metro to thank unknown strangers for their good deeds—turning in lost wallets or helping them when they tripped and fell. I liked knowing good deeds were happening all around me in London.

I smiled at Dave and agreed to detour to the pub. We had nearly finished packing. In our three months in London, we had both enjoyed dozens and dozens of chats with Brits in grocery stores and libraries, on the trains and buses, and most often, in pubs. It was easier to plunge into the life of a country and to feel connected to a place and to a people when you understood the language. *If only I could package up the sense of connection we feel in London, put it in my suitcase next to the inflatable mattress, and bring it with us to Venice,* I thought. Soon we would be in Italy, back to being verbal outsiders. A night at the pub was exactly what we both needed.

Dave brought my beer to our table in the pub and went back to the bar to get his. Sitting at the table, I watched him stand at the bar talking to the barman. *Probably talking beer stats,* I thought with a smile. In London, Dave had switched to only drinking dark stout Guinness beer. He had tried asking for other stout beers but more than one bartender told him "You don't need any other stout."

Taking a sip of my beer, I put down the newspaper and thought about leaving London. So many images passed through my head, not just museums, restaurants, and art galleries, but also the late-night trip to the hospital emergency room. That was a vivid image.

I should have called my doctor for advice before I went back to using the insulin pump. Why didn't I call her?

Wiping the condensation off my beer mug, I easily answered my own question—pure exhaustion. Almost from the moment I stepped on English soil, I had been battling blood sugar numbers that were all over the place, and I had no idea why. My allergies were acting up a little. Was that causing weird numbers? My insulin pumps were failing more frequently than usual. Had I gotten a bad batch of Pods? I spent almost two weeks nursing my sore ankle after tripping on a cobblestone. Was the stress from that injury ratcheting up my numbers? I didn't have problems with my blood sugar numbers every day, but it happened far more than usual.

Somewhere along the way in the last few months, I had become worn down dealing with the turbulence of high/low numbers—day after fricking day—so I just started coasting, putting in the minimum effort. I lost motivation to manage my diabetes, began testing less often and guessing at carb counts in food. Calling my doctor for advice about switching from shots to the pump seemed like too much effort. I knew "diabetes exhaustion" was a real thing that affected many people with diabetes; it had just never happened to me before.

As a diabetic, day-to-day life was hard enough without fighting random, unexplained battles with out-of-control blood sugar numbers. Testing my blood sugar was the first thing I did every morning and the last thing I did every night. Everywhere I went, I carried a pouch of supplies that had to be protected from getting too hot, too cold, lost, or stolen. The edges of my fingers were sore from being poked and pricked. I had dry skin, thinning hair, and weight gain, courtesy of diabetes. I had to remember to check my feet because a cut or sore could lead to infection and possible amputation. Every scrap of food or drink that went into my mouth left me hesitant, thinking about the effect on my blood sugar. If I walked a lot, I spent extra time checking blood sugar. It. Just. Never. Stopped. Diabetes burnout had slowly crept up on me during our time in London, leaving me frustrated and defeated. The beer in my hand was getting warm as I sat thinking, trying to remember exactly when I had thrown up my hands at the constant, daily, hourly effort of it all. *Things have to change. What I want to leave behind as we leave London is my defeated attitude. I have to pull myself together and get back on track.*

My thoughts were interrupted by a couple of ladies sitting down near me.

"Do you need that chair?" one of them asked me.

"No," I said. "You can have it."

"Oh, American! Where are you from?"

And so it begins, I thought, *a night of chatting at the pub*. I was going to enjoy it while I could. In just a few days, we were going to our final stop, three months in Venice.

> *TIP: In London, our apartment's plugins included "on" and "off" switches. So after plugging in an appliance, we also needed to turn "on" the plugin, using a little switch on the face of the plug-in itself.*
>
> *TIP: Take the time to check in with yourself as you travel. There is so much external stimulation and activity, and it is easy to forget this one simple thing.*

PART V: VENICE

• SOUL CITY •

I believe in soul cities. Venice, Italy, is my soul city.

After stumbling on an article about Venice when I was in middle school, I couldn't get the pictures of sunshine glittering on water, canals, boats, palazzos, and bridges out of my mind. It didn't seem like it could be a real place that existed in the same world as me, living landlocked in small-town Missouri. At that age, I had never seen an ocean in person, so I could barely comprehend a city built on water. With no roads? No cars, buses, trucks? The article said Venice was sinking, slowly, into the lagoon it was built on, and someday it would be underwater. I wanted to get there before it disappeared.

In 2002 when I traveled alone to Venice, I prepared by memorizing the guidebook. I had no cell phone in those long-ago days, no travel blogs to consult, no internet, and no Google Maps. In my backpack, I carried paper maps, guidebooks, and lists—including phone numbers I might need in an emergency, a list of my plane and hotel reservations, and copies of my credit card and passport. If there was some way to be prepared for any situation, I was going to do it.

The trip got off to a rocky start when the plane taking me from Kansas City to New York had some random airline problems and I missed my flight to Venice. The travel insurance policy I had bought covered things like missed airline flights due to illness, so I got "sick" visited a doctor to document my "illness" and then bought another ticket, leaving the next evening. The travel insurance later reimbursed me for the extra ticket.

On the plane, I didn't sleep for even one instant. I couldn't. It was all new and exciting. I studied the guidebook and read and re-read Rick Steve's precise advice for getting from the airport to Venice: "Walk out of the west door of the airport, turn right and walk for 200 yards, then wait for the blue bus." With explicit directions like these, I didn't think I could possibly have a problem. To be safe, I memorized the directions.

Once safely on the blue bus to Venice, I was hugely disappointed. The bus passed buildings that looked like old deserted factories leftover from World War II. I saw dry, brown land filled with weeds and surrounded by falling down fences. We passed through a town, and there was graffiti covering the walls and scrawny dogs waiting outside tiny, dingy-looking stores. The sun was hot. The bus didn't have air conditioning.

When the bus arrived at the end of the line, everyone got off, but I could see there had been a mistake. This was a parking lot. This was not Venice. This didn't even look like any pictures of Italy I had ever seen. If I squinted, I could imagine myself in a Greyhound station in Kansas City.

Not knowing what to do, I followed the streams of people walking away from the bus, and when I turned the corner, I saw it. Venice—the glittering water of the canal, the stone palazzos and churches lining the water, the boats filled with people and produce, moving in all directions. It took my breath away. I swear a stream of light came out of the clouds and shone on the scene in front of me like a spotlight. In an instant, I was in love. This was my soul city.

There is no way to be absolutely certain when you have found your own soul city, but there are some common signs that you may have found "The One." In Venice, my soul city, I was alone, so there was no one to distract me from my silent communion with the city. Venice communicated with me in mysterious ways. One day, lost and wandering down a narrow alley (one of the thousands in Venice), I heard the lyrics of a song I knew well by the rock music group Pink Floyd called "Time." The song came from the open window of some nearby apartment like it was waiting for me to walk by. I stood in the alley and sang along softly with the lyrics; about how when you are young, life seems so long; then it goes by in a flash, and you find yourself in middle age, decades older, and looking back at your younger self.

For me, this song was a cautionary tale, a reminder that life is brief and flies by faster every year. I came to Venice alone to grab ahold of life—every bit of it. This haunting song found me in the alleyway, and I knew Venice was speaking to me.

Once I arrived in Venice and dropped my bags at my small hotel, I began to wander and got immediately lost. Venice is a labyrinth of twists and turns. Often a sidewalk will dead end on a canal, and there is no choice but to backtrack. Normally I hate getting lost. It's a waste of time and makes me feel anxious and nervous. In Venice, it was different and I had no fear or nervousness. The old stone walls around me had seen everything. They had been witness to wars and death and plague. I was comfortable and confident I would find my way, eventually, and in the meantime, being lost felt like a dizzy dance between Venice and me.

Years later, I would visit Florence and Rome and, again, Venice. In the years between visits, I discovered I could navigate life, function, grow, and explore on my own. I built a life. I found Venice still spoke to me, comforted me, and wrapped me in her arms, unlike any other city. Florence undoubtedly has more art, and Rome has its own unique history as the former capital of the civilized world. Still, Venice and I connected on a deeper physical and psychological level. It was, simply, my Soul City.

Now I was going back for a longer sojourn in Venice. This was going to be a very good three months.

• ARRIVAL •

When Dave and I arrived in Venice, we skipped the slow bus through the dusty countryside and bought tickets on Alilaguna. This lagoon boat taxi brought people from Marco Polo Airport directly to Venice and the other larger islands of the lagoon. For a reasonable fee of €54, the boat took us, heavy suitcases and all, directly to Fondamente Nove on the northwestern side of the island of Venice where Leonardo, our landlord's son, met us. A short walk later and we arrived at the apartment that would be our home for the next three months.

The apartment was a nice size. Not as large as our apartment in Greenwich but bigger than the ones in Rome and Split. There was one large living/dining/kitchen combo room. Off the main room was one door to the bedroom and another separate door to the bathroom. *Thank goodness our summer guests don't have to access the bathroom through our bedroom,* I thought. I had been looking at the apartment pictures for weeks, trying to figure out the layout.

The kitchen cabinets and appliances were modern, with a gas cooktop and an oven. Although not full-size (it only reached to my shoulders), the fridge was bigger than a dorm fridge.

"This apartment is beautiful," I said to Leonardo as he watched us explore the space.

"Yes, it belonged to my grandmother," he said. "After she died, my father divided it. This is a rental. Next door is my Great-Aunt. She is very old and you will not see her often."

My mind flashed back to sweet Lucia, our neighbor in Croatia. It didn't sound like our new neighbor would be bringing us cookies.

"Look at this, Dave—a washing machine." The washing machine was behind the modern kitchen cabinetry. The Airbnb description of the apartment referenced a "shared washer on the premises for a fee." I had pictured a smelly, dank, dark basement with a community washing machine, and it was a happy surprise to find we had our own washer. There was no dryer, of course, just a hanging rack.

There was a lovely air conditioner on the living room wall, a big reason I had chosen this apartment. Dave opened the heavy wooden shutters on the tall south-facing windows. He leaned out onto the small Juliet balcony filled with plants and looked right and left. "Alleys. Lots of alleys. I predict we will get lost," Dave said.

The furniture in the apartment was antique, but the appliances and finishes were all modern, and I loved the mix of styles. This was the most elegant apartment we had rented so far and, for €2,500 a month, the most expensive. But it was summer and it was Venice. Any place we lived in the busy summer travel season would cost a lot, and in Venice, all those lovely canals made transporting goods expensive. It didn't matter. We were here, and that was worth everything.

Leonardo gave us a small map and tried to explain where the grocery store was. "You leave the building and turn left, then right, over the iron bridge to the dead end, then left and over a stone bridge, then past a tabacchi shop, and twenty steps ahead to the building on the right. That is the grocery store." *Every direction in Venice involves bridges,* I thought.

Leonardo left, and we explored the apartment alone before heading out to take care of our usual "get settled" check-list. Our first stop was the ACTV (Venice's local transit authority) office at the Piazzale Roma bus station, where we bought our monthly transportation passes. In Venice, most transportation was on foot, but we would also get around using water buses, called "vaporetto." The *daily* rate to use the vaporetto was a crazy, obscenely expensive €20. The monthly passes were only €37 a month. There was an upfront fee of €50 each to activate our passes, but that was a one-time fee. Going forward, we would have endless rides on the vaporetto and some buses on the nearby island of Lido for only €37. At the ACTV office, I just filled out a form, showed our passports, and left with passes in hand.

On the way home from the ACTV office, we hit the grocery store. It was much the same as the grocery stores in Rome, very small with lots of pasta options, and we stocked up. I found a new Venetian pasta called bigoli that I had to try. We barely used Google Translate and I felt like an old pro at Italian grocery shopping.

Leaving the store, I noticed a bulk wine store across the street. These stores, called "vino sfuso" (translated as "loose wine"), existed everywhere in Italy, but when we lived in Rome, there hadn't been one we could get to easily. So I knew what they were but had never been inside of one.

"Oh, man. We have to go in there," I told Dave. He squinted at the store dubiously. It did look dusty and the window wasn't exactly clean.

"What is it? Can we come back later? After dumping all these groceries?"

"Oh, believe me. You're going to like this place."

Dave and I walked inside with our bags of groceries for a look around. He immediately understood what it was. Behind the counter of the small room were rows of large round plastic containers, each holding probably 30 gallons of wine. A label on each container identified the wine inside. A plastic hose and sprayer came out of each container's top, and on the side-wall were dozens of empty bottles of different sizes. I decided to give my Italian a spin.

"Buongiorno signore," I said to the genial, smiling, middle-aged man behind the counter.

"Buongiorno," he replied

"Vorremmo del vino," (We would like some wine.)

"What kind of wine?" He asked—in English. *Oh well. I was on a little roll with the Italian,* I thought.

Dave decided to get involved. "Can we try the wine?" he asked.

"Yes, of course."

As we sipped two or three reds and an equal number of whites, we exchanged names. Roberto had been in the wine business for decades.

"These wines are young wines. Giovane. They are no..." he paused to think of the English word but failed. "They are senza conservanti." I would have to look that one up, but I nodded encouragingly and took another sip. (Conservanti=preservatives. Vino sfuso wines have no preservatives.) There were many wine varieties in the shop, some completely unfamiliar: Raboso, Pinot Rosso, Tocai. All were delicious. Although we had picked up a few bottles of wine at the grocery store, I couldn't go home without wine from our own neighborhood vino sfuso shop, so we bought two bottles there—one excellent Cabernet Franc and the other a dark Pinot Nero. The cost was only €2.70 a liter, about half of what we'd just paid for a bottle at the grocery store.

Dave was still doing most of the family cooking and grocery shopping, and during our time in Venice, he became a regular at the vino sfuso shop. The owner gave him a wine sample whenever he entered, so he eventually tried every wine in the store. Dave told me he seemed to run into the shop owner all over Venice, and when they met in the streets and on the vaporetto, they exchanged the friendly nods of fellow wine lovers. It wasn't as good as chatting at the pubs in London, but it was a small, warm connection in our new city.

TIP: Vaporetto ticket prices are high. A single ticket valid for 75 minutes will cost €7.50. Other ticket options are 24 hours (€20), 48 hours (€30), 72 hours (€40), or seven days (€60). During our three month stay, we paid only €37 per month (plus a one-time activation fee) for unlimited rides on the vaporettos after buying and activating our Venezia Unica "frequent user" card. This card also gave us a 50% discount on Alilaguna boats to the airport. There is a separate "tourist" version of the Venezia Unica card that is primarily used for access to museums and churches but which can also be loaded with money for city transportation. www.veneziaunica.it

• FAMILY VISITS •

After being in Venice for only a week, and despite still getting lost on a daily basis, we were expecting our first visitors.

My daughter Vanessa and granddaughter Aubree also lived in Colorado, not too far from our house, and before leaving for our year of traveling we saw them often. Aubree, at almost seven, was a curious, sweet, chatty, imaginative, energetic girl. We were excited to see both of them again after being gone so many months and knew Aubree, especially, would love Venice—gelato on every street!

Vanessa found a cheap flight to Rome and planned to spend the night there before attempting the four-hour train ride to Venice. I traveled to Rome to meet them and to help manage the suitcases and a jet-lagged Aubree. When they finally made it through customs and we saw each other, there were many tears and hugs. Aubree had lost a few teeth since I had last seen her, but even with no front teeth she was still all smiles and hugs.

When the three of us arrived in Venice the next day, Dave already had their "bedroom" set up. The inflatable air mattress purchased in London fit on the floor in one corner of the main living space, and we pushed the dining table to the center of the room. There was still space to walk around the apartment, the bathroom served as their dressing room, and everyone was comfortable.

After settling in, we left the apartment for our first stop—the local gelato shop. Before leaving the U.S., Dave and I had promised Aubree that if she visited us in Italy, we would make sure she ate gelato every day. She made us keep our promise. At the gelato shop, she eyed the choices. "What kind is that?" she asked, pointing at a very bright blue gelato. It was called "puffo." Google translated this as "Smurf," and it was the same neon blue as Papa Smurf in the old 80's cartoons. Aubree wasn't having it. We went through the other flavors, naming the ones we recognized and trying to translate the ones we didn't. After all our efforts at translation, she played it safe and settled for strawberry—"fragola." Dave and Vanessa each picked a flavor, and I looked on—trying to decide what to do. I could get gelato for myself and take extra insulin, but it was hard. I spent every day trying to limit carbs and lower my insulin intake. Lucky for me, I don't have much of a sweet tooth and much prefer savory flavors. Gelato wasn't hugely enticing to me, but to see my family eating it right there made my mouth water.

While Vanessa and Aubree were in Venice, we kept our promise and bought Aubree gelato every day—multiple times every day. Menta, stracciatella, nocciola, pistacchio, caffe, cioccolato, melone, arancia, lampone, and more fragola—Dave, Aubree and Vanessa tried them all. I compromised by getting a small plastic tasting spoon from the gelateria and taking a taste from each of them. It was just enough for me.

Our five days in Venice with Vanessa and Aubree were a whirlwind. At the nearby island of Murano, we looked at the colorful glass for sale and watched a glass-making demonstration. As the glassblower puffed air into one end of a metal tube, the liquid, molten glass on the other end expanded. When it was the size he wanted, he changed the shape by spinning and rotating the tube and pinching the glass with pliers, creating a fanciful glass horse. Surprisingly, this demonstration bored Aubree, and afterward, she needed a gelato to cheer up.

Later, when we were inside the Basilica San Marco, the golden mosaics on the ceiling and walls immediately captured everyone's attention until I realized we had lost Vanessa.

"Where is Vanessa?" I whispered to Dave as we began to edge through the church.

He is taller and can usually spot people in a crowd. He spun around, slowly searching the mass of people. "I'll backtrack and look for her if you and Aubree stay here."

It was crowded in the Basilica and we were being pushed forward in a slow-motion shuffle. I pulled Aubree to one side to wait. After a few minutes, Dave and Vanessa caught up with us.

"What is that?" I asked Vanessa, eyeing some bulky white gauze paper wrapped around her waist.

"Modesty," Dave said.

She had been stopped and forced to buy the paper cover on her way into the Basilica because her shorts were deemed too short to be "decent."

We finished our Basilica tour and made our way to the Rialto Market. I wanted us to arrive like real Venetians, so we climbed into a narrow wooden boat called a traghetto to cross the Grand Canal. The Grand Canal is Venice's main highway, and overcrowded vaporettos constantly zig-zag its length, somehow avoiding collisions with gondolas, private boats, delivery boats, and water taxis. Standing on the little traghetto boat as it bobbed its way across the canal felt thrillingly unsafe.

The fruits and vegetables in the stalls at the market looked and smelled freshly picked, but the rows of fish were far more interesting.

"What is that!" Aubree screeched, pointing at a quivering blob of squishy grey flesh.

"Octopus?" I guessed, making out tentacles and the suction cup disks on the bottom of each tentacle.

"Gross." Aubree scrunched her nose and backed away.

The market was full of new things. There were lots of tiny sardines, ordinary salmon, tuna, shrimps, and a huge swordfish. All the food made us hungry, so we found a restaurant near the market and chose a table in the shade. Besides drinks and pizza, Dave ordered an octopus salad appetizer. When it arrived, Aubree held her nose.

"How about one bite of octopus salad now and gelato after lunch?" Dave gently bribed Aubree. We both loved food—loved trying new food—and wanted Aubree to love it too.

"One bite of octopus and *two* gelatos." She liked to negotiate and we predicted she would grow up to be an attorney.

"One bite of octopus and no gelato," Dave countered.

She could tell things were going the wrong way, so she settled for the "one bite octopus-one gelato" agreement. Twirling a piece of hair, she speared the tiniest bit of octopus and tentatively put it to her lips. Dave, Vanessa, and I went back to our glasses of wine and started talking but watched her out of the corner of our eyes as she finally put the piece of octopus in her mouth and chewed. As she swallowed that bite, her fork searched for another piece of octopus. She ate that and took a sip of her soda. "I like it," she offered as she ate another piece. Dave and I ate some of the octopus before she gobbled it all down, and it was fantastic—drizzled with olive oil, a little splash of lemon, and some spices I didn't recognize. It was cooked perfectly. From then on, we ordered octopus salad whenever we ate out and became experts on the best and worst octopus salads in Venice. The good salads had a grilled crust, salty sea taste mixed with olive oil. The bad salads were rubbery.

Florence was only a two-hour train ride away, and Vanessa wanted to go, so I booked a small apartment for one night in Florence, and we took a train there early one morning. Our first day in Florence didn't work out as planned because the kid's "Secret Passages" tour of the Palazzo Vecchio was sold out, and I hadn't reserved tickets. Tickets for the Palazzo tour were available the next day and I grabbed them. Luckily I did have reserved tickets to see Michelangelo's sculpture of *David* that first afternoon, so we walked over to the Galleria dell'Accademia. The statue is 14 feet of gleaming, glistening white marble. *David* is focused, concentrating on some distant figure, as he loosely holds his rocks and a sling. *David's* physique, his muscles, capture your attention, and his neck is so detailed and perfect I imagined I could see a pulse throbbing in his neck.

Aubree noticed he was nude. "Why don't the people have clothes on?" she asked, coming up to my side in the crowded room.

"You mean the statues?" There were several statues other than the *David* in the Galleria.

"Yes."

I thought for a minute. *Why is David naked? Surely he wouldn't have actually fought without any clothes on. He would have worn a loincloth or a cloak, or maybe there would be an animal skin covering him. But in the gallery, there were many other statues of all types of people and they were naked also.*

"I think in the olden days people thought the human body was beautiful and they weren't embarrassed by people with no clothes on," I finally said.

She silently digested my explanation, then shrugged and moved on. I made a mental note to tell Vanessa that Aubree might have some questions later about the difference between boy bodies and girl bodies.

The next day, the kids' tour of the Palazzo Vecchio's secret passages was a big hit with all of us. The guide led us from the lower courtyard up the stairs to a room full of maps. It looked like an ordinary room until she moved to one sidewall and opened a secret, hidden door, and our group stepped through. The kids were thrilled and began chattering—instant friends. The guide led everyone to a display of old toys, tools, and clothing that the kids were allowed to handle and play with. Further down the corridor, they all played dress up in kid-sized Renaissance-style clothing while the tour guide told them about Florence's history. She explained the power struggles in early Florence and how those in power used the hidden passages to escape their enemies and run away. I stood near an open window and fanned my sweaty neck with a museum leaflet while the kids played. It was a relief to finish the tour and step out into the slightly cooler air outside. Later that day, we returned to Venice on the train.

Vanessa and Aubree stayed with us for five days before Vanessa returned to Rome to meet up with her fiancé Eric. Then Dave and I would have Aubree to ourselves in Venice for a few extra days before taking her to Rome to fly home with Vanessa and Eric. Besides daily trips to get gelato, we made lots of plans for Aubree.

One day we took her to the Lido and spent a day at the free beach. The beach was such a big hit we went back another day. It isn't Venice without a gondola ride, so that was another afternoon. There aren't many parks and playgrounds in Venice, but we found them all. We struggled a few times with the lack of public restrooms in Venice—a chronic problem for both adults and kids with small bladders. Dave and I had quickly learned to duck into restaurants and buy a quick glass of wine or espresso just so that we could use the restaurant bathroom.

All too soon, it was time to take Aubree to Rome and meet up with Vanessa and Eric. They had been busy going to Pompeii, the Colosseum, and all the usual sights. On this final day in Rome, they wanted to pick up souvenirs, so Dave and I took Aubree to the Borghese Gardens. It was a sweltering hot June day, and on the way to the park, I couldn't help moaning about the heat. "Why can't they air-condition the buses?" Dave was used to my grumbling and complaints about the heat and just ignored me. Aubree was excited to be riding the bus.

The park was a relief—shady and breezy. *This place won't be too bad*, I thought. We found a vendor renting bikes and picked a big multi-person bike with electric assist. As we started exploring the park, I noticed the bell on our bike wasn't working.

"Aubree. We need your help," I told her as we navigated a narrow road/sidewalk on the bike. She was riding on a seat on the front of the bike. "The bell on the bike isn't working. You need to yell at people to move if they get in front of the bike."

"What do I yell?" she asked. Good question. "Watch out" wouldn't work in Italy.

"Yell ATTENTO!" I told her. And she did. Whenever people wandered in front of our bike, she yelled, "Attento!" and we all giggled a little as people dodged out of our way. The park spread over several acres and we made it from one end to the other, lingering over the panoramic views of Rome from the Pincio Terrace. As we ate lunch at a park cafe, we fought off the birds diving for our food and, of course, ordered yet another gelato.

That evening Dave and I took Vanessa, Eric, and Aubree to dinner at one of our favorite restaurants in Trastevere before the three of them caught a cab to an airport hotel to wait for their early morning flight leaving the next day. Dave and I spent one final night in Rome before returning home to Venice.

§ § §

In the few days we spent with Aubree, Dave and I both noticed many changes in her. She had always been a very chatty, sweet-natured, kind, with a big imagination. Now, in Venice, she was only seven, but she seemed to have grown up a lot. We hadn't seen her in ten months. She paid more attention to her surroundings; she watched people, listened, and asked questions about what she saw. She made her own connections and comparisons between parts of her world instead of waiting for an adult to tell her what things meant. She used to be a little anxious, a little clingy, but nothing seemed to make her uneasy in Venice. Not the crowds or the crooked, dark alleys, or the complete and utter unfamiliarity of everything around her. Once we told her the winged lion was the symbol of Venice, finding lion symbols became a competition, and her sharp eyes and concentration won the contest every day. We were both fascinated by the watchful and observant child who now replaced the dreamy, fanciful Aubree we had left behind.

But then, I had changed too.

In the beginning months of our trip, I had almost daily mini bouts of anxiety as I watched our surroundings, the traffic, the weather, the people, always poised to react—to what, I didn't even know. Whatever came our way, I was on alert. Now, ten months later, I had joined Dave to become a calmer and dreamier person. We wandered Venice with no schedule or timetable. I was okay with starting the day aimlessly, just tossing books and water bottles into a backpack and setting out in the general direction we wanted to go just to see what we could see, not knowing where we might end up. Sometimes we would go to the nearby Fondamente Nove and jump on whichever vaporetto came along first. We'd jump off at an unfamiliar stop and wander until we got hungry or hot and then found a café for lunch. We wandered in quiet out-of-the-way corners of Venice that we would never find again, where no one spoke English and where the alleys smelled of ripe tomatoes and Nonna/Grandma making lunch. Each day slipped easily by.

If Aubree had become more observant and alert, I had undoubtedly become more dreamy and inattentive.

TIP: There are apps you can download to help find public bathrooms anywhere in the world. Dave downloaded one called "Flush" on his phone, but we often didn't have Wi-Fi while out and about in Venice, so it was pretty useless. The app is worth having when visiting other cities.

• THE ESSENTIAL VENETIAN VAPORETTO

•

After only a month in Venice, I could say with certainty that I had seen more lost people there than in all the other cities we had visited— combined. I was constantly amazed by the sheer number of people I saw every single day who simply did not have the slightest clue where they were. Nearly every day that we wandered out and about, someone would come wildly rushing onto a vaporetto/water bus stop asking, "Train station?" *No. This vaporetto doesn't go to the train station. You and your large suitcase might miss your train because this vaporetto goes to The Lido, and THAT isn't even close to the train station.* It was not unusual to see clumps of people with suitcases headed to the train station but getting on a vaporetto going the wrong direction. More than once, I overheard people at vaporetto stops arguing loudly with each other because they didn't know which stop they were at. When I could, I tried to help until I noticed that people invariably ignored me and went in the direction they wanted to go. *Tourists.*

Venice is hard. It is worth doing a little more research before arriving. In Venice, a certain amount of getting lost is inevitable and normal. The entire city is a twisting maze of alleys after all, but a little time spent preparing before arriving does make a visit there easier. There are some cities where you can fly by the seat of your pants, but I don't think Venice is one of them.

When we arrived I hadn't done advance research, and spent the first few days looking at the vaporettos and studying the piteously small map Leonardo had given us. Scouring the official Venice transportation site, called the ACTV, (ACTV at www.actv.avmspa.it) didn't help much. Finally, in English, I found a site giving me all the information I needed to figure out the vaporettos, and I used it every day. It was www.visit-venice-italy.com. This site is what you would get if you could combine Google Maps and Moovit, only it was for vaporettos. It also has information about things to do in Venice—very handy.

On the site, there is a section for "Water Bus and Taxis." If you click on "Lines," all of Venice's vaporetto lines are shown. If you choose a specific vaporetto line, like the 5.1, a map shows each stop of the entire 5.1 line. There are very accurate timetables. Best of all, for my aging eyes, I could enlarge the map on my phone and see it in more detail. Still, there is a lot to learn about using the vaporettos, and most of it can only be learned by trial and error.

For anyone seeking detailed information about using vaporettos, I have included a detailed, step-by-step example of how to use the vaporetto for the first time after arriving in Venice—from buying tickets to getting on and off the boat, on the website for my book (www.bravingtheworldbook.com). One thing I can't emphasize enough is that you must validate your vaporetto ticket *before* you get on the boat.

One sunny afternoon Dave and I were sitting on the coveted back seat of a vaporetto going down the Grand Canal. The view from the stern is the best, and we shared the back seats with a nicely dressed, very tan couple.

I nudged Dave. "Look." I inclined my head toward the interior of the vaporetto. Inside, two ticket inspectors were making their way down the boat. They were easy to spot because they each held electronic devices, about the size of a small shoebox, to scan tickets. People on the vaporetto patiently handed over their tickets to be scanned.

"Do you have your ticket?" Dave asked as he reached for his wallet for his. Each of us carried plastic monthly passes with our pictures on the front. I grabbed my purse to pull out my pass and have it ready for the inspectors. When an inspector got to the back of the vaporetto, Dave and I handed over our passes, which the inspector scanned and handed back. The couple next to us handed over their paper tickets, but they were not given back.

"This ticket is not valid," said the inspector. He spoke perfect English, probably a requirement of the job.

"What? Yes, it is. I just bought it ten minutes ago. It is a valid ticket," said Tan Man.

"This ticket has not been validated by the machine. All tickets must be validated by the machine." The inspector turned over Tan Man's ticket and pointed to the written directions explaining ticket validation. There was also a sign in the front of the vaporetto, in multiple languages, that explained how to validate a ticket. I had seen similar signs at vaporetto stops while waiting for a boat to arrive. They were everywhere. Still, I felt sorry for Tan Man and his girlfriend.

"This is ridiculous. We have paid for a ticket. If there is a problem, we will get off at the next stop and validate our tickets." Tan Man stood up, prepared to stand his ground. I did think it was poor planning not to have the validating machines *on* vaporettos instead of only on land at the vaporetto stops.

"That will not be possible. The tickets are not valid and the fine for this is €67." The inspector's face was impassive and calm.

"No way! I will not pay €67 for a simple mistake." Tan Man was furious, and the silent girlfriend now got into the action to plead with the inspector. The second inspector, seeing the disagreement, came to the back of the boat to stand shoulder to shoulder with the first. They all argued back and forth for several minutes and then I heard the inspectors mention the police. Suddenly silent, but clearly fuming, the man jerked a credit card out of his wallet and shoved it at the inspector. The final fee: €67 for EACH of them—a very expensive lesson. Validate your ticket—merely having the ticket is not enough.

TIP: The vaporetto system has a lot of signs. They are outside the vaporetto stops, inside the vaporetto stops, and outside (and inside) the vaporettos themselves. I don't think I paid particular attention to the signs on my first visits to Venice, but once I noticed them, my skills navigating around the city took a leap forward.

• VENICE VISITORS •

We specifically planned our year of travel to end in Venice in the summer, so friends and family would be more likely to visit us. Of course, I wanted to show everyone my beautiful and enchanting Venice. Vanessa and Aubree were our first visitors in June. In July, our friend Michelle came for a visit with her son Jonathan and his girlfriend Ali. Jonathan and Ali would be using our air mattress while Michelle stayed at a nearby Airbnb.

They rented a car at the airport and drove over Venice's causeway, where Dave and I met them at Tronchetto, a large parking lot on the edge of Venice near where the cruise ships docked. First, we all stopped by Michelle's rental so she could drop her bags. Then Dave and I led them to our apartment for dinner and to plan our time together. Michelle was excited to take us to the village where her grandfather had lived before immigrating to the U.S.

"My grandfather left his family and traveled to the U.S. alone in 1909 when he was 19 years old. He had $50 in his pocket for his new life. He ended up in Pittsburg, Kansas," she said.

"Can you imagine traveling for weeks on a boat, all alone, to a country where you couldn't speak the language? Where is his village in Italy?" I asked.

"The village is Imer, about two hours north of Venice, in the Dolomite mountains. I have the car for two more days so all of us can drive up there, spend the night and then come back to Venice."

Michelle had visited Imer years before with her father, and now she wanted to take her son and show him where their family lived before immigrating. Dave and I were happy to tag along. The next day we loaded up the car, and with Michelle at the wheel and son Jonathan navigating, we all sped along the highway and up into the Dolomite mountains toward Imer. After almost a year of not being in a car, it felt great to be cruising through the green countryside.

We arrived in Imer in time for lunch and then explored what little was open in the small town.

"There isn't even an ATM here," said Ali.

"It's pretty dead. Everything is closed for the siesta. Most places in Venice don't close down like this," I said.

Michelle found the house where her family had lived many decades before, and then drove us to a neighborhood church. Next, she drove to the top of the nearby mountain called Passo Rolle. In the winter, everyone here would be skiing, but it was summer, and she dodged bike riders as she navigated the narrow twisting roads. We explored the small restaurant/shop/bar at the top of the mountain, bought souvenirs and drinks, and admired the blue skies, snowcapped peaks, and stunning views.

Back in Imer, we checked into our B&B to get ready for a special dinner in the mountains at a place called Malga Canali. Michelle had visited before and remembered a little bit of how to get there and the restaurant owner gave her directions when she called to make reservations. Still, we got a little lost. I closed my eyes and squeezed the blood out of Dave's hand when we had to turn around on a narrow mountain road.

From the outside, the restaurant looked like a hut stuck on the side of a mountain. The sound of birds and the occasional cowbell filled the air.

Everything was very, very green. The interior was small, with only five tables, and very rustic, decorated with old kitchen and farm implements. The floors and walls were solid stone. After we were seated, the waitress came over with a pitcher of water and glasses.

"The food for tonight, for il primo, you can have soup—onion or mushroom. Il secondo there is, uhmmm, sausages or beef," the waitress explained. No pre-printed menus were offered because they only served what was fresh each day. We looked at each other, quickly decided what to eat, and ordered a carafe of wine to share. Michelle filled us in on the history of the tiny restaurant.

"The same family has owned the farm for generations and the restaurant has been operating for decades. Most of the food they serve is grown or raised on this farm," she told us. It was truly a farm-to-table experience.

"Do you see the cauldron on the fire in the corner?" I pointed. "They are making our dinner on the fire." I watched as polenta was scooped from the cauldron and added to plates that the waiter carried to a table near us.

The scent of food in the room was overwhelming, and when the waiter brought bread and homemade cheese with our carafe of wine, all of us pounced on it. I looked around the cozy, warm room. People filled every seat in the place.

"You are Americans?" asked a man at a table next to us.

Dave was closest, so he explained. "Yes, we are staying in Venice and drove to Imer today."

"We are also from Venice," said the man, with a pronounced Italian accent. At another table, everyone was speaking German. As I looked around the room and reached for another piece of bread, I knew I would never find this place again, no matter how hard I tried. I wanted to memorize this once-in-a-lifetime experience.

The next day we all returned to Venice in time for the Festa del Redentore, a city-wide celebration of the end of the plagues that hit Venice around 1575. The plagues killed one out of every three Venetians, so when the epidemics ended, Venetians celebrated by building the magnificent Chiesa del Santissimo Redentore, the Redentore church, on the island of Giudecca. Today the Festa Del Redentore is still celebrated during the third weekend in July, but since Venice has enough churches and no available land, they celebrate with fireworks, parades, and gondola races.

It was drizzling when Michelle, Jonathan, Ali, Dave, and I gathered close to the Doge's Palace, with thousands of other people waiting for the fireworks to begin over the water of Saint Mark's basin. We huddled together in the doorway of a closed shop.

"My feet are wet," Ali said.

"Should we fight our way through the crowds to get a better view?" I asked. If we were going to huddle in a doorway, maybe we should go home.

Everyone agreed to take the plunge, and with umbrellas, hoods, and ball caps, we mostly stayed dry as we oohed and aahed at the fireworks reflected in the canal. Lovely but exhausting, and it was long past midnight when we finally arrived back to our beds.

The next day started late. Michelle, Dave, and I trekked across Venice to the Redentore church, built when the plagues ended. The church dominated one end of the island of Giudecca and the large white dome was visible from a long distance. Usually, Dave and I rode a vaporetto over the canal to Giudecca, but today, because of the festival, there was a temporary pontoon bridge linking Venice and Giudecca.

"We missed the big parade this morning," I told Dave and Michelle as we crossed the pontoon bridge. I was gripping the handrail to keep my balance while the bridge bounced and bobbed on the water.

"What big parade?" Dave asked. I explained the Festival included a morning mass at Redentore church, usually attended by hundreds of people who paraded across the pontoon bridge.

"I wouldn't want to be on this wobbly bridge with a crowd," Dave said. "Besides, this looks like more fun." He was talking about the rows of gondolas lined up on the canal for a gondola race.

We sat in the sun, watching the brightly dressed gondoliers maneuver their boats down the canal. At lunchtime, we found a table on the canal and sipped glasses of wine. The rain was gone and had taken some of the wicked heat of July away with it. When the day was over, and it was time to return home, we were all red and a little sunburnt—one more perfect day in Venice.

• CHURCH ART •

After Michelle and her family left us to return to the U.S., only a few weeks remained of our time in Venice, so Dave and I stepped up our explorations of the city. It was August, and on more than one sultry afternoon, we ducked into the cool darkness of an open church to escape the summer sun. There are hundreds of churches in Venice, and although some of them are very pretty, in general, the neighborhood churches are mostly ordinary. The outside walls are often just stucco or plain brick. The pictures inside the churches are usually dark and hard to see, made worse by dim lighting. At some churches, a person collected entrance fees, while other churches were free. They all seemed to be open at different hours, though they usually closed around lunchtime. If there was an event, a wedding or funeral, the visiting hours might be canceled without notice.

One day we set out to explore churches tucked away in our Cannaregio neighborhood. Closest to our apartment was the Church of Santa Maria Assunta (known as I Gesuiti). The outside had dozens of statues in wall niches, with more statues on top of columns reaching into the sky and even more statues along the roof-line. "They overdid the statutes a little," Dave muttered as we approached the church.

Inside I Gesuiti, the ceiling was adorned with golden frescos and one very dark painting by Titian, *The Martyrdom of St. Lawrence*. I was interested in the picture and made a note to find out more about it, but I was more captivated by the church's green and white tile walls.

"I can't reach that," I said to Dave, pointing at the pulpit/lectern above my head. "What is it made of?" The pulpit looked like it was covered by fancy, flowing, fluffy brocade *fabric* billowing over the sides. But the columns and walls that were the same style, color and design as the pulpit were cool to the touch, and I was certain they were stone.

Dave reached up and felt the area I was pointing at. "It is stone. It just looks like cloth." The hard, cold marble had the shape of heavy draped fabric. The spectacular marble effects and the soaring gold and white ceiling made this one of my favorite churches in Venice.

A short vaporetto ride away, we found the Madonna dell' Orto church, a much simpler, light, and comfortable church, with a dark wood ceiling and yellow and white marble floors. The outside was plain brick, but in one corner of the church was the tomb of the famous Venetian artist Jacopo Robusti, known as Tintoretto. This had been Tintoretto's neighborhood church, where he worshipped, and several of his paintings were still there. We lingered inside for over an hour, soaking up the quiet and looking at the art.

From Madonna dell' Orto, it was a long zig-zag walk to the final stop in our tour of churches in Cannaregio—Sant'Alvise.

"This church only managed to get one statue," Dave said, looking at the small figure over the doorway.

"Is this a warehouse or a church? Plain brown brick and hardly any windows—I don't see any stained glass." I stood in the shade of a nearby building, hoping to catch a small breeze off the canal.

"Is it worth going in?"

"We finally found the place. We can at least go inside and cool off," I said.

The interior was a huge surprise. For almost an hour, we craned our necks to stare at the ceiling. After traveling for so many months, I expected that every church in Venice, every church in Italy, would have a ceiling decorated with wooden beams or gold-colored glass or painted frescos. The painted fresco ceilings routinely contained figures from the Bible or from mythology. The ceiling at Sant'Alvise Church was different. The artist had used a trompe l'oeil technique to give a curved look to the flat ceiling. From below, it looks as if the ceiling is arching away from the ground, and it boggles the mind to imagine Pietro Antonio Torri and Pietro Ricchi creating the frescoed ceiling some 400 years ago and somehow getting the angles and dimensions to work. If you are not on the typical tourist death march through Europe, you may want to make your way to Sant'Alvise and ponder the ceiling.

After leaving Sant'Alvise, we walked until we found a small restaurant with tables in the shade, ordered lunch and drinks, and talked about the art in all the churches we had explored in Rome and Venice.

"How many paintings by Caravaggio did we seen in Rome?" Dave asked, pulling off his ball cap and running his hands across his head. "How many Madonna portraits?"

"Dozens of Caravaggios and hundreds of Madonnas. Going into a church in Italy is like going to an art exhibit in the U.S. But don't you think a lot of the paintings here in Venice are dark and grimy looking? And the salt air can't be good for them." I was reading some information about St. Lawrence as I spoke to Dave, looking for information about the painting by Titian we had seen in I Gesuiti.

"Maybe the churches get help from the state to take care of the art."

"Maybe," I said doubtfully. "I do love that there are so many paintings. A picture can tell a story better than a sermon. Did you notice the painting of St. Lawrence at I Gesuiti? In the painting he was lying on a grill over a fire—a gruesome death. After seeing that painting, I won't forget how St. Lawrence died."

Our pizza arrived, and as I bit into a piece, I thought about the neighborhood churches all across Italy that are full of paintings, statuary, and mosaics. Art was part of everyday life here—accessible, commonplace, and familiar. Maybe Italians took it for granted as part of the typical background of life, or maybe they became curious, like me, and looked for the stories behind the paintings and statues. Why was St. Lawrence grilled to death, and did he really say, "I'm well done on this side. Turn me over." Curiosity about art led to explorations of history, which fed into questions about political power. In the case of church art, that led to examinations of religion. Looking at art was like pulling a loose thread on a sweater; the more you followed the thread, the more things became exposed.

In art and in travel, there were layers, slices, chunks, fragments— pieces, places, and people waiting to be exhumed, explored, and examined. And sometimes after a bout of digging deep, an idea opened a door, a painting told a story, something inside shifted, and beliefs and opinions slipped a little sideways and changed. It was magical.

TIP: Of course, the Basilica of Saint Mark is the most famous church of Venice and is described in great detail in every Venetian guidebook. It has paintings, golden-colored mosaics, statues, icons, and maybe even the body of Saint Mark. If your time is short, this is the one church you must see. It is well worth paying a €3 fee through www.venetoinside.com for tickets to avoid the lines outside the Basilica. Unfortunately, this won't help you avoid the slow, crowded shuffle of tourist hordes inside the church, but bring your guidebook to read as you shuffle through.

• SCOTLAND AND THE FRINGE FESTIVAL•

When we walked out of the airport in Scotland, I took a deep sniff of the refreshing, wet, brisk air. It was heaven, after hot and sultry Venice. Our savings from Croatia financed only one trip from Venice—and this was it—the Fringe Festival in Edinburgh, Scotland.

As soon as the Uber dropped us at our Airbnb, I could see we had landed in the middle of a raucous city-wide party. The Fringe was similar to Oktoberfest in Munich, that city-wide drinking party involving dancing on the benches in beer halls, but the Fringe Festival in Edinburgh is so much more. It is a city-wide party that includes comedy shows, theater, dance, circus, cabaret, literary pub crawls, and conga lines of people dancing in the streets (and yes, drinking). The population of this city of 500,000 people more than doubles every year during August, the month of the annual Fringe Festival, a 70-year-old city tradition.

Our Airbnb rental was in the middle of the city, where everything was crazy, chaotic, and crowded, but that was a small problem. A far bigger issue was how to decide what to do out of the overwhelming number of possibilities. A catalog in our rental listed over 400 pages of events. Dave was the one who wanted to go to the Fringe, and I had turned over trip planning to him. He had already bought online tickets to a few shows. After dropping suitcases at the rental and grabbing the catalog of events in the apartment, we made our way to a nearby square filled with people. Some were mingling, some passing through, and some handing out flyers for different shows and events. I quickly had a handful of flyers.

"What do we do first?" I asked, laughing as a line of dancing clowns streamed past. Dave was holding the catalog open, looking with glazed eyes at the offerings. "I think beer is always a good place to begin," I said. "Let's sit over there." I pointed to a café on the square with outdoor tables.

After we both had a beer in hand, we turned to the catalog.

"What tickets have you bought?" I asked.

Dave pulled out his wallet and laid four tickets on the table. "We have tickets to a show tomorrow afternoon and then another tomorrow night." He pushed them toward me. I looked at them and then at the catalog table of contents.

"Are you interested in theater? Or comedy? Or dancing?" I asked, reading the categories.

"Not dancing. The tickets I have are for theater, so maybe we mix it up and look for comedy?"

"Okay, but before we leave, you know I have to see the Vermeers at the National Gallery of Scotland."

Dave smiled and pulled out his phone to show me an article he had saved. "I've already checked their hours. We can go there tomorrow morning before our two theater shows."

"You have done some planning," I said, pleasantly surprised. My only contribution to this particular trip had been booking the air travel and the Airbnb. The rest was up to Dave. I pushed the tickets and catalog over to his side of the table. "That all sounds great. Tomorrow is planned. We can go to comedy shows the day after." We spent the rest of our first day in Edinburgh wandering the city and watching random, unscripted, impromptu comedy, dancing, and magic shows on street corners. After a dinner that did not involve either pizza or pasta, we finished our first day in a pub.

The next morning at the small National Gallery of Scotland, I quickly found Vermeer's painting of *Christ in the House of Martha and Mary*. Since we came to Edinburgh from Venice, I wanted to look over the museum's works by Italian painters Titian and Tintoretto. Titian's *Diana and Actaeon* and Tintoretto's painting of *Christ Carried to the Tomb* were very different from paintings I'd already seen by Titian and Tintoretto in Venice. The paintings in Scotland were in warm colors, blues, and reds, the skin tones bright and pale. Nothing was dark and dull. *Do the paintings in Venice just need a really good cleaning?* I wondered.

That afternoon we finished the first of two shows Dave had booked and afterward found an open space filled with booths selling food and drink. Dave went to get beers while I looked for space at one of the communal picnic tables set up in the square. Two spots opened up, and I put down my jacket to save the spaces as I stood and looked around for Dave. He soon saw me and carried over our drinks. We both sat and I smiled at two older ladies sitting across the table.

"Cheers," I said tentatively, raising my glass.

They raised their glasses. "Sláinte mhath." (Slan-ge-var.)

"You must be Scottish," I said. We introduced ourselves and began talking about the Fringe.

"How do you like having your city explode with people like this?" I gestured around at the crowds.

"Ach, we do this every year, come out and do the Fringe. It is part of our year," one explained.

"My sister won't leave her house all month." The other lady laughed. "But it is part of the city and changes every year. I always see something new." There was time to talk over another beer before Dave and I left to make our way to our next show.

Most of the next day, we spent at a stand-up comedy club called The Stand. Each room there showcased a different comedian, so we just looked at the board and picked a show. When that was over, we consulted the board and picked another. While waiting in line, we struck up conversations with people, and everyone had a Fringe story to tell. I don't think there is one "right" way to do the Fringe, and no two people would, or could, ever have the same Fringe experience.

Between the shows, the National Gallery, a visit to the Holyrood Palace, and a half-day at Edinburgh Castle, we had no trouble filling three days. Our apartment was in the center of town, an easy walk nearly everywhere, while Uber worked perfectly for the longer trips. We hit BrewDog where Dave drank a Cocoa Psycho stout and Jerimiah's Tap Room for a Williams Black Ball Stout. I stuck to wine. Scotland offered us a welcome break from pizza and pasta, and we even tried a Scottish dish called haggis, which was amazingly good. The description of haggis was off-putting (a pudding made of the diced liver, heart, and lungs of a sheep, mixed with seasonings and packed into a sheep's stomach), but I always try new foods if the opportunity presents itself, no matter how odd.

On the way back to Venice, I held Dave's hand as the plane took off.

"I could get used to this," I said, "having trips planned by someone else."

"No, you couldn't. You love planning things—being the boss."

Well, he's right, of course.

"You did a great job. You get four stars out of five. I would only tweak a thing or two."

"Yeah, like buying tickets in advance was a mistake," Dave said. "When a show got a good review and took off, we already had tickets to something else."

"Next time we come to Fringe Fest, we'll know all the tricks. Somehow we have to figure out how to be in three places at once." I settled back into my seat—*next time. I like the sound of that.*

There was only one hiccup on our Scotland trip. The minute we landed in Edinburgh, my phone quit working. Dave's phone was fine. He tried trouble-shooting my phone problem and googling remedies, but nothing worked. The Vodafone store in Edinburgh couldn't help since we set up our phones in Italy. I only became worried after we returned to Venice and my phone still didn't work. Tech man Dave took the phone to the nearby Vodafone store in Venice and quickly solved the problem. I had somehow agreed to buy a game on my phone, and at €6 per week for the game, I didn't have any money left in my phone account. Once Dave canceled the game and added money to my account, the phone worked again.

When we started on this adventure, we wondered and worried about so many things: would we like the food, would the apartments work out, did we pack enough clothes, and, of course, would our phones work. Now, in our last weeks of travel, Dave was clearly the rock star of technology for keeping our phones working, almost perfectly, for an entire year. My travel tip? Always travel with your own personal tech specialist.

• THE END OF THE LINE •

Our life in Venice took on a rhythm very different than the other places we had lived in Europe. There was a quietness about our days. Instead of the giddy thrills that were there at the beginning of our journey when all our adventures were ahead of us, now we could see the end. Venice rent was pricey, and other than a short trip to Edinburgh, there wasn't money in our budget to go flitting around Europe like we did when our travels began. While living in Venice, we stayed there. In between visits from friends and family, we settled in.

The summer was hot, so most days began early with a quick breakfast. Then we would just wander, maybe to a gallery or museum we had walked by but hadn't stopped to look at. Maybe we would go to the Fondamenta de La Sacca de San Girolamo on the northwest side of Venice with a book and a picnic and sit in the shade on the red benches watching the trains travel from the mainland and the boats on the water. Sun sparkled, the air smelled of salt, and there was always a fresh breeze.

Some days began with a vaporetto ride to a distant section of Venice where we would get off and explore for hours, and other days we explored surrounding islands. We rented bikes on the Lido and browsed the flea market. In keeping with our tradition, we found a craft beer bar (Il Santo Bevitore in Cannaregio). In the evenings, we could open our windows for fresh breezes from the Adriatic Sea before leaving the apartment to walk around the back alleys and look for new spots to watch the sunset. The sunsets were routinely spectacular, in shades of yellow, orange, and purple, and we saw them from the back of vaporettos, from neighboring islands, from the tops of bridges, and the edges of the fondamente. We began to know the turns and twists of the alleys and which ones led somewhere and which ones were dead ends. We rarely got lost anymore.

At lunchtime, we walked to the nearby Fondamente Nove and ordered a sandwich at the little Caffegelato sandwich shop where the vaporetto drivers stood and drank espressos after their shifts ended. We chatted with the waiters, who recognized us and never charged us the €3 table fee they charged the tourists. Another favorite eatery just a few steps down the fondamente was the Ristorante Pizzeria Da Alvise, where we could sit on the deck over the water and eat a carbonara pizza complete with a lightly fried egg in the middle. We found a favorite restaurant in nearly every section of town—the bar with great sandwiches near the Guggenheim museum, the hostel on Giudecca with a bar and large pool table, the gelateria near the Jewish ghetto neighborhood in with the hard-to-find almond caramel gelato. We laid down memory markers all over the city with food.

The free beach on nearby Lido island became the highlight of our week. Despite the heat, neither of us wanted to sit in our air-conditioned apartment, and there was no better place than the beach to relax and people watch. We alternated cooling off in the water, soaking in the sunshine, reading in the shade of our rented umbrella, commenting on neighbors and passersby, and debating whether to get a massage from the Asian ladies working the beach doing massages for bargain prices.

Every week there was a new batch of beach people to watch—families with kids, couples of all ages, and young people of all nationalities. The women were mostly topless, as was allowed, and the men mostly wore tiny speedos, which I felt shouldn't have been allowed in some cases. We saw only one regular beachgoer from week to week—an older woman—always alone and always topless, lying completely motionless like a statue tipped over in the sand. She must have been at the beach every day because we watched her tan progress from beige to a dark mahogany leather color as the weeks passed.

This was our life in Venice. Each day eased by slowly.

In our last week, the sense of everything coming to an end grew larger and larger. Foreboding sat like a dense fog in the air of the apartment. Sitting on the side of the bed, I looked at half-packed suitcases lying open. Taking a deep breath, I felt a lump in my throat grow, and my eyes blurred from unshed tears. Rubbing my throat, I looked away from the suitcases. *It's almost over.*

"I'm going to run to the store," I called to Dave, jumping up and grabbing my keys. Almost running down the stairs, I got out the building door and pulled it shut behind me. Turning away from the familiar route to the store, I began walking quickly. Without a plan or a destination, I zig-zagged through unfamiliar cool shadowy alleys, places I'd never been before. Venice was somehow always new.

How can I hang onto this trip? If only I could somehow dig my fingers into time itself and hold it still. I wish I could snap my fingers and be standing in Greenwich Market eating oysters, or click my heels and be in Rome walking on Palatine Hill and looking down at the Colosseum.

Finally, the tears came, and I rubbed them away—feeling angry, lost, sad, tired. It was ending. We had lived our crazy dream—from country to country, city to city, to Europe and Africa and back again. There wasn't one thing I would change.

When will we ever come back?

I walked on, not seeing or hearing or feeling anything around me, my mind slipping backward in time, just following the shade. Gradually I noticed the smell of sharp tomato ragù and the perfume of oleander blooms. I heard the blare of a TV, a dog barking, and voices raised in conversation. There was so much life being lived all around me. I breathed deeply to soak it in, to imprint it on my heart. The bumpy stone walls were warm to the touch, and I dragged my fingers over them, memorizing the roughness.

I sat on the steps of a church, my breathing calmer and my head clearer. This place was my place. It would always be part of me, and I would always be part of it. I would return to Venice. Someday. I was sure of it.

• PARIS •

We left Venice early one morning for five days in Paris before our planned flight home to Denver. Paris was a buffer. Paris gave us time to make the mental shift from being residents of Europe to being visitors in Europe. It eased our way home. In Paris, we were tourists, with limited time and a lot of things we wanted to see, things we missed on our honeymoon years earlier. So we did go to the Louvre, to the top of the Eiffel Tower, to the Arc de Triomphe, and floated down the Seine on a boat. But we also idled away time in cafés over lunch, lingered in the Luxembourg Gardens listening to music, lounged on a bench outside the Louvre for a picnic, and wandered through an outdoor market near our apartment ogling the cheese, meat, and vegetables. We had learned a new way to travel, a new way to be. We didn't make it to the Moulin Rouge or the Cathedral of Notre Dame. Neither of us had the least desire to cram the days full or cross destinations off a list. That would have gotten in the way of searching for the best French onion soup or kept us from strolling along the Seine at sunset. On our last day, we locked up our Paris apartment, made a final trip to the corner bakery for coffee and fresh pastries, and said goodbye to Europe…just for now…before getting an Uber to the airport.

PART VI: RE-ENTRY

• HOME AGAIN •

Re-entry was brutal. We left Paris on a Monday at 2 p.m. and arrived in Denver on the same Monday at 4 p.m. It was a ten-hour flight, but we went backward through eight time zones. To our bodies, it was midnight. To beat jet lag, we stayed on our feet as long as possible, and when I finally collapsed in bed at 10 p.m. that first evening, I was certain I would sleep for a week.

It was still dark early the next morning when I rolled over in bed, eyes wide open and staring at the ceiling, blinking and trying to remember where I was. I could tell Dave was awake in the other twin bed in our guest room. All our other furniture was still stuffed into the garage. Our dog was with Aliciah, temporarily, at the new home Aliciah had bought and moved into weeks earlier. "What time is it?" I asked Dave.

He picked up the alarm clock beside his bed. "Four-thirty a.m."

"Are you hungry?"

"No. I don't know. Maybe."

"I need coffee. Did the coffee pot turn up yesterday?" We had done some halfhearted unpacking. "Never mind. It doesn't matter. There is no coffee in the house."

Both of us dragged ourselves upright and pulled clothes from our suitcases to get dressed in the peculiar fog of jet lag—wide awake exhaustion. The sky was pitch black and the street lights still on when we left the house in search of coffee. The lights of the nearby Village Inn were warm and welcoming. I stirred my coffee, adding ice to cool it off quickly and listened drowsily to the loud banter of a group of men at a table near us.

The waitress kept bringing refills of coffee and I kept gulping them down. By the time our breakfast arrived, I was reasonably alert.

"Can you believe this bacon?" I held up a piece for Dave's examination. "Thick, crisp, perfectly cooked *bacon*."

He was cutting his pancakes, doused in syrup and butter.

"What was that stuff they called bacon in Europe?"

"Pancetta," I said. "Pancetta is not bacon." We couldn't help making comparisons between our old reality and new reality.

The first week, both of us woke up every morning in the dark, but we got a lot done during the long days. Boxes were unpacked at a record rate. It took no time at all to buy a car, set up insurance, choose cell phone, cable, and internet service, re-start our mail and newspaper delivery, and stock the fridge, freezer, and pantry. After only five or six days, everything was back in its old place.

As I unpacked boxes and re-stocked our closets, I was stunned by how much stuff we owned. We had traveled for a year with only four suitcases. Those suitcases became our wardrobe for clothes and shoes, filing cabinet for papers, medicine cabinet for drugs, and kitchen cabinet for holding essential things hauled from one apartment to another (a good knife, ice cube trays, and spatula). While traveling, we pared down life to basics, but now I was home, with closets and shelves brimming with clothes, appliances, towels, books, dishes, shoes, and blankets, the usual overflow of everyday life in America.

Many things were very familiar. It was easy to go back to driving a car, and I remembered the layout of my neighborhood grocery store. The selection in the airport-sized grocery store was dazzling. In Rome, there had been only *three* choices of shampoo. Here the choices were overwhelming. I wandered the long aisle of *just* hair products (about a quarter the size of an entire grocery store in Rome) and wondered if we needed so many choices: shampoos, conditioners, foams, volumizers, gels, sprays, and mousses. The products contained pearl proteins, caviar extract, blackberry quinoa protein, antioxidants, passion fruit, and mango extracts. They promised to smooth, texturize, straighten, fluff, and curl my hair, making it fresh, glossy, shapely, airy, rumpled, sleek, or, my favorite, "sexy." One product claimed to be "like a wellness retreat for stressed out hair." After the shampoo aisle, I was the one who was stressed out. *Does all of this choice make our lives easier?*

There were some moments of pure, head-scratching "unfamiliarity." Our refrigerator/freezer seemed a thing of miracles after a year of mostly dorm-sized fridges. When we first arrived home, I struggled to get ice. I saw a bin of ice in the freezer and looked for a latch or handle I could use to open it and grab ice. After pushing, pulling, and tugging at the bin, I finally gave up and closed the freezer door—where I saw the ice and water dispenser *on the door.* I had forgotten ice came out of the freezer door—no more ice cube trays for me. I was home.

There were other differences. Everywhere we traveled in Europe, I had bought a box of insulin pens (without using our health insurance) at a very affordable price of about $50. After we returned home, I refilled my insulin prescription at my local Walgreens. My co-pay was $50, but the pharmacy note on the refill said that "insurance saved you $594.79 on this prescription." Without insurance, the same box of insulin pens I bought all over Europe for $50 was more than ten times more expensive in the U.S. That. Is. Just. Insane.

§　§　§

The emotional re-entry was as hard in its own way as the physical re-entry. In the beginning, after arriving home we were elated and excited to be back in our own bed, surrounded by familiar things and people. The possibilities seemed endless. We made visits to family, and over the first Christmas holidays, our house was loud, crazy, and overflowing with children and grandchildren.

But when Christmas was over, everything slowed down, winter arrived, the days were short, and the possibilities not so endless. On our travels, every day was filled with museums, parks, walks, churches, markets, side trips, shops, pubs, and restaurants. Even on a simple trip to the grocery store, there was always something new and unique to see, examine, and discuss. After the constant variety, after being surrounded every day by unfamiliar scenes, people, smells, and foods, life at home felt flat. I thought I had seen enough churches to last several lifetimes, but now I'd give anything to have one more afternoon sitting on a pew of a stone church looking around me, seeing the light through the stained glass windows. I was like a drug addict whose drug had been taken away. Now at home, the world seemed drab and uninteresting. A slow creeping sadness began settling in.

I could still feel the hot sun in Rome, smell the salt air from the beach at the Lido near Venice and see Diocletian's old stone palace in Croatia. Part of my mind and my heart was still in Europe, wandering and exploring, but my body was very much in Colorado. The tension between the two states of being kept growing the longer I tried not to think about it.

"I feel….sad, in a funk," I said, finally, to Dave. "Remember the *Wizard of Oz* movie, before the colors exploded on screen? That feels like life now. Colorless."

I felt guilty to feel this way and even guiltier talking about it. We were lucky to have lived this once-in-a-lifetime trip. Expecting more was greedy.

Dave, the homebody, surprised me though. He agreed with me. "I know," he said. "Doesn't it seem like we have seen everything in Denver more than once?"

"Remember the beach in Venice and the pasta in Rome?"

"And the pubs and beer in London."

I was glad we both felt the same way and I wasn't alone. We began to talk about our future life and future travel. Home was terrific, we were glad to be back, but we both also wanted to travel again. Could we make another year-long trip? Did we want to? We talked about South America and Dave's dream of going to New Zealand. I heard parts of Africa were beautiful. Botswana? Besides going back overseas for longer trips, we wanted to spend time exploring our own country. There are over 60 national parks in the U.S. and I've been to only three of them. I've never been to New York City, Savannah, Georgia, or Portland, Oregon.

"So, where do you want to start?" Dave asked as we stood around the kitchen island, wine glasses in hand (of course), looking at maps and destinations and possibilities on our phones.

"We've only been back in the country a year. There is a lot of exploring to do here in the U.S., and those trips don't involve long flights over the ocean. Maybe stay in the U.S. this year and go overseas next year? It will give us time to save money." I was still keeping an eye on the budget.

Life was going to be full of adventures and our travel days were far from over. I was thrilled and definitely had a new spring in my step. A few months later, on a family visit to Kansas City, we convinced Dave's brother and his wife to join us on a trip to Paris, including a side trip to drink wine in Bordeaux. I imagined the four of us in France touring a vineyard in the hot sun, drinking lots of French wine, and eating in small cafés. It was thrilling to begin researching and planning a trip, even one that was a year away.

It is thrilling and exciting to know that there will be more traveling in our future, with time for family/friends and to relax at home thrown in for good measure. Life has more to offer and I am ready for the adventure and the journey to continue.

France 2020!

• AND THEN LIFE CHANGED ...A COVID STORY •

Boy, how it changed. In one fell swoop, almost overnight, as Covid 19 spread across the world with stunning speed. While I sat writing and revising this book, travel bans sprang up between countries, and borders closed. People were confined indoors for months.

The future of travel is unknown, the timeline of when things will return to "normal" is unknowable, and there is a lot of fear, isolation, death, sickness, financial struggle, chaos, and anxiety. The Fringe Festival was canceled. Oktoberfest in Germany will not happen in 2020. Museums, churches, and monuments closed.

As events unfolded and I kept working on the draft of my book, the irony of what I had written near the end of my book kept running through my head. *"It is thrilling and exciting to know that there will be more traveling in our future..."* But of course, our 2020 trip to Paris was canceled. When I saw the email canceling our flight, I burst into tears.

In the grand scheme of all the pain and upheaval that so many people are experiencing, it is petty to mourn the loss of a trip to France. The entire world is fighting an unseen enemy in a battle that will last many months. But I was mourning the loss of more than one trip. I was mourning the loss of the world as it was, and all that we had and took for granted.

People will travel again. I believe that. We are in a "pause," and someday, people will roam, wander, and navigate the world again. I don't know when and I don't know how and I don't know what it will look like—probably very different—but that is okay. I am hopeful. Until the world re-opens, I have gone back to "traveling" the way I started, many decades ago in my small, landlocked, Midwestern town—with books. Life goes on. The world will be new and we will see it in new ways. All of us will brave the new world—one day.

EPILOGUE: BEFORE AND AFTER

When we left for our year of travel, I wondered how our lives would be different when we returned. I could not have imagined how many things would change for us.

Before leaving for Europe, work, home and family "busyness" consumed us. We spent entire weekends keeping the household up and running—repairs, lawn care, cleaning, and grocery shopping, and in the evenings, we crashed in front of the TV. I think we were both stuck in a rut, where days blurred together and neither of us put much time or energy into new things. Nothing was inspiring us anymore. Simply retiring didn't shift us out of our ruts; it just changed the boundaries. After retirement, there was more free time, but our interests were no longer interesting; hobbies had become stale, and we had quit trying anything new. I'll just say it. We were boring. Probably we weren't much different from other couples our age.

Our year of travel upended our old roles, rhythms and routines. For an entire year, we were never apart for more than a few hours. We were on the same path every day, sharing the same experiences, and we relied on each other. Dave became the family cook while I planned our sightseeing. I became the family navigator and arranged our excursions around town, but more than once, Dave's extra pair of eyes kept us from jumping on the wrong bus/train or one going the wrong direction.

We connected more strongly through our individual strengths. I booked our side trips around Europe, compared prices, and watched the budget. Dave kept our computer, Kindles, and phones working. I scoured the local newspapers for things to do, and Dave kept his daily backpack supplied with water, snack bars, and emergency soda in case my blood sugar went low.

When challenges came up, we navigated them together. When the bus/train/subway was a no show, we jumped in a cab or called an Uber. We got lost together in Pompeii, navigated the political unrest in Barcelona, and shared water restrictions in Egypt.

Traveling for a year also blew up our familiar habits, gave us a glimpse of what we could do differently, and showed us what we were missing.

In Europe, we walked miles every day and were in constant motion. Once we got settled back home, Dave took our bikes in for an overhaul, and we began taking longer and longer rides, sometimes loading the bikes on the back of the car to explore different neighborhoods.

I was even more curious about places, people, history, customs, and foods than before we left. After we returned, Dave and I became a dinner club of two, searching for new restaurants and cuisines. Maybe we would never travel to Ethiopia, but we found Ethiopian restaurants to try—a bit of culture on a fork.

Taking risks and trying new things was easier. Inspired by a spark of adventure from our travels, we rented electric scooters and zipped through the streets of downtown Denver. I thought we had seen everything in the city but made it our mission to seek out new, unknown nooks and crannies.

We brought home new habits from our year of travels—a love of long leisurely lunches, like we had in Croatia, and lounging in shady parks with a picnic and a book, like our life in Rome.

After we returned, we were different people. We were closer, more connected and our relationship had grown. After a year of dealing with unexpected obstacles, unfamiliar hurdles, things outside our ordinary experience while in a different country, without support from friends or family, surrounded by strangers, and without speaking the local language, *we were a team*. We had jumped into the deep end of the pool together. I found a new appreciation for Dave, who quietly and constantly watched out for me, working behind the scenes to make our life flow every day.

It was hard at first, but we learned how to navigate time together and time apart and discovered that our time apart complemented and enhanced our time together. Our relationship regained its spark and energy, and we rediscovered how to have fun together. After we returned home, we did another double pinkie swear promise. Every birthday gift, every anniversary, Christmas, and Valentine's gift going forward would be a new experience we could do together. I imagined all the gift cards to comedy clubs, golf lessons, balloon rides, and cooking classes in our future. We promised to hold onto the fun we had found.

Myself, my nervous, list-making, hyper-vigilant self, had finally relaxed. It took time before I realized everything worked out, somehow, one way or another. No matter what obstacle popped up, we could fix it or survive it. Many outcomes can't be controlled, and all of my list-making, worrying, and advance, excessive planning couldn't prevent problems from happening. That was a slowly dawning realization for me. I can't say I overcame all of my nervousness about the unexpected and the unplanned, and I will still insist on being at the airport for a flight way too early. Still, it was a revelation for me to see things work out, over and over, time after time.

My whole outlook on diabetes changed. London had been hard, with too many days of crazy blood sugar numbers, and I was disheartened and frustrated. In Venice, I got my diabetes "mojo" back and my blood sugar numbers settled down. When Vanessa visited us in Venice, she brought me a new box of Pods and none of them failed. There are not many gardens and parks in Venice and the fresh sea air eliminated my allergy problems. The motivation I lost in London returned and I tried harder. I drank more water, tested more often, and checked the number of carbs in my food instead of guessing. Strangely, despite my trip to the emergency room in London, I felt more in charge of my diabetes and more capable of steering my way through it. Usually, I waited for my endocrinologist to make changes to insulin doses or to recommend changes to my routine. But as we traveled, I hadn't seen an endocrinologist once. I was the one making all the decisions about adjusting doses and figuring out what was going wrong when my numbers went crazy. And that was okay. I could handle diabetes.

§   §   §

My *dream*, when we left the country, was to live like a local, "*to get to know a neighborhood, to eat where the locals ate, learn new things, and watch one season replace another.*" Things didn't turn out exactly the way we thought they would. The grocers and shopkeepers in our neighborhood didn't learn our names. Dave and I are both a little reticent and shy, and language barriers plagued me in Italy. But we saw the seasons change, and everywhere we lived we created a home, and from that home, we interacted with people around us and connected with strangers, if only temporarily. It didn't happen often enough, but when it did, it was exhilarating and magical.

We shopped in small, local markets and ate local food—tripe in Rome, oysters in London, haggis in Scotland, and fresh fish in Croatia. We weren't tourists snapping up souvenirs or rushing through each day. We stopped, focused, settled in, explored, and navigated the backroads and out-of-the-way places never mentioned in guidebooks.

Besides the personal adjustments we experienced, our year of travel was eye-opening on a broader level, and I came to realize just how similar people are. Most of the people we met and talked to just wanted to live their lives in peace, with friends and family, meaningful work, safe communities, and good food and wine. Just like Americans, they cared about their families, their cities, and their environment. Ana, our landlord in Split, worked to save beautiful Marjan Park from developers. Protestors in London blocked the bridges in their fight against climate change. Our Venetian landlord Roberto worried the thousands of day-trippers dumped into Venice by the cruise ships for only a few hours changed the neighborhoods and culture of the city in a way that longer-term visitors did not. Cab drivers, Uber drivers, people we met in pubs and bus stops had the same universal complaints about traffic, roads, politics, and their kids' schools.

Despite the worry and complaints, I didn't sense hopelessness in anyone we talked with, rather the opposite. The people I talked with were optimistic about their personal lives. They loved their city, were proud of their country's history, and were eager to give us tips about places they wanted us to experience. I am a die-hard news junkie, and sometimes it seemed the news headlines became more ominous every day. But I realized after our year-long trip that the best, sweetest and finest parts of daily life go on unnoticed, every day, among people in every country around the world, *despite* the news headlines. I came home more optimistic about the world and the people in it. That was the best discovery from our year away from home.

NOTE FROM THE AUTHOR

If you enjoyed reading Braving the World: Adventures in Travel and Retirement, I hope you will take a few minutes of your time and leave a review on Amazon. Amazon reviews are rare and important things to authors AND to other readers. Please share your thoughts.

ABOUT THE AUTHOR

Pam Saylor grew up in the landlocked Midwest, reading books and dreaming of travel. While on a year-long trip visiting nine countries and two continents, she managed to control her Type 1 diabetes and reconnect with her husband. A former paralegal turned contented retiree and travel addict, Pam lives with her husband Dave in Colorado. Pam and Dave are currently busy trying to agree on their next adventure. Braving the World: Adventures in Travel and Retirement is her first book.

To see pictures of their year of travel, visit Pam's website.

Website: https://www.bravingtheworldbook.com

Email: bravingtheworldbook@gmail.com

ACKNOWLEDGMENTS

I want to thank my daughter, Kate Rado, for her encouragement and a terrific book cover. I owe many thanks to my friend Michelle Riley who read the first draft and gave me valuable input and advice. Finally, I also wish to thank "Alexa" for endlessly playing my favorites playlist.